ICSA Study Text

Foundation Programme

ICSA Study Text

Foundation Programme

**Doug Armour, Santhie Goundar,
Kelly Padwick and Lee Roach**

The Governance
Institute

First published 2018
Published by ICSA Publishing Ltd
Saffron House
6–10 Kirby Street
London EC1N 8TS

Typeset by Paul Barrett Book Production, Cambridge

British Cataloguing in Publication Data
A catalogue record for this book is available from the British Library.

ISBN 978 186072 733 7

Contents

How to use this study text

This study text has been developed to support ICSA's Level 4 Foundation Programme for the ICSA qualifying programme and includes a range of navigational, self-testing and illustrative features to help you get the most out of the support materials.

The text is divided into three main sections:

- introductory material
- the text itself
- additional reference information.

The sections below show you how to find your way around the text and make the most of its features.

Introductory material

The introductory section includes a full contents list and the aims and learning outcomes of the qualification, as well as a list of acronyms and abbreviations.

The text itself

Each part opens with a list of the chapters to follow, an overview of what will be covered and learning outcomes for the part.

Every chapter opens with a list of the topics covered and an introduction specific to that chapter.

Chapters are structured to allow students to break the content down into manageable sections for study. Each chapter ends with a summary of key content to reinforce understanding.

Features

The text is enhanced by a range of illustrative and self-testing features to assist understanding and to help you prepare for the examination. You will find answers to the 'test yourself' questions towards the end of this text. Each feature is presented in a standard format, so that you will become familiar with how to use them in your study.

These features are identified by a series of icons.

The text also includes tables, figures and other illustrations as relevant.

Reference material

The text ends with a range of additional guidance and reference material, including a glossary of key terms, a directory of web resources and a comprehensive index.

Stop and think

Test yourself

Worked examples

Case law

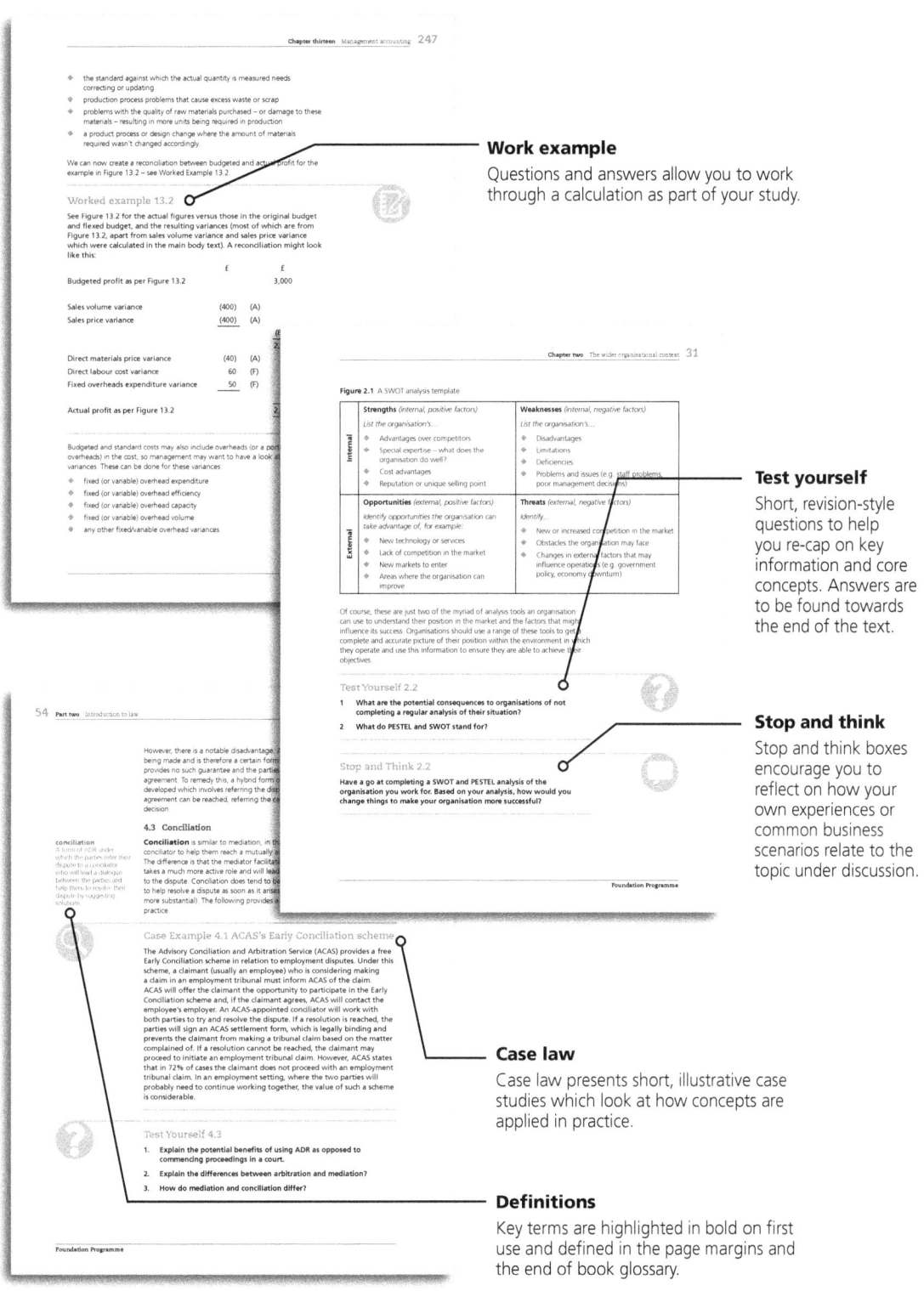

Work example

Questions and answers allow you to work through a calculation as part of your study.

Test yourself

Short, revision-style questions to help you re-cap on key information and core concepts. Answers are to be found towards the end of the text.

Stop and think

Stop and think boxes encourage you to reflect on how your own experiences or common business scenarios relate to the topic under discussion.

Case law

Case law presents short, illustrative case studies which look at how concepts are applied in practice.

Definitions

Key terms are highlighted in bold on first use and defined in the page margins and the end of book glossary.

Syllabus outline

Qualification outline and aims

The path to becoming Chartered begins with the ICSA Foundation Programme. It is your first step on the path to a career as a governance professional or company secretary.

The programme provides a broad introduction to businesses, how they are governed, maintained and financially managed and the laws to which they must adhere. The knowledge and skills you will gain through this programme will also help prepare you to meet the demands of Part One of the ICSA qualifying programme – the next stage in the path to becoming Chartered.

Part one – Introducing the Business Environment – 10%

This part provides an overview of how organisations are structured and managed and how the external environment affects business activities and influences decision making.

Learning outcomes

After completing this part, you will:

1 Know about types of organisations and their objectives
2 Understand how organisations are structured to achieve their objectives
3 Know the stakeholders who influence and affect organisations and their activities
4 Be able to analyse the external factors that may impact achievement of organisational objectives.

Part two – Introduction to Law – 35%

This part provides an introduction to business law, including its purposes, administration, and sources. In order to fully understand the law and identify which areas of the law are most applicable to businesses, it is important to understand where laws come from, the different types of laws that exist (and how they interrelate), and how the law is administered and applied.

Learning outcomes

After completing this part, you will:

1 Understand the purposes of business law, and how the law is classified
3 Understand how the law is administered and applied
3 Understand the sources of law and how law is created
4 Understand the UK's company law and corporate governance frameworks
5 Know which areas of law principally impact upon businesses.

Part three – Principles of Company Compliance and Administration – 25%

This part examines the historical origins of modern company law and introduces the legal process that has to be followed to create a corporate entity or company (known as incorporation). It will also cover the administration side of incorporation and the obligation for companies to be transparent when providing information about their activities and financial status.

Learning outcomes

After completing this part, you will:

1 Understand the different legal structures available for companies
2 Know how companies are incorporated
3 Understand the routine compliance and governance obligations placed on companies
4 Understand the ownership and management structures and the decision making processes for shareholders and directors.

Part four – Introduction to Finance and Accounting – 30%

This part introduces the components of financial documentation and the principles of financial decision-making. It provides an overview of basic accounting terms and concepts and examines the importance of financial reporting. It then covers how financial statements and reports can be analysed to help inform the decision-making activities of both internal and external stakeholders, such as management and investors.

Learning outcomes

After completing this part, you will:

1 Know about costs, revenue and profit
2 Understand principles of accounting and financial reporting
3 Understand principles of management accounting
4 Understand principles of financial decision making and the impact of financial decisions on businesses.

Acronyms and abbreviations

ABC	activity-based costing method (in management accounting)
ACAS	Advisory Conciliation and Arbitration Service
ADR	alternative dispute resolution
BEIS	Department for Business, Energy and Industrial Strategy
CA 2006	Companies Act 2006
CEO	Chief executive officer
CFO	Chief financial officer
CIMA	Chartered Institute of Management Accountants
CJEU	Court of Justice of the European Union
CMA	Competition and Markets Authority
COGS	cost of goods sold
CoJ	Court of Justice
CPR	Civil Procedure Rules
Cr	credit (in accounting/bookkeeping)
CSR	corporate social responsibility
CVP	cost–volume–profit (analysis)
DPP	Director of Public Prosecutions
Dr	debit (in accounting/bookkeeping)
EBIT	earnings before interest and tax
EBITDA	earnings before interest, tax, depreciation and amortisation
ECHR	European Convention on Human Rights
ECJ	European Court of Justice
ECtHR	European Court of Human Rights
EEA	European Economic Area
EEC	European Economic Community
EU	European Union
FRC	Financial Reporting Council
FRS	financial reporting standard
FRSSE	Financial Reporting Standard for Smaller Entities (now superseded)
FSMA 2000	Financial Services and Markets Act 2000
GAAP	Generally Accepted Accounting Practice
HMRC	Her Majesty's Revenue & Customs
HRA 1998	Human Rights Act 1998
IA 1986	Insolvency Act 1986
IAS	International Accounting Standard

IFRS	International Financial Reporting Standards
IIRC	International Integrated Reporting Council
IP	intellectual property
IR	integrated reporting
KPI	key performance indicator
LLP	limited liability partnership
NED	non-executive director
NPV	net present value
P&L	profit and loss
Plc	public limited company
ROA	return on assets
ROE	return on equity
SI	statutory instrument
SID	senior independent director
SME	small- and medium-sized enterprises
SME	small and/or medium-sized entity
TEU	Treaty on European Union
TFEU	Treaty on the Functioning of the European Union
WACC	weighted average cost of capital
WIP	work(s) in progress

Acknowledgements

Douglas Armour
I would like to take this opportunity to thank the staff at ICSA for their encouragement and patience during the writing of this study text. In particular Kelly Padwick, Tom Young and Sheida Heidari whose assistance was invaluable.

Santhie Goundar
I would like to thank the team at ICSA for their invaluable support, patience and advice while writing this book. In particular, I would like to thank Kelly Padwick for her guidance and feedback and incredible organisation, as well as Emma Chafer, Tom Young, Sheida Heidari, Mark Jenkins, Danusia Wysocki and Jenny Robertson. Last, but not least, I would like to thank my husband Adrian Rogers, whose support and encouragement and assistance proved essential.

Kelly Padwick
I would like to send huge thanks to my ICSA colleagues for all the help and support throughout this development, in particular Dan Macdonald, Emma Chafer, Tom Young and Sheida Heidari. Also, grateful thanks to all of the excellent writers and reviewers who have helped to make this complex project a reality. I would also like to thank my folks and my husband Geoff Johnston for the unwavering support and encouragement. This is for you Mum – you always said I would, and I finally did.

Lee Roach
I would like to thank the team at ICSA for all their hard work and support, including Kelly Padwick, Tom Young, Sheida Heidari, as well as the technical reviewers whose comments were of tremendous help.

Part one

Introducing the business environment

Overview

Part One will unravel the complex puzzle that is the organisation and the environment in which it operates. These first two chapters will introduce the concepts that underpin later parts of this study text in terms of how organisations are structured, managed and the factors that influence their operations.

Chapter 1 will explore how organisations are categorised according to the economic sector they operate in and the size and scope of the organisation. It will then look at some of the different types of legal ownership structures available to organisations, the objectives that might be pursued and how organisations structure and manage the workforce to help them achieve their objectives.

Chapter 2 will examine the wider issues organisations need to consider when trying to achieve their objectives, including the influence of stakeholders on the activities of organisations and how to analyse the potential impact of external factors that may affect efforts to achieve their objectives.

Learning outcomes

At the end of this part, you will be able to:

◆ Understand types of organisations and their objectives

◆ Understand how organisations are structured to achieve their objectives

◆ Know the stakeholders who influence and impact upon organisations

◆ Understand how organisations can analyse the potential impact of the external business environment on achieving their objectives

◆ Be able to use methods of external analysis to understand an organisation's external environment and identify ways it can potentially adapt to changes

Chapter one
Introducing organisations

CONTENTS

1 Introduction

An organisation is a complex machine, with no two the same, and whilst we can draw many similarities from different organisations and categorise them, each have their own unique set of needs and objectives. The purpose of this chapter is to understand the economic sectors in which organisations operate and their 'shape' in terms of size, scope and legal ownership. We will then look at the objectives that organisations might pursue and how they can structure and manage the organisation, including its workforce, to achieve those objectives.

2 Sectors of business activity

The economic activity of a nation can be divided into three sectors: primary, secondary and tertiary. It is within one of these three sectors that all organisations within that economy operates and each sector represents the type of economic activity organisations are engaged in. The sectors form a continuum that represents increasing distance of raw materials from the earth. It starts with sourcing raw materials (primary) through manufacture (secondary) to providing finished goods and services (tertiary).

Examples of activity within each sector include:

- Primary – extraction and harvesting of natural products from the earth (e.g. farming, fishing, mining and forestry).
- Secondary – manufacturing goods from raw materials, such as making plastics from oil and building/constructing and assembling products such as houses and roads.
- Tertiary – organisations that provide services (e.g. banks and other financial institutions, retail and sales businesses, transport and distribution, restaurants, leisure and tourism).

Although most economic models divide the economy into only three sectors, some models divide it into four or five sectors. The quaternary and quinary sectors represent activities that are closely linked to the activities of the tertiary sector, as follows.

- Quaternary – also known as 'the knowledge economy', representing organisations involved in intellectual services linked to technological innovation (e.g. scientific research and information technology).
- Quinary – representing the highest-level decision makers in an economy or society (e.g. the top executives/officials in government, universities, not-for-profit organisations, media, police and fire services). Some economists also classify domestic activities such as childcare and housekeeping as quinary sector activities as they contribute to the economy by providing a service for free that would have otherwise had to have been paid for.

3 Organisational size and scope

Different countries have different criteria for categorising organisations in terms of size, but number of staff and turnover are often used as the main defining criteria. Micro, small, medium and large enterprises are the four main categories used to describe organisational size and whilst there is no generally accepted formula that is used by everyone, a rough guide to categorising according to number of employees is as follows:

- Micro – 0–9 employees
- Small – 10–49 employees
- Medium – 50–249 employees
- Large – 250+ employees

micro, small- and medium-sized enterprises
Categories for defining the size of an organisation. The criteria differs between countries, but as a general rule, these are categorised into <10 employees (micro), <50 employees (small) and <250 employees (medium).

Categorising organisations according to size helps to inform government policy, such as tax rates for businesses and eligibility criteria for subsidies. It is also a useful measure when analysing the impact of different types of business on the economy. In the UK and European Union (EU), **micro, small- and medium-sized enterprises (SMEs)** make up around 99% of all businesses, so they are an important part of the economy.

However, defining organisations according to size can be problematic as a general measure, as the criteria for categorising size varies so widely. Depending on which definition is followed, an SME can have between 0 and 500 employees and turnover of between £6.5 million and £50 million. Different departments of the UK Government define organisation size according to different parameters and for different purposes, so it is good to be mindful of this fact when looking at published information relating to organisation size.

Stop and Think 1.1

How many employees does your organisation have? Look up some different definitions of organisation size – does this affect the category your organisation is placed into?

4 Legal ownership structures

Different organisations are set up to do different things for different sectors of business. Most fall under one of the three main sectors of the economy – public, private and the voluntary sector.

This section looks at the purpose of these different types of organisation, how they are controlled, financed and what they produce and provide.

4.1 Private sector organisations

The private sector consists of organisations that are owned and run by private individuals. These are not under direct government control and are run with the intention of generating a profit for the owners of the business. Examples of private sector organisations include:

- Sole traders (also known as sole proprietors)
- Partnerships
- Limited companies
- Parent and subsidiary
- Unincorporated association
- Cooperatives.

Sole traders

This is a business that is owned by one, self-employed, individual who may or may not employ other staff on a full- or part-time basis. Often financed using the owner's personal funds (and sometimes topped up with borrowed funds, e.g. a bank loan), any profits made accrue to the owner. The owner will often reinvest a significant proportion of these profits back into the business, which can help to ease any debts that the business may have accumulated (e.g. paying off a previous bank loan). Whilst being eligible to receive all the profits is definitely an advantage for the owner, one significant disadvantage is that if the business makes any losses, the sole trader is personally responsible for them. Since this type of business does not have a **separate legal personality**, the owner has **unlimited personal liability** for its debts and liabilities. This means that the owner's personal assets can be seized to pay off any debts

separate legal personality
The company is set up as a legal 'person' to delineate the actions of company from that of its owners.

unlimited personal liability
The owner of the business is personally responsible for any debts and liabilities accrued by the business.

if they do not have funds from the business available to settle them. Despite being personally liable, there are more sole traders in the UK than any other business type because of the ease with which the business can legally be established. They are attractive as they have fewer document filing requirements as compared to other, larger, businesses and afford privacy for the individual as the accounts for the business are not publicly available.

Partnerships

A partnership is established when two or more individuals combine money, resources and skills to operate and manage a business and share in the profits and losses of that business. A partnership is defined by the Partnership Act 1890 as 'the relation which subsists between persons carrying on a business with a view to profit'. The benefits of partnerships is that they are easy to establish and combine the skills and resources of the partners involved. There are various partnership arrangements to choose from; we will cover general, limited liability and limited partnerships, below.

In a general partnership the owners have unlimited personal liability jointly and severally for any losses and liabilities incurred by the business. This means that each individual owner is personally liable for the whole debt and can have their personal assets seized to settle it. Other partnership arrangements involve having a written, legal arrangement in place which limits the liability of partners in the business. This may involve agreeing to share liabilities and losses or one or more partners having limited liability for losses. Similar to a sole trader, general partnerships benefit from non-public disclosure of the accounts of the business, affording privacy for the partners.

Limited liability partnership (LLP)
Each partner is not liable for another partner's misconduct or negligence (e.g. a partner in a law firm being sued for malpractice) or personally responsible for losses and liabilities beyond what they have invested in the business.

A **limited liability partnership (LLP)** is popular with businesses that carry out a trade or profession and is often the preferred legal structure of professional firms such as accountancy, law and architecture firms. In the event of one partner being sued for misconduct or negligence (e.g. malpractice) the assets of the other partners are not put at risk.

A limited partnership (LP) combines the principles of a general partnership and a limited liability partnership. It involves having a least one general partner who has unlimited personal liability for the debts of the business and one or more partners with limited liability who are only liable for what they have invested in the business. In this arrangement, the general partner is involved in the day-to-day management of the business while the limited partners (also known as silent partners) are not. The limited partners can only have the privilege of limited liability if they are not involved in the day-to-day management of the business.

The law surrounding partnership arrangements varies between different jurisdictions, so individuals wishing to set up a partnership should seek legal advice before entering into such an agreement.

Limited companies

According to law, a company is a corporate association with its own legal identity that is separate from that of its owners. In essence, the company is set up as a 'legal person' in its own right. This means that company property and assets belong to the company and not its members (the shareholders), but the personal assets of the members do not usually belong to the company. Having a separate legal identity means that if the company goes into **insolvency**, the company is liable for its debts and each member is only liable for the amount they originally invested in the business. The shareholders delegate the responsibility of the day-to-day running of the company to the board of directors, who act on the shareholders' behalf in this capacity.

These companies have undergone the process of incorporation – the process by which a new or existing business registers as a limited company. They are limited by shares or guarantee.

A **company limited by shares** involves the shareholders having a right to share in the profits a business makes through dividends and also having the right to vote. The amount they receive depends on how much they have invested, meaning the more they have invested, the larger the dividend they receive. In a public limited company (plc), shares can be offered to the general public and traded on the stock exchange, whereas in a private limited company, they cannot.

In a **company limited by guarantee** there are no shares and the company is owned by the members (known as guarantors) instead of shareholders. Guarantors often appoint themselves as directors and must guarantee to contribute a fixed sum of money in the event of the **winding up** of the company. These private companies limited by guarantee are usually non-profit businesses and charitable organisations and surplus income is commonly used to further the non-profit or charitable aims of the business, rather than being distributed to the owners as personal income in dividends.

Parent and subsidiary

A subsidiary company is a company owned or controlled by another company, referred to as the 'parent' or 'holding' company. Generally, the parent will own 50% or more of the subsidiary but remains a legally separate entity. Companies might form or purchase subsidiaries for expanding business operations or to spread the risk of liability when engaging in new lines of business.

Unincorporated association

An unincorporated association is an organisation set up through an agreement between a group of people who come together for a reason other than to make a profit (e.g. a voluntary group or a sports club). This type of association does not need to be registered with Companies House (hence the term unincorporated) and it doesn't cost anything to set one up, however individual members are personally responsible for any debts and contractual obligations.

Co-operatives

A co-operative is an organisation owned and run by its members, which can be, for example, the employees, the customers, local residents or suppliers. They are not run for the benefit of the shareholders and operate in the interests of the members, who have an equal say in how the business is run and decide how

insolvency
The situation in which a company or individual can no longer pay back the money owed to outside lenders (e.g. a loan from a bank or other financial institution).

company limited by shares
Shareholders usually receive a share of any profits the business makes (dividends). Shares can be kept private or, if a public limited company, offered to the general public and traded on the stock exchange.

company limited by guarantee
A company owned by the members (known as guarantors) instead of shareholders.

winding up
The process of liquidating the assets of a limited company. The company will stop doing business and employing people and assets are used to pay off its debts with any money left going to shareholders. The company won't exist once it has been dissolved (either 'struck off' or 'liquidated') and removed from the companies register at Companies House.

its profits are used. Co-operative organisations range from multi-billion pound businesses to small community enterprises and offer a wide range of products and services, including healthcare, housing, renewable energy, retail products, sports and social care.

4.2 Public sector organisations

The public sector is the part of the economy that is controlled by the government. Organisations in this sector are mostly financed by using the taxes people pay to the government. The government uses this money to provide essential public services for citizens.

Central and local government

To provide essential services, the public sector is split into two distinct parts – central government and local government. Central government (e.g. Parliament in London) provides nationwide services such as police, defence, healthcare, prisons, roads and social security. Local government (e.g. local borough councils), provides services for their local community such as social services, council housing, refuse and recycling collections, primary and secondary education and parks and recreational services. Some services are free (e.g. schools) and some are provided with a charge (e.g. fees to use leisure facilities such as a public swimming pool).

In contrast to the private sector, these organisations are run without the intention of generating a profit. However, some public sector organisations – public corporations and municipal enterprises – more closely resemble private sector organisations.

Public corporations

Companies owned by central government are known as public corporations. A chairperson and board of directors are appointed by a government minister to run the company on behalf of the government. An example of this is the BBC in the UK, whose board and chairperson are appointed by the Secretary of State. The organisation is financed through grants from the government and from raising finance through charging the general public a fee for a TV licence.

Municipal enterprises

These are businesses owned and operated by local government for the purposes of generating revenue. Examples include running the car park of a local hospital where visitors are required to pay to park or running a local community theatre and charging visitors for its services, such as ticket fees for events and use of theatre facilities such as the theatre bar/café or for hiring the venue.

Significant advantages of this type of enterprise is that it creates jobs and provides services for local communities without having to rely on funds generated from taxes to run the enterprise. They can offer lower rates for services than a private sector equivalent might as they are run for the benefit of shareholders. However, the idea of local government running a business that is usually regarded as a private sector enterprise is controversial. Critics have argued that money generated from taxes should not be used to provide the capital to start these enterprises and cast doubt over whether local governments possess the skills to run them effectively and economically.

4.3 Voluntary organisations

The purpose of voluntary organisations is to help a particular cause and benefit and enrich society. They are often set up without profit as a motive and instead of returning any profits made to its owners, any money raised or earned is usually invested back into the community or the organisation itself. Unlike public sector organisations, voluntary organisations are independent of government and are often referred to as non-governmental organisations (NGOs).

These organisations can have a mix of paid and volunteer staff (e.g. most charities) or be composed entirely of volunteers (e.g. a community group). Their defining characteristic is their voluntary nature, whether in governance through a trustee board, in finance through donations and grants or in resources through the help of volunteers.

Examples of voluntary sector organisations include:

◆ Charities: Red Cross, RSPCA, Samaritans

◆ Foundations: David Suzuki Foundation, Bill and Melinda Gates Foundation

◆ Advocacy groups: Privacy International, World Wildlife Fund

◆ Faith-based organisations: churches, mosques, temples

◆ Community groups: Neighbourhood Watch

◆ Recreational sports: running clubs, tennis clubs.

These organisations are not owned by any individual people, but someone (e.g. an individual or a board of trustees) is responsible for ensuring that the organisation sets targets and budgets and does what it is set up to do. In order to survive they normally must at least **break even** (i.e. spending no more than they are taking in through fundraising, grants and donations). Legal forms of voluntary organisations can include charitable companies, Charitable Incorporated Organisations (CIOs) and Community Interest Companies (CICs).

break even (or breaking even)
The point at which income is equal to costs and the business is making neither a profit nor a loss. Spending no more than you are taking in.

5 Organisational objectives

All business organisations pursue different objectives for different reasons; these can change over time as the organisation changes and evolves. The objectives an organisation pursues is also dependent on a number of factors, including the business sector the organisation operates in, its legal structure and the goals of the stakeholders involved.

5.1 Sector differences

Organisational objectives vary between business sectors. In the private sector, for example, a new sole trader may be focused on **breaking even** and establishing its place in the market to survive and keep the business going. However, a larger, more established, private sector organisation may be interested in generating large profits for shareholders or pursuing growth to dominate the market. In contrast, a voluntary sector organisation such as a charity is motivated to generate revenue to fund projects that meet its charitable purposes. For example, by providing facilities for the local community to play tennis, netball and football, a local sports charity might be fulfilling its charitable purpose to advance amateur sport for the public benefit.

5.2 Influence of legal structure

The legal structure of an organisation also has an influence over the types of objectives it can pursue as some objectives may be incompatible with its legal structure.

For example, a co-operative business is set up as its members wish to create a business that embeds social goals such as job creation, co-operation and democracy into its day-to-day activities. If the organisation pursued an objective of maximising profits, this would be in direct conflict with its legal structure; to maximise profits, it needs to minimise costs and one way to cut costs is by creating job losses.

5.3 Influence of stakeholder goals

Objectives are also influenced by the goals of different stakeholders in organisations. For example, in a public limited company where ownership is separated from control, the goals of the owners (shareholders) may differ from those of the directors responsible for the operational management of the business. Shareholders may have the goal of maximising profits to get the best return on their investment, whereas the directors may be pursuing their own individual goals such as increased personal rewards or enhancing their career status. This conflict between the goals of directors and shareholders could result in differences of opinion over priorities and objectives for the organisation, adversely affecting the success of the company if the conflict is poorly managed. Stakeholders will be covered in more detail in Chapter 2.

6 Vision, mission and values

Being able to communicate to your wider stakeholders why the organisation is doing what it's doing (its mission), where it's trying to go (its vision), and how it's going to go about it (its values) is an important step in strategically planning how the organisation is going to achieve its objectives.

Developing and communicating statements to tell stakeholders what the business is about and what it hopes to achieve serve a variety of purposes, some of which are explored below.

6.1 Mission statement

A mission statement is designed to communicate how an organisation plans on achieving its objectives. It is very much focused on the present – what the organisation is doing, how it's going to do it and why it's doing it.

Large organisations often spend a lot of money and effort creating an effective mission statement, which can involve hiring external consultants to help managers develop just the right statement to describe the mission of the business.

6.2 Vision statement

A vision statement is designed to communicate where an organisation wants or aspires to be in the future. An effective vision statement does not focus on the current state of the organisation but articulates a realistic vision of the organisation's mid- to long-term goals. The language used in vision statements is often inspirational in nature and may set out an organisation's plans for the future in terms of blocks of time (e.g. where it wants to be in three, five and ten years' time).

6.3 Potential uses of vision and mission statements

Mission and vision statements can be used for different purposes, both inside and outside of an organisation.

Inside of the organisation by:

◆ assisting senior management in the development of strategic plans

◆ developing performance measures, also known as Key Performance Indicators (KPIs)

◆ motivating and focusing employees by providing common goals

◆ assisting the development of an ethical framework.

Outside the organisation by:

◆ encouraging support from third parties (e.g. generating funding and endorsements)

◆ creating closer links to, and better communication with, customers, suppliers and other external stakeholders

◆ serving as an effective public relations tool.

Test Yourself 1.1

What is the difference between mission and vision statements?

6.4 Core values statement

A companion statement to accompany vision and mission is a core values statement. This statement declares how the organisation will behave during the process of realising its mission and vision. It articulates the principles and values the leaders will follow when carrying out the activities of the organisation.

7 Organisational structures

Understanding what the organisation wants to achieve is only part of the puzzle. It also needs to be structured in a way that will best enable it to achieve those objectives.

hierarchy
Another term for chain of command.

In its simplest definition, an organisational structure should set out the **hierarchy** within an organisation, define each job role and how each role fits into the work of the whole organisation. It outlines how roles in the organisation are delegated, controlled and coordinated. The internal structure of an organisation can be represented visually through an organisational chart or diagram which also illustrates how information and work flows through the business. Understanding the shape of an organisation can help management to make more effective decisions on how to change or adapt the organisation to achieve its objectives and business goals.

7.1 Structuring the workforce

The best structure for an organisation is very much dependent on the type of business and how complex its operations are. Each of the common types of organisational structure has its advantages and disadvantages and, as we shall examine, the choice of structure has wide-ranging implications for the success of the business, from efficiency of operations to culture and future growth.

The first things to examine when looking at organisational structure are the layers of management required and where the authority for key decision making is concentrated within the organisation.

7.2 Layers of management – tall versus flat hierarchies

Organisations are divided horizontally and vertically. Vertical divisions are the layers of management and horizontal divisions manifest as departments. How those divisions are structured themselves will differ according to the business needs of the organisation.

There are many layers of management in the hierarchy of a tall structure, usually with a chief executive officer (CEO) at the top making decisions and then delegating authority to lower-level managers. Tasks are easily designated in this structure as employees and departments have well-defined responsibilities. However, an efficient tall structure depends on strong leadership at the top. If leadership at the top is weak, poor decision making can ripple down through the organisation, which can lead to low staff morale, poor productivity and inefficiency.

In contrast, a flat structure has fewer layers of management and day-to-day operational decisions may be delegated to higher-level managers who interact with employees directly. Higher-level managers have more control over their area of operations, are given more authority over decisions and are more empowered to make decisions than their counterparts in tall structure organisations.

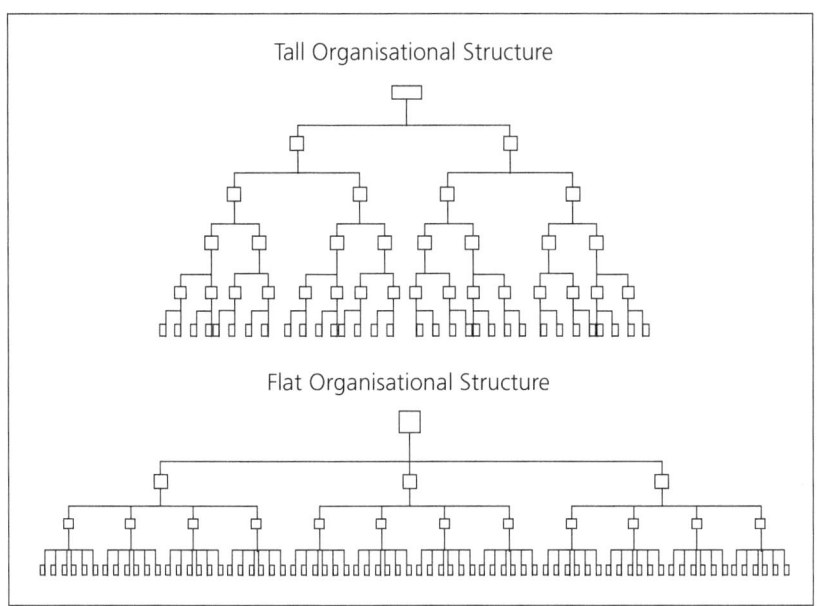

Figure 1.1 Tall versus flat organisational structure

Flat structures often have higher employee morale than tall structures as employees are more in control over everyday decisions There are also fewer layers of management to go through to get to the ultimate decision maker, resulting in a faster response to issues, which can be ideal for customer-facing organisations such as shops and hotels.

Flat structures also cost less to run than tall structures as there are fewer management salaries to pay for, but there are limited opportunities for promotion as there are fewer levels available to climb in the organisation. Flat structures are more transparent, as information can get more muddled the more layers it has to get through, but employee roles and responsibilities may also be less well-defined, which can make it difficult to delegate tasks. It can also be a difficult structure to maintain if an organisation grows and needs more centralised control over its operations.

7.3 Authority for decision making

In a **centralised structure**, authority for key decisions rests with the senior management at the centre of the business who then delegates authority to implement these decisions to middle- and lower-level managers in the **chain of command**. In a **decentralised structure**, however, power is distributed away from the centre of the business. Authority for key decision making is delegated across a larger group, including managers, lower down the chain of command as well as individual business units or trading locations.

centralised structure
Authority for decision-making rests with the senior management in this structure.

chain of command
This defines who reports to whom in an unbroken line from the very top of the organisation (senior management) to the bottom (operations).

decentralised structure
Authority for decision making is distributed across a larger group within the organisation. For example, day-to-day operational decisions may be delegated to middle and lower-level managers, leaving only major decisions to the remit of senior management.

Organisations such as the military or large, multi national businesses with global brands such as McDonalds and Burger King operate with a centralised structure and well-defined chain of command. Key decisions are mostly made by senior management at the top of the hierarchy and disseminated to the rest of the organisation. This structure is useful for large organisations which need to retain control and maintain consistency across areas such as operations, customer experience and quality as standard policies and practices can be decided at the top and implemented throughout the rest of the organisation. It is easier to show strong leadership in this type of structure. Decision making is able to happen quickly (particularly in times of crisis) as the authority rests in one place – with the senior management team. Communication and reporting is easier as all the information is stored in one place and it is easier to coordinate and control aspects of the business if they are kept centralised (e.g. budgets and financial decision-making). Maintaining control is particularly important in businesses run by a single individual/owner as this individual is able to control everything that is going on within the business.

However, having a centralised structure can be more bureaucratic, less flexible when responding to local customer needs (as decisions are made centrally rather than locally) and demotivating for managers lower down in the hierarchy who have less control over decisions that affect their teams and projects. While there would inevitably be a certain amount of minor, decentralised decision making in organisations operating in different locations, the amount of control and flexibility managers have over these decisions would be minimal when compared to the powers of managers in a decentralised structure.

Hotel chains and large supermarket chains (e.g. Sainsbury's or Tesco) often operate with a decentralised structure. Each individual trading unit has a hotel/store manager who has the authority to make decisions about areas that directly affect the business, such as staffing and sales promotions. Decisions can be made with the local market in mind. This promotes good customer service as the manager has the power to make quick decisions to resolve customer problems and complaints without having to contact a central team for a decision. Being given the authority to make such decisions is more empowering for managers lower down in the organisational hierarchy. It is also more motivating for staff as there are more opportunities for development and decisions can be made that are directly relevant to their location rather than disseminated down from a 'faceless' central hub that may not fully understand the needs of that location or its customers.

function
The main departments of a business (e.g. finance, human resources, sales, operations).

Having more autonomous business units in a decentralised structure reduces bureaucracy as individual units are more self-sufficient, but costs can be increased as some **functions** are duplicated throughout the different locations. Decision making may benefit the local market, but the thinking behind the decisions made by individual managers may not be strategic, with less attention paid to the overall impact the decision may have on the wider organisation. As standardised policies and procedures are less likely to be implemented in a decentralised structure, quality across different locations may vary. This may prove detrimental in businesses that rely on customer service (e.g. hotels) as customers may prefer consistency between different trading locations. It is also harder for senior management to retain a tight control over the business as decisions are being made away from the centre. This can mean areas such as financial control can be harder to maintain and could result in issues such as spiralling costs.

7.4 Creating a structure to meet business needs

Deciding on how many layers of management and where the authority for decision making lies in the organisation is just the beginning when it comes to strategically planning to achieve objectives. Organisations also need to ensure that they are structured in the best way to help meet their business needs. Below we examine three ways organisations can do this, through organising themselves by their functions, divisions or by combining the two into a matrix structure.

Functional structure

A functional structure involves dividing an organisation into smaller groups or departments based on the specialised function they perform (e.g. IT, finance, marketing and human resources (see Figure 1.2)). Each functional unit has its own priorities and objects and reports directly, usually via the departmental head, to senior management. It is then the responsibility of senior management to coordinate the activities of each functional area to ensure the organisation works as a cohesive whole to achieve its overall business purposes.

This type of structure works for small companies and start-ups and in larger companies which concentrate on a single product or service. It is ideal in situations where the external business environment is stable and not prone to rapid changes that would involve the organisation responding with a change in business strategy. A functional structure promotes efficiency and cost-effectiveness as all employees with similar, specialised knowledge are grouped together in one place.

However, this type of structure can be more bureaucratic with complicated communication and decision-making processes, leading to less flexibility and innovation. While a functional area may have efficient and expedient internal operational and decision-making processes, these are usually slower and less efficient between functional areas, resulting in difficulties when co-ordinating cross-departmental projects as each area is not accountable to other functional areas, just itself and senior management. A functional structure can therefore result in **silos**, with departments unwilling to share information, duplicating work and working to different priorities. A lack of transparency between departments and lack of collaboration and challenge on projects can lead to poor decision making and a tendency towards **groupthink**. Constructive challenge is an important part of good governance in an organisation; groupthink can therefore be a barrier to good governance practices.

silo effect
Members of a discrete department communicate and collaborate efficiently within their group but have limited interaction with other departments.

groupthink
A psychological phenomenon that can occur when the desire for harmony, conformity and consensus within a group results in irrational or dysfunctional decision-making processes (e.g. suppressing dissenting opinion, not allowing group members to constructively challenge decisions or propose alternatives and isolating themselves from outside opinion).

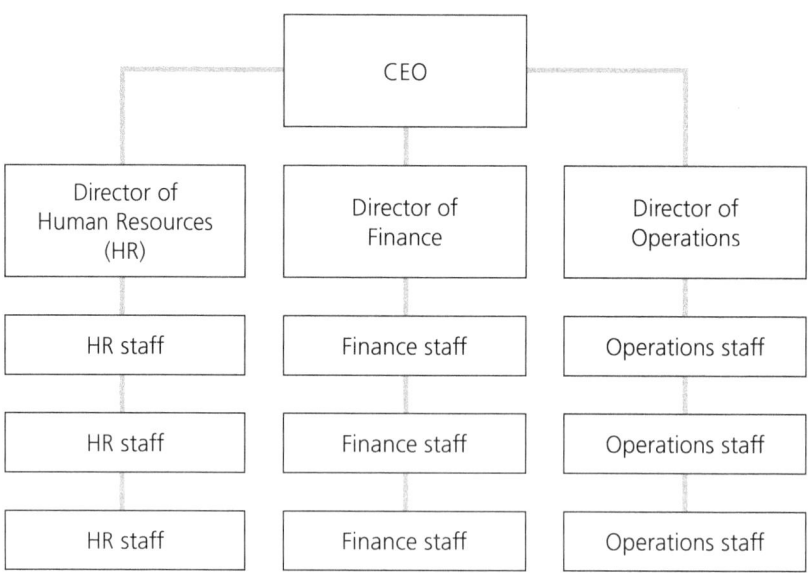

Figure 1.2 Functional organisational structure

Divisional structure

Organisations with a divisional structure are usually large and dynamic, operating over a wide geographical area and often with more than one product line or service. They typically consist of smaller organisations (divisions) under an umbrella or 'parent' group (see Figure 1.3). Each division is a discrete

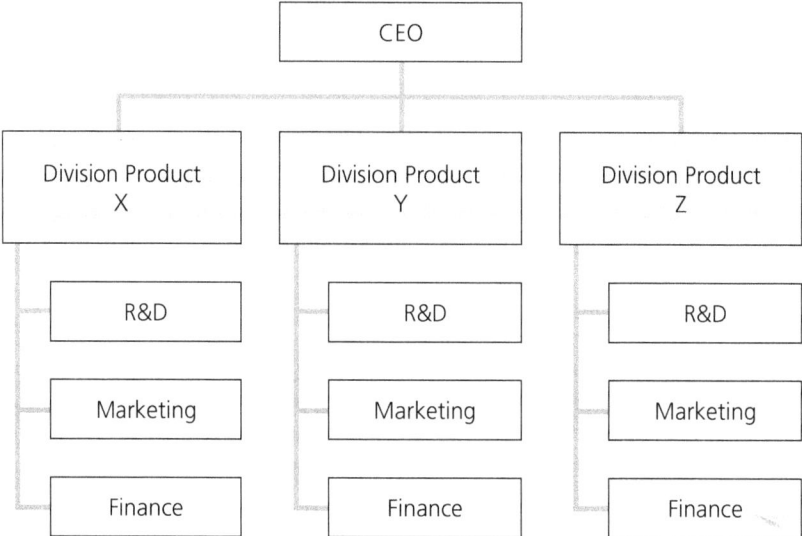

Figure 1.3 Divisional organisational structure

operating unit with its own complete set of departmental functions – IT, HR, finance, marketing, etc. For example, Virgin Holidays and Virgin Mobile are all subdivisions of the Virgin Group and all subdivisions operate as separate businesses. Each division is usually led by a general manager or division chief who has autonomy for the division and is responsible for its day-to-day activities. The general manager/division chief reports directly to the top management of the umbrella group and is accountable for the performance of their division. This structure is ideal for rapidly responding to local business needs and is more flexible for a changing external business environment. Staff can concentrate on the product line or service provided by their division with a management structure that supports their organisational objectives. However, a divisional structure can be costly as resources (IT, HR, marketing, etc.) are duplicated.

Effective senior leadership is crucial in a divisional structure. Senior management needs to fully understand what each division is doing and provide effective guidance to general managers/division chiefs on how to implement new strategies and partner across divisions. Senior leaders also need to make strategic decisions on allocating resources across divisions to prevent office politics being the basis of decisions, resulting in one division undermining another.

Matrix structure

In a matrix structure, products are managed horizontally and functions are managed vertically, with each product line having its own functions (e.g. finance, sales, marketing). Therefore, employees usually report to both the project/product manager and head of their function (see Figure 1.4).

This type of structure helps to minimise the likelihood of a silo effect developing across teams, as often seen in organisations with a functional structure. It is more dynamic than a functional organisational structure, with fewer barriers to communication between teams. Employees also have more opportunities to

	Marketing	Operations	Finance	HRM
	Marketing Manager	*Operations Manager*	*Finance Manager*	*HR Manager*
Project A (Team Leader)	Marketing Team (A)	Operations Team (A)	Finance Team (A)	HR Team (A)
Project B (Team Leader)	Marketing Team (B)	Operations Team (B)	Finance Team (B)	HR Team (B)
Project C (Team Leader)	Marketing Team (C)	Operations Team (C)	Finance Team (C)	HR Team (C)
Project D (Team Leader)	Marketing Team (D)	Operations Team (D)	Finance Team (D)	HR Team (D)

Figure 1.4 Matrix organisational structure

increase their specialised knowledge working on different projects across the matrix and the organisation can maximise efficiency of delivery of projects by selecting the most capable employees to work on them. Duplicating functions in every geographical location the organisation is based offers more flexibility in terms of meeting local customer needs, meaning the organisation can reach a wider audience and operate on a global level.

A major disadvantage of a matrix structure is its complexity in terms of chain of command. The manager-to-employee ratio is usually higher in a matrix structure and having more than one manager to report to can result in a conflict of employee loyalties and difficulties in deciding how to prioritise work. Having blurred lines of authority can also mean that decision making can be slower, particularly where managers in different parts of the matrix disagree, resulting in a deadlock and difficulties when it comes to conflict resolution.

The complexity of the matrix structure benefits large organisations with a complex operational structure (e.g. an organisation offering multiple products or taking on different projects across different geographical locations that requires a lot of cross-department communication and interaction). It is also a very costly structure to implement due to duplicated functions across the structure. Smaller companies with a simpler operational structure would not benefit from implementing a matrix structure due to its complexity and cost. Senior management also need to have a good understanding of the organisation's structure to allocate resources efficiently across the matrix. Poor resource allocation can lead to slowing down of processes and difficulties in delivering projects to time and on budget.

Stop and Think 1.2

How is your organisation structured? Draw a chart that visually represents how your organisation is structured. From this diagram, can you identify:

◆ **If it is a tall or flat structure?**

◆ **If decision-making is centralised or decentralised?**

◆ **If it is divided by functions, divisions?**

8 Managing an organisation – the board of directors

Many organisations are managed by a board of directors, often appointed or elected by the shareholders to run the business on their behalf. Organisational success depends on effective decision making and responsibility for high-level decision making in organisations rests with the board of directors. The size and composition of a board will vary between different types and sizes of organisation and approaches to how a board should be structured or function differs between countries. This means that there is no single agreed approach to how a board should be formed and who should serve on it.

To prevent the risk of power and information being concentrated in one or a few individuals, boards need to have a balance of different members. This is to ensure that matters and issues are discussed and examined from a variety of perspectives leading to more effective decision making that will benefit the organisation and its stakeholders.

For the purpose of this section, we will focus on examining the most common boardroom roles and their function.

8.1 Board roles

In a large public company in the UK, the board typically consists of:

- a chairperson
- possibly a deputy chairperson
- a chief executive officer (CEO)
- executive directors
- non-executive directors (NEDs)
- a senior independent director (SID) (who often acts as deputy chairperson).

Other types of organisation will have a mixture of these roles depending on their size and decision-making needs. We will examine the function of each of these roles below.

8.2 The chair

The chair leads the board and is responsible for ensuring its effectiveness as a decision-making group. The chair sets the agenda for board meetings and acts as a liaison between the shareholders and the board, ensuring that shareholders are kept informed of board decisions and that the board are aware of shareholder concerns. The role can be fulfilled by a non-executive or executive director.

8.3 The chief executive officer

The CEO is ultimately responsible for the day-to-day running of the organisation. The CEO leads the development and execution of the organisation's long-term strategy and is responsible for implementing short- and long-term plans created to help fulfil that strategy. The CEO acts as a liaison between the board and management team and communicates on behalf of the company to shareholders, staff, other stakeholders and the general public.

8.4 The importance of separating the role of chair and chief executive

It is good practice to have different individuals fulfilling the roles of chair and CEO on the board. If one individual occupies both roles, it increases the chances of this one individual dominating the board. This can diminish the objectivity of board discussions and make it more difficult for other board members to provide constructive challenge during discussions, leading to poor and ineffective decision making that may negatively impact the organisation and its stakeholders.

8.5 Executive directors

Executive directors are full-time employees and usually work for the organisation in a senior capacity, often being responsible for functional areas of the business such as finance or marketing (e.g. the chief financial officer (CFO) or head of marketing) or for areas of strategic importance, such as the director of policy. They are often the highest earners in the organisation. Other executive directors may be representatives of, for example, an institutional investor or a union. Many executive directors also choose to pursue non-executive director roles on boards in other organisations.

8.6 Non-executive directors

Non-executive directors (NEDs) act as independent advisors to board. They are not part of the executive management team and are not employed by the organisation (they may however, be paid a flat fee for their services similar to a consultant) or involved in its day-to-day activities. To remain objective, they should not be affiliated with the organisation in any way or have a financial stake in its success or failure. They are usually chosen on the basis of their independence, impartiality, wide experience, specialist knowledge and the personal qualities they can bring to the mix of board members. NEDs are appointed to provide a balancing influence and help to minimise conflicts of interest.

A NED's primary function is to improve the effectiveness of the board by providing objective challenge and criticism in board meetings. A board filled with directors who have a direct personal stake in the organisation would not always be objective, leading to bias in their decision making, so it is important to have objective viewpoints to help the board understand matters and issues from a variety of perspectives. They should not get involved in the day-to-day running of the organisation and should focus solely on board matters, as well as acting as mentor to the chairperson and CEO, providing advice and guidance when issues arise. NEDs also serve on the board's committees (e.g. helping to make decisions on directors' pay and benefits packages on the remuneration committee).

While there are differing opinions over the number of NEDs a board should have, it is generally accepted that one-third to one-half of a board's directors should be a non-executive.

8.7 The senior independent director

In larger, publicly listed organisations, the board often appoints a senior independent director (SID) from among their independent non-executives.

The role of the SID is to:

- provide support for the chairperson, acting as a sounding board where appropriate
- act as an intermediary for other directors if and where necessary
- be an alternative point of contact for investors who feel that their concerns have not been adequately addressed via the chairperson, CEO or finance director
- meet at least annually with other non-executives (without the chairperson) to appraise the chairperson's performance
- meet with major shareholders regularly to gain an understanding of their issues and concerns
- intervene and act as a mediator between the chairperson and CEO if a serious disagreement or dispute occurs.

8.8 Board size and composition

It is important to balance the board, having the right mix of skills and abilities, plus an appropriate level of objective challenge. Unfortunately, there isn't a magic formula for defining board-size and composition, although company law in some jurisdictions specifies a minimum and/or maximum number of directors for different types of organisation. In the UK, for instance, the Financial Reporting Council (FRC) advises that the board 'should be of sufficient size that the requirements of the business can be met' and there should be a 50% split of executive and non-executive directors to ensure that one group does not dominate board discussions and decisions. In general, large organisations (such as Tesco plc or Swire Pacific Ltd) have more than ten board members and smaller organisations less than ten (typically six to eight).

Stop and Think 1.3

How many board members do you think it takes to make decision making effective in an organisation? Does having larger numbers of board members necessarily mean board decisions are faster and more effective?

Have a look at some studies on board effectiveness to see how the size of a board can affect discussions and decision-making.

8.9 Board structures

In an organisation with a one-tier or unitary board, day-to-day business is delegated by the board to the CEO and senior management team who run the business on behalf of the owners (usually the shareholders). The board itself comprises both executive and non-executive members and the board makes decisions as one unitary group. This model is popular in the UK, USA, Australia and South Africa.

In other countries, a two-tier, or dual board system is preferred. This system separates those responsible for supervision from those responsible for operations (the executive board). The supervisory board (usually consisting of NEDs representing the shareholders) oversees the executive board. This board structure can be seen in many countries in continental Europe.

Case example 1.1 – Volkswagen emissions scandal

German carmaker Volkswagen became engulfed in its worst scandal since the organisation began more than 80 years ago. In the pursuit of an objective to grow to become the largest car manufacturer in the world, it admitted to manipulating emissions test data on its diesel vehicles in the US and Europe. The vehicles were marketed as more environmentally friendly than they actually were when it was revealed that the cars were emitting as much nitrous oxide as an articulated lorry. The emissions resulted in the deaths of nearly 50 people in the US.

The board of directors followed a two-tier structure with major shareholders represented on its supervisory board who were paid for their input, meaning they were not independent. As Hans-Christoph Hirt, a director of Hermes Equity Ownership Services and adviser to pension fund investors in companies including VW commented, 'VW's supervisory board is short of people with relevant experience and skills and – significantly – independence'. Also, the appointment of a long-standing executive to the role of chairman created, as Mr Hirt commented, a 'serious conflict of interest'.

Worth €80 billion before the scandal, VW suffered a loss of €25 billion to its share stock overnight. Whilst €16 billion has since been recovered (as of July 2017), the company is still worth €13 billion less than in its pre-scandal days.

A two-tier board structure with plenty of subject expertise, but a lack of independence, created a culture where challenge of ideas was less likely to happen. This led to a strategy that resulted in loss of life, as well as massive losses to the company and its reputation. Whilst unitary and two-tier boards each have their advantages and disadvantages, it's the composition and balance of the types of members on the board(s) and the creation of a culture of constructive challenge that are key elements to creating effective strategies that achieve organisational objectives.

Sources: www.ft.com/content/e816cf86-6815-11e5-a57f-21b88f7d973f and ICSA Annual Conference session 'VW Case Study: A Moral Failure' by John Armour, Hogan Lovells Professor of Law and Finance, Oxford University (July 2017)

Test Yourself 1.2

1 **Why is it important that the chairperson and chief executive roles are fulfilled by separate individuals?**

2 **What are the benefits of having non-executive directors on the board?**

3. **What is the difference between a unitary and a two-tier board structure?**

Chapter summary

◆ Economic activity in a nation is categorised in a continuum that represents increasing distance of raw materials from the earth. The main sectors are called the primary (extractive industries), secondary (manufacturing goods from raw materials) and tertiary (providing services) sectors.

◆ Organisations are categorised in terms of size according to the number of staff employed and often according to their turnover. The criteria differs between countries, but as a general rule, these are categorised into <10 employees (micro), <50 employees (small) and <250 employees (medium) and >250 (large).

◆ Private sector organisations are owned and run by private individuals with any profit made accruing to the owner(s). The financial liability of individual owners differs according to the legal structure chosen for the organisation.

◆ Public sector organisations are controlled by the government and are mostly funded by money collected from taxes to provide essential services such as roads, schools, hospitals and waste disposal services.

◆ Voluntary organisations are set up to help a particular cause, are independent of government and are often set up without profit as a motive.

◆ The objectives an organisation pursues are dependent on a number of factors including business sector, legal structure and influence of stakeholder goals.

◆ Organisations need to understand what they are doing (their mission), where they are trying to go (their vision) and how they are going about it (their values).

◆ While there is no one best way to structure the workforce, there are a variety of different structures organisations can implement to help them achieve their objectives and meet their business needs. This can mean dividing the organisation by its functions, divisions or a combination of the two (matrix structure).

◆ Organisations are managed by a board of directors, often appointed or elected by the shareholders to run the business on their behalf. To be effective, boards need to have a balance of different members and can be structured in more than one way, with a one-tier or two-tier approach being the most common.

Chapter two
The wider organisational context

Contents

1. Introduction
2. Stakeholders
3. Analysing the business environment

1 Introduction

Chapter 1 looked at how organisations might structure themselves to achieve their strategic objectives and purposes. This chapter delves into the wider issues that organisations need to consider when trying to achieve those objectives. This includes the influence of different types of stakeholder and the effects of the external environment on the organisation.

2 Stakeholders

Stakeholders are individuals, groups or organisations that have an interest or 'stake' in a business. They are affected by the activities and policies of a business and, in turn, can influence decision making within the business. Stakeholders are often grouped and defined according to their perceived proximity to the business (known as internal or external stakeholders) or by their connection to it (primary and secondary stakeholders).

2.1 Internal stakeholders

Internal stakeholders are individuals or groups within a business (e.g. owners, employees and shareholders). They actively participate in the management of the business and are directly affected by its activities. For example:

shareholders
The owners of a business. They are individuals, groups or a business that legally own one or more shares of stock in a business.

◆ **shareholders** invest money in the business and are directly affected by how much profit it makes

◆ workers/employees invest their labour in the business and are impacted by decisions that affect their salaries and job security.

2.2 External stakeholders

External stakeholders are individuals or groups outside of the business and even though they are not employed by the business, they are still affected by its activities. It is useful to note that while internal stakeholders are aware of and involved in internal matters of the business, external stakeholders will not be. Some examples of external stakeholders and their interest in the business or influence on it are as follows.

Customers

Whether it's consumers buying products/services from the business or another business buying products/services for business use, the provision of quality products and services at reasonable prices is the primary concern of most customers. Effective management of customer expectations is crucial to the financial success of a business and careful thought should be made to the impact of business decisions on attracting and retaining customers.

Suppliers

Suppliers have an interest in the financial success of a business as they expect to be paid what they are owed and want the business to keep buying their products or services.

Creditors

Creditors provide a source of finance for business ventures. This could involve banks or mortgage lenders providing capital for the business to buy a new factory, or a supplier providing products on account for the business to sell. These stakeholders have a financial interest in the performance of the business as poor decision making or other activities (e.g. excessive borrowing) may result in the capital they have lent to the business not being paid back on schedule or in some circumstances, not at all.

Debtors

Debtors are individuals or other businesses who owe money to the business (e.g. if they have bought products on account from the business). Ineffective management of collection of monies owed by debtors on schedule could have a serious impact on the financial success of the business

Government

Businesses must comply with government rules and regulations, such as paying taxes or applying for permits which will have cost implications for the business. Changes in government and government policy (e.g. increasing taxes) directly affect businesses by increasing costs and limiting investment opportunities.

Local and national communities

Communities often rely on the goods and services provided by large businesses and can be affected by decisions the business makes (e.g. utility companies providing a constant supply of gas, electricity or water or a rail organisation providing transport for commuters). Local communities also rely on businesses to provide jobs for members of their community.

Trade unions

Employees of a business may be members of a trade union. Trade unions will often attempt to develop working relationships with businesses to help protect (e.g. through representing members during a disciplinary action) and advance the interests (e.g. through negotiating higher salaries) of its members in the workplace.

Pressure groups

Pressure groups seek to secure the interests of their members and supporters in businesses by attempting to influence government policy through activities such as protests and demonstrations. Examples of pressure groups affecting businesses are trade unions, consumer rights groups and animal welfare groups.

Stop and Think 2.1

Who are the internal and external stakeholders in your business? How are they affected by your business's activities and what influence do they have over decision making?

2.3 Primary and secondary stakeholders

Stakeholders can also be grouped according to their interest in the business and its success. Primary stakeholders can be defined as anyone who has a functional or financial interest in the business (e.g. customers, employees, shareholders and suppliers). The primary responsibility of the business is towards these stakeholders as its actions have a direct impact on them.

Secondary stakeholders are those who have an influence on the business, but may not be directly involved in its day-to-day activities.

2.4 Stakeholder interests and conflicts

Stakeholder groups will have different interests and expectations and will be affected by the decisions made by a business in different ways. Stakeholders may have conflicting interests in the activities of a business which may result in the board having to compromise when making decisions to meet the needs of each stakeholder group. Examples of conflicting interests are:

◆ owners having an interest in generating high profits may be reluctant to pay employees high wages

◆ directors deciding to make the pursuit of higher sales a top priority over owners' wishes of generating higher profits

◆ making a business decision to move customer service operations overseas to reduce costs that may result in customers suffering if they receive a poorer service.

2.5 Stakeholder theory

Stakeholder theory suggests that a business should make decisions that consider and create value for all its key stakeholders and don't just satisfy the needs of its owners or shareholders. Key stakeholders may include, for example, customers, investors and employees.

The theory also considers the role of businesses in society and the responsibilities businesses have to society as a whole. Some businesses are so large and have such an influence on society that it could be argued that they should be accountable to their wider stakeholders for what they do. This part of stakeholder theory supports arguments in favour of **corporate social responsibility (CSR)**.

corporate social responsibility (CSR)
The measures taken by a business to assess and take responsibility for their effect on the environmental and social wellbeing of the wider society influenced by their activities.

Test Yourself 2.1

1. **What is the difference between internal and external stakeholders?**

2. **What is the difference between primary and secondary stakeholders?**

---

3 Analysing the business environment

The business environment is the context within which business takes place. Organisations need to understand both the internal and external factors that affect their own situation and activities to align their own capabilities and resources with that environment.

The external environment concerns factors outside of the organisation that may affect the way it operates (e.g. customers, companies, suppliers, competitors and partners). The internal environment concerns the factors inside the organisation (e.g. how it is structured and the resources it has available to carry out its activities).

The business environment changes continuously, so to remain relevant within their environment, organisations need to periodically analyse their situation within that environment.

3.1 Reasons for analysing the business environment

To be able to develop strategies to help achieve business purposes and objectives, organisations must have a thorough understanding of the context in which they operate. Therefore, by understanding their current product, market, opportunities and challenges, organisations can devise a clear path from their current situation to their desired position. In other words, effective **situational analysis** is crucial in helping organisations realise their vision by identifying factors that may impact on their current mission activities.

situational analysis
A collection of methods used to analyse an organisation's internal and external environment to understand its capabilities, potential customers, and factors that may influence or impact upon its activities.

Effective analysis enables organisations to develop the capacity to identify potential issues and anticipate changes that may affect their activities so they are able to respond accordingly. There are a variety of ways an organisation can analyse the business environment it is operating in and each method examines different factors that may influence the organisations and its activities.

Since the business environment changes constantly, organisations need to constantly analyse their environment to develop the capacity to identify potential issues and anticipate changes that may affect their activities and be able to respond accordingly.

3.2 Consequences of not understanding the external environment

Insufficient analysis of the internal and external business environment can have detrimental effects on an organisation and its survival. Not having an understanding of the context in which an organisation is operating can result in senior management developing and implementing unrealistic or inappropriate business strategies that cause issues such as a decline in profitability, loss of market share, reputational damage, a decreased level of sales or even causing the organisation to fail completely. Similarly, being slow to respond to issues identified in an analysis of the business environment, not developing an appropriate response, or failing to respond at all, can also cause an organisation to miss out on opportunities or eventually fail.

3.3 Types of situational analysis

Organisations need to gather useful information about their product and the market they sell it in, including its size, their competitors and the customers who purchase it. An effective situational analysis involves adopting a variety of different methods of analysis that give senior management a thorough understanding of the current business situation the organisation is in and where there is potential to change and grow.

This section covers two of the most common methods of situational analysis organisations used to understand the business environment:

◆   PESTEL and LoNGPESTEL used to understand an organisation's external environment.

◆   SWOT analysis used to understand the interconnection between an organisation's internal and external environment.

3.4 PEST/PESTEL analysis

While an organisation has some degree of control over its internal environment (e.g. how it structures its workforce and allocates resources to undertake its activities) it has very little control over its external environment. However, if the organisation regularly analyses the external factors that may impact on its operations, senior management can use this information to inform decision making, redirect resources and develop and implement strategies that allow the organisation to adapt accordingly.

To understand the external factors that will potentially influence its operations, the PEST or PESTEL framework is a useful tool to examine those factors. The purpose of this analysis is to identify the external political, economic, social/ sociocultural, technological, legal and environmental factors that might affect an organisation's operations. Examples of these factors are outlined below.

- **Political** factors look at the government regulations and legal issues affecting an organisation's activities that can only be changed by political parties. For example, tax policies, copyright and property law enforcement, political stability, trade regulations, social and environmental policy, employment laws and safety regulations. Everyone must abide by and work within these laws or face legal consequences. Organisations also need to be aware of potential shifts in the political landscape (e.g. a change of political party in power).

- **Economic** factors are anything that influence the economy (e.g. taxes, inflation rates, stock market trends, wage costs).

- **Sociocultural** factors mainly revolve around consumer behaviour and potential customers (e.g. buying trends, demographics, population growth rates, age distribution) Attitudes towards work and job market trends affect how consumers spend their money. As most organisations need customers, this part of the PESTEL analysis is extremely important when trying to understand the organisation's external environment.

- **Technological** factors consist of levels and advancements in technology. Changes that impact how organisations can use technology to sell products and communicate with consumers will be of particular interest in a PESTEL analysis and technological factors will be the most important factors to understand for IT-based organisations.

- **Environmental** (or ecological) factors look at issues such as climate change, weather patterns and ecological-friendliness of products. The leisure and tourism, forestry, and agriculture industries and any organisations whose business is often dependent on the weather are affected by these factors more than other industries. Bad weather can affect revenue and profits (e.g. large outdoor events being cancelled or experiencing low turnout due to poor weather).

- **Legal** factors often overlap with political factors, but these factors specifically affect how an organisation operates, facilitates business and handles product demands (e.g. obtaining a patent to ensure a competitor doesn't copy a product). Legal factors also include laws covering consumer protection, health and safety and data protection.

A PESTEL analysis does not take into account the geographical context in which the organisation operates. To do this, an organisation can extend its analysis to look at the PESTEL factors that may influence their business according to their geographical relevance – locally, nationally or globally. A LoNGPESTEL analysis gives organisations a deeper understanding of the PESTEL factors as it considers these influences at the geographical level at which they impact on an organisation. In this context therefore, geographical level is defined as:

◆ Local level – the organisation's home town, city or region.

◆ National level – the organisation's home country.

◆ Global level – any region beyond the local or national level.

Used in isolation however, a PEST/PESTEL/LoNGPESTEL analysis is limited as it doesn't consider the organisation's internal or competitive environments. The external environment can change extremely quickly so should be used in conjunction with other situational analysis tools to ensure that decisions being made are not based on tenuous assumptions derived from outdated information. To get the most value out this type of analysis, organisations can combine their findings with a SWOT analysis to gain an overall picture of the organisation and the environment it is operating in.

3.5 SWOT analysis

PESTEL and LoNGPESTEL analysis considers the impact of external factors in isolation of the current picture within an organisation. SWOT analysis, however, is taken from the perspective of the organisation by identifying sources of Opportunities and Threat (its external environment) and analysing the organisation's Strengths and Weaknesses (its internal environment).

This type of situational analysis can be used to examine the organisation's current and future situation to help plan strategies to help the organisation react effectively to changes in the business environment. By building on current strengths and reducing current weaknesses, organisations can develop the capability to respond to opportunities in the market, whilst reducing the impact that any threats within the market may have on the organisation, its activities and future success. An organisation has control over its strengths and weaknesses and, with work, can change them over time. However, as opportunities and threats are external, organisations have no control over them or the power to change them. For example:

◆ **Strengths** describe the positive attributes, tangible and intangible, internal to the organisation that are within its control.

◆ **Weaknesses** are aspects of the organisation that detract from the value it offers in the market or that place the organisation at a competitive disadvantage. Weaknesses need to be enhanced to compete effectively in the market.

◆ **Opportunities** are external attractive factors that represent reasons the organisation is likely to prosper.

◆ **Threats** are external factors beyond the organisation's control that could place its strategy, or the organisation itself, at risk. Even though the organisation has no control over these factors, it is beneficial to have contingency plans in place to address them should they occur.

Figure 2.1 A SWOT analysis template

Internal	**Strengths** *(internal, positive factors)* *List the organisation's…* ◆ Advantages over competitors ◆ Special expertise – what does the organisation do well? ◆ Cost advantages ◆ Reputation or unique selling point	**Weaknesses** *(internal, negative factors)* *List the organisation's…* ◆ Disadvantages ◆ Limitations ◆ Deficiencies ◆ Problems and issues (e.g. staff problems, poor management decisions)
External	**Opportunities** *(external, positive factors)* *Identify opportunities the organisation can take advantage of, for example:* ◆ New technology or services ◆ Lack of competition in the market ◆ New markets to enter ◆ Areas where the organisation can improve	**Threats** *(external, negative factors)* *Identify…* ◆ New or increased competition in the market ◆ Obstacles the organisation may face ◆ Changes in external factors that may influence operations (e.g. government policy, economy downturn)

Of course, these are just two of the myriad of analysis tools an organisation can use to understand their position in the market and the factors that might influence its success. Organisations should use a range of these tools to get a complete and accurate picture of their position within the environment in which they operate and use this information to ensure they are able to achieve their objectives.

Test Yourself 2.2

1 **What are the potential consequences to organisations of not completing a regular analysis of their situation?**

2 **What do PESTEL and SWOT stand for?**

Stop and Think 2.2

Have a go at completing a SWOT and PESTEL analysis of the organisation you work for. Based on your analysis, how would you change things to make your organisation more successful?

Chapter summary

◆ Stakeholders in organisations are typically classified as internal (owners, employees, shareholders) or external (individuals not involved in the organisation's activities but still affected by them).

◆ Stakeholder groups will have different interests and expectations and will be affected by the decisions made by a business in different ways. This may result in conflict depending on the interest of the individual stakeholder or stakeholder group.

◆ Organisations can better understand the business environment they operate in by regularly analysing the factors that may influence their activities and impact on their operations. Organisations should use a variety of methods of analysis (such as SWOT and PESTEL) to gain an informed understanding of the environment they are operating in and how they might adapt effectively to changes within it.

Part two

Introduction to law

Overview

Part Two of this text aims to provide you with an introduction to business law, including its purposes, administration and sources. To fully understand the law, it is vital that you also understand where laws come from, the different types of laws that exist (and how they interrelate) and how the law is administered and applied. It is also important to be able to identify which areas of the law are most applicable to businesses.

At the end of this part, you will be able to:

- Explain the purposes of business law;
- Understand the various different ways in which the law is classified;
- Understand how the law is administered, including demonstrating an understanding of the UK courts and tribunals structure, the role of ADR, and the persons who administer the law;

- Discuss the various sources of domestic and European law;
- Explain the key sources of company law and corporate governance recommendations; and
- Identify which legal subjects are most relevant to businesses.

Chapter three
Purposes and classification of the law

CONTENTS

1. Introduction
2. The purposes of business law
3. Classifying the law

1 Introduction

Much of your study will focus on understanding and applying individual laws that affect businesses. However, a full understanding of these laws can only come about if you understand the overall purposes behind these laws, how they fit into the legal system and the type of liability they create. Accordingly, this chapter will discuss the purposes of business law and the various different ways in which laws can be classified.

2 The purposes of business law

One of the difficulties involved in regulating businesses is the number of (sometimes competing) purposes that business law has. Here, the principal purposes are set out. How the law strives to achieve these purposes is discussed elsewhere in this text and in other units you will study.

2.1 Accountability

Perhaps the key purpose of business law is to ensure that businesses are held to account for their unlawful acts and omissions. As a result, a system of regulation has been devised to regulate business of all types which includes sole proprietorships, partnerships, limited liability partnerships and limited companies. Bearing this in mind, consider the following.

FTSE 100
The largest 100 companies
in the UK, as measured by
market capitalisation.

market capitalisation
A company's share price
multiplied by the number of
shares it has issued.

Case Example 3.1

At the time of writing, the largest company in the **FTSE 100** is Royal Dutch Shell plc, with a **market capitalisation** of over £210 billion. It operates in over 70 countries and has over 90,000 employees. In 2017, its global revenue was just over $305 billion, and it holds assets worth over $400 billion.

Businesses range from multinational giants like Royal Dutch Shell (and there are many companies significantly larger than Shell) to a single self-employed person with an annual turnover of hundreds of pounds. Holding such massive entities to account is a central challenge of business law.

2.2 Transparency

Linked to the notion of accountability is the need for transparency. From an accountability perspective, requiring businesses to disclose certain information has two notable benefits:

1. It enables regulators and stakeholders to hold businesses to account. A business cannot be held to account if it fully conducts its business in secret.

2. Businesses, knowing that they will be required to disclose certain information, will take steps to ensure that they are conducting themselves in a lawful and proper manner.

Of course, the effectiveness of transparency in attaining these goals will depend upon the accuracy of the information being disclosed. Unfortunately, there are numerous examples of businesses disclosing false or misleading information to avoid scrutiny (perhaps the most obvious example is Enron, which engaged in accounting practices designed to hide the fact that it was making significant losses). To discourage this, it is appropriate that business law imposes criminal liability on those who fail to disclose required information or disclose inaccurate or misleading information.

Transparency also helps stakeholders make decisions relating to the company. An obvious example is a company's annual accounts and reports, which will be used by numerous stakeholders (e.g. investors, when deciding to purchase shares; creditors when deciding to trade with the company; employees). However, it is important that disclosure does not become overly burdensome and onerous as it can impose unnecessary costs on the business and discourage stakeholders from engaging with the information.

Case Example 3.2

Between 2012 and 2017, the average length of a **FTSE 350** company's annual accounts and reports increased by 25% from 148 pages to 186 pages, with some reports being much longer (e.g. the 2015 Annual Reports and Accounts of HSBC Holdings plc were 502 pages long, although subsequent years' reports have been considerably shorter). It is likely that the significant length of such documents will discourage certain stakeholders from engaging with them fully, if at all.

FTSE 350
The largest 350 companies in the UK, as measured by market capitalisation.

2.3 Flexibility and autonomy

Accountability is undoubtedly a key purpose of the law, but the quest for accountability should not unduly prevent businesses from engaging in risk-taking activity that can benefit society. Laws must therefore exhibit a flexibility that allows businesses to react to new opportunities without undue restriction. Business law provides flexibility in two different ways. The first way is by providing businesses with a significant amount of autonomy. As Lord Devlin stated in *Kum v Wah Tat Bank Ltd* [1971] 1 Lloyd's Rep 439 (PC), '[t]he function of commercial law is to allow, so far as it can, commercial men to do business in the way they want to do it'. This principally arises via the use of contracts which, as noted at p 84, constitute a major source of business law and allow businesses to effectively draft the rules by which business transactions will be conducted. The courts will strive to give effect to the contractual rules that the parties have agreed upon and will not lightly cast them aside. However, especially in relation to laws affecting consumers, party autonomy is not absolute and statute does provide significant limitations on the use of certain contractual terms (e.g. exclusion and limitation clauses, which are regulated strongly by the Consumer Rights Act 2015 and the Unfair Contract Terms Act 1977).

The second way in which the law provides flexibility is by allowing businesses to draft certain rules by which their business is to be run. For example, although the Companies Act 2006 (CA 2006) is an extremely lengthy and detailed piece of legislation, it does not provide an exhaustive account of company law and says nothing regarding many areas of internal company regulation. Many internal rules by which a company is run (e.g. rules relating to appointment and remuneration of directors, rules relating to the conduct of board and general meetings) are a matter for the company's **articles of association**. Upon incorporation, companies are free to draft their own articles and so can determine their own internal rules. These articles can be amended at any time in order to respond to the needs of the company.

articles of association
The principal constitutional document of a company that sets out the company's internal rules.

2.4 Efficiency

When devising laws, Parliament and the courts should consider the cost and impact that the law will have upon the business. Laws that impose excessive costs or which unduly impede a company's ability to conduct business will be extremely unpopular and companies will try to avoid them. A law that is suitable for one type of business might detrimentally affect the efficiency of another. The following example demonstrates how the law recognises this.

Case Example 3.3

Y-Corp Ltd is a small, family-run business. The company has three directors who, between them, own all the shares in Y-Corp. Y-Corp's annual turnover is around £200,000 and it has four employees. Under the CA 2006, many standard company law requirements (e.g. holding general meetings, having audited accounts) would serve no purpose and may impose unnecessary costs on the company. Accordingly, the CA 2006 provides that certain types of company are excluded from certain company law requirements (e.g. private companies do not generally need to hold general meetings, small companies can prepare abridged accounts and need not have their accounts audited).

For larger companies that are listed, the 'comply or explain' approach adopted by the UK Corporate Governance Code (discussed at p 87) also enhances efficiency as companies can justify non-compliance with the Code if compliance would adversely and unduly affect their efficiency.

2.5   Certainty and predictability

In *Vallejo v Wheeler* (1774) 1 Cowp 143, Lord Mansfield stated '[i]n all mercantile transactions, the great objective should be certainty … ' However, the desire for certainty creates a tension in the law. Businesses want the law to be flexible, but it is also important that they can rely on it, so it needs to be certain and predictable. Laws that are certain can be inflexible and laws that are flexible can be broad and vague. Striking a balance between certainty and flexibility remains one of the great challenges of business law. It is important that business law is certain and predictable for several reasons:

- Businesses must be able to rely on the law and they cannot do this with confidence if it is unclear or uncertain.

- Laws must adapt and evolve, but they should not be amended excessively frequently nor changed without good cause. If the law is amended too frequently, there is a danger that businesses will struggle to stay up-to-date with the changes or that ensuring compliance with the ever-changing new laws will impose unacceptable costs upon the business.

- The application of business law should be predictable. This allows businesses to conduct themselves in a manner that does not breach the law, and so reduces the need to engage in costly litigation. If litigation does arise, clear and predictable law should allow for the dispute to be resolved more quickly and cheaply.

2.6 Acting in the business's interests

It is important that those who act on behalf of businesses act in the interests of the business. This is not a problem in a sole proprietorship as the sole proprietor and his business are one and the same. However, those who run other types of business may be tempted to run it in a way that is of benefit to themselves, not the business itself. This can be especially problematic in companies as these intermediaries (notably the directors) may seek to use the company to benefit themselves at the company's expense. The law's response to this is usually to require specified persons to act in the interests of the business (e.g. CA 2006 s. 172(1) requires directors to 'promote the success of the company for the benefit of its members as a whole').

2.7 Dispute resolution

As noted above, business law should try and minimise the need for costly litigation. However, disputes will arise, so it is important that the law provides an effective and efficient system of dispute resolution. In some cases, the parties themselves can determine how a dispute is to be resolved (e.g. by including a specific term in a contract). In other cases, litigation may be unavoidable, so the parties need access to a dispute resolution system that is quick and inexpensive. There are three systems for this:

1. The traditional dispute resolution mechanism is to commence legal proceedings in a court. This is the principal form of dispute resolution and is extremely important. However, cases involving businesses (especially complex commercial and corporate cases) can be extremely costly and lengthy.

2. A case could be taken to a tribunal (discussed at p 51).

3. The expense of legal proceedings has contributed, in part, to the increased importance of Alternative Dispute Resolution (ADR, discussed at p 52) in the business world. ADR mechanisms are seen as being more cost-effective forms of dispute resolution, especially if the disputing parties wish to continue to engage in business in the future.

2.8 Preventing disaster and failure

Business failure can have significant adverse impacts upon those who work for, and transact with, the business. If the business is large enough, it can even have local or national consequences. Accordingly, business law does try to prevent business failure in several ways:

◆ Businesses and their employees who act in an unlawful manner can cause significant amounts of damage (e.g. the unlawful actions of Nick Leeson caused the collapse of Barings Bank, one of the largest and most well-established banks in London). Business law seeks to prevent or minimise such occurrences by prohibiting certain conduct and by promoting good governance.

◆ In some cases, the law seeks to help failing businesses. For example, the Insolvency Act 1986 (IA 1986) provides a number of rescue mechanisms (e.g. administration, company voluntary arrangements) that are designed to try and help financially struggling companies survive and return to profitability.

Where business failure cannot be avoided, then the law should provide a system under which the affairs of the business can be efficiently concluded and its existence brought to an end.

Test Yourself 3.1

1. Identify the eight purposes of business law.

2. What are the benefits of requiring businesses to act in a transparent manner?

3. Why is it important that laws are certain and predictable?

4. What are the three main forms of dispute resolution?

3 Classifying the law

Different types of law can be classified in a number of different ways. Obviously, there are numerous legal subjects that are relevant for businesses (e.g. company law, commercial law, employment law etc.) and these are discussed in Chapter 7. Here, we are focusing on the five principal ways that the law can be classified.

3.1 Criminal law and civil law

civil law
Civil law can refer to (i) the body of law that pertains to civil wrongs (e.g. the law of torts, contract law) and do not impose criminal liability; or (ii) those legal systems that are largely based on Roman law.

criminal law
Criminal law refers to those laws that impose criminal liability on a person.

The distinction between **civil law** and **criminal law** is perhaps the most important classification of law. Acts that breach the law will either amount to a civil wrong or a criminal act (although it is possible for a single act or omission to breach both civil and criminal law). Criminal law and civil law have differing aims, procedural rules, and consequences (which are set out in Table 3.1) so it is important to understand the distinction between them.

The distinction between a civil wrong and a criminal act lies not in the act itself, but in the legal consequences that flow from the act. For example, if a person commits an unlawful act and the consequence of that act is that the person is sued and required to pay compensation, then the act will likely be a civil wrong. If the act results in its perpetrator being prosecuted and imprisoned, the act will be a criminal act.

Table 3.1 The differences between civil law and criminal law

	Civil law	Criminal law
Parties involved	The person who sustained the loss (the **claimant**) sues the person who caused the claimant's loss (the defendant).	The State (denoted by the letter '*R*', which is short for *Regina* (Queen) or *Rex* (King)) prosecutes the defendant for the alleged criminal act.
Usual first-instance courts	County Court or High Court.	Magistrates' court or Crown Court.
Burden of proof	The burden of proof is usually placed upon the claimant.	The burden of proof is usually placed upon the prosecution.
Standard of proof	The claimant must prove his case on the balance of probabilities.	The prosecution must prove the case beyond reasonable doubt.
Outcome	If the claimant's case succeeds, he will be awarded a remedy (e.g. compensation, injunction). If his case does not succeed, no remedy will be awarded.	The defendant is either guilty or not guilty. If guilty, the defendant will be punished (e.g. imprisoned and/or fined).

3.2 Common law and civil law

The phrase '**common law**' has three different meanings. Here, it is referring to those legal systems that have historically based their legal system on that of England (e.g. Australia, Canada and the USA). Common law legal systems tend to have a number of features:

- the bulk of the law is found in case law;
- the judiciary's principal role is to interpret law, but common-law judges also create law;
- common-law systems have a well-established system of precedent in place;
- members of the judiciary are normally recruited from the ranks of legal practitioners.

As noted in 3.1, the phrase 'civil law' is used in relation to laws that do not impose criminal liability. The phrase 'civil law' also has a second meaning and refers to those legal systems that are largely based on Roman law (e.g. Republic of Ireland and most Continental European countries). Such systems have converse features to common law systems, namely:

- the bulk of the law is found in a series of written documents known as 'codes';
- the judiciary's role is to interpret law in line with the relevant code, not to create law;

claimant
A person who commences a civil legal action.

common law
Common law can refer to (i) those legal systems that have based their legal system on that of England; (ii) the body of laws and decisions created by judges and applied via the doctrine of precedent; or (iii) the unified system of law that arose following the Norman Conquest and still exists today.

- civil law systems often place great weight on the decisions of senior judges, but tend not to have a system of binding precedent; and
- civil law systems tend to have a career judiciary where judges are trained straight from university.

3.3 Common law and statute law

The second meaning of 'common law' refers to the body of laws and decisions created by judges in decided cases and subsequently applied via the doctrine of precedent. The phrase '**statute law**' refers to laws created by Parliament, with such laws also being known as 'legislation'. Case law and statute law are discussed more in Chapter 8.

statute law
Laws created by Parliament.

3.4 Common law and equity

The third meaning of 'common law' refers to the system of law that emerged following the Norman Conquest and still exists today. To understand the phrase 'common law' in this context and how it differs from '**equity**', it is necessary to briefly look at how our legal system evolved.

equity
The supplementary system of law based on fairness and justice.

Prior to the Norman Conquest in 1066, each area of England had its own set of laws. In the 150 years following the Norman Conquest, the legal system in England underwent a process of unification with judges following a body of laws derived from Westminster. The people of England were, for the first time, all subject to a single body of law that was common to all (hence the 'common law'). Unfortunately, such a broad system soon came to be unwieldy and resulted in injustice in individual cases. At first, the law's response was to allow persons to petition the King directly for a remedy, but soon this function was delegated to the Lord Chancellor. These petitions to the Lord Chancellor were, unlike common law cases, not based upon following precedent and strict procedures, but were based upon fairness and justice in the individual case. Accordingly, this supplementary system of law became known as 'equity'.

injunction
A court order restraining an act or requiring an act to be performed.

Both the common law and equity still exist today (although there are no separate courts for each system, as used to be the case). In order to achieve fairness, equity developed new remedies, notably **injunctions** and **specific performance**. The two systems generally co-exist harmoniously, but tensions can arise and, in the event of a conflict between the common law and equity, equity prevails (Senior Courts Act 1981, s. 49(1)).

specific performance
A court order requiring performance of an act, normally to fulfil a contract.

3.5 Public law and private law

public law
Laws that regulate the relationship between the state and persons within the state.

Public law refers to laws that regulate the relationship between the state and persons within the state. Obvious examples of public law subjects would be human rights law (persons who have had their human rights breached may sue the state) and criminal law (the state prosecutes those who have committed crimes).

private law
Laws that regulate the relationship between persons (i.e. the state is usually not a party to the legal proceedings).

Private law refers to laws that regulate the relationships between people (i.e. the state is usually not a party to the legal proceedings). The vast majority of laws applicable to businesses are private laws and include company law (which

regulates the relationship between companies, directors, shareholders etc.),
contract law (which regulates the rights and obligations of contracting parties)
and employment law (which regulates the relationship between employers,
employees and workers).

Test Yourself 3.2

1. **Explain the three meanings of the phrase 'common law'.**

2. **Explain the two meanings of the phrase 'civil law'.**

3. **Explain the differences between civil law and criminal law.**

4. **Explain the difference between public law and private law and
    provide examples of each type of law.**

Chapter summary

◆ Business law seeks to hold businesses to account for their actions and
   also requires certain businesses (notably companies) to disclose significant
   amounts of information.

◆ Laws should be certain and predictable, but they should also be flexible.
   Striking a balance between flexibility and certainty is a significant challenge
   of business law.

◆ Civil law refers to acts that amount to civil wrongs and have civil
   consequences (e.g. the payment of compensation). Criminal law refers
   to acts that are crimes and result in a sentence being imposed (e.g.
   imprisonment).

◆ The phrase 'common law' can refer to (i) legal systems based on that of
   England; (ii) the body of laws created by judges; and (iii) the unified system
   of law that arose following the Norman Conquest.

◆ The phrase 'civil law' can refer to (i) legal wrongs that result in the
   imposition of civil remedies (e.g. compensation); and (ii) those legal systems
   based on Roman law.

◆ 'Equity' refers to the supplementary system of law that is based on
   achieving fairness and justice.

◆ Public law refers to laws that regulate the relationship between the state
   and persons within that state, whereas private law refers to laws that
   regulate the relationship between persons.

Chapter four
Administration of the law

CONTENTS

1. Introduction
2. The courts system
3. Tribunals
4. Alternative dispute resolution
5. The judiciary, the law officers, and the legal profession

1 Introduction

It is important to not only understand what the law states, but also how it is administered and enforced in practice. Accordingly, this chapter looks at the administration of UK law, including an examination of the UK court structure, the functions of tribunals, the role of alternative dispute resolution, and a discussion of some of the key personnel involved in the administration of the law.

2 The courts system

The courts are the most integral component in the administration of the law and it is vital that you understand the role of each court. Courts can have a first instance and/or appellate jurisdiction

first instance
The first time a case is heard by a court, it is said to be heard at first instance.

1. **Courts with a first instance jurisdiction**: when a case is first heard by a court, it is said to be 'heard at **first instance**'. Some courts (e.g. magistrates' courts) primarily hear first instance cases.

appeal
A challenge to a legal decision in a case (usually by the person who lost the case).

2. **Courts with an appellate jurisdiction**: the losing party in a case heard at first instance may have the right to apply to a higher court (or, in some cases, the same court) to seek to have the first-instance decision overturned. This is known as an '**appeal**' and some courts (e.g. the Court of Appeal) only hear appeals.

Most courts have some form of first instance and appellate jurisdiction, and most courts also have some form of criminal and civil jurisdiction. Figure 4.1 sets out the differing appeal routes for civil and criminal cases. Each court will now be discussed in turn below.

Figure 4.1 Appeal routes in criminal and civil cases

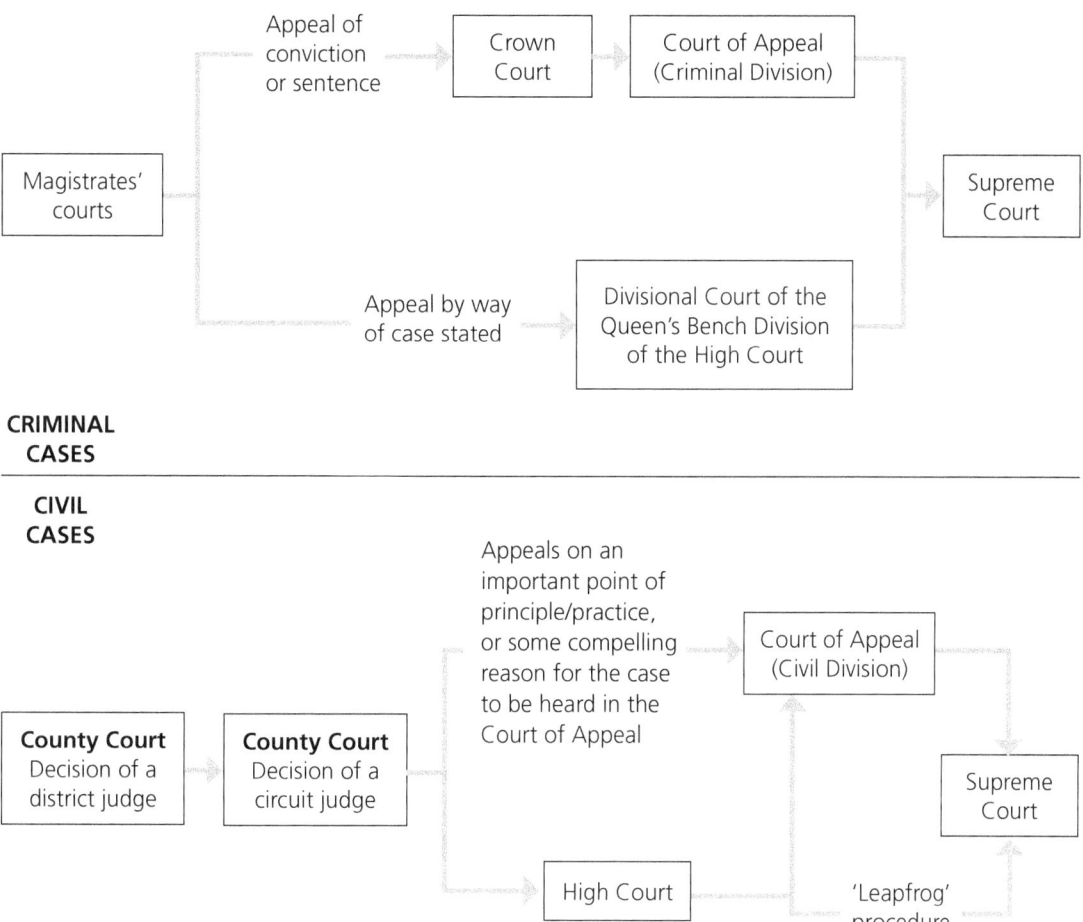

2.1 Magistrates' courts

Magistrates' courts are notable because, unlike all the other courts which are comprised of legally qualified judges, the vast majority of magistrates (or 'Justices of the Peace' as they are formally known) are not legally qualified (however, they do have a legally qualified clerk to advise on the law). The rationale behind having cases decided by laypersons is that it allows members of the community to become involved in administering justice. It should be noted, however, that cases in magistrates' courts can also be heard by district judges (although the vast majority are heard by magistrates). Magistrates' Courts primarily hear first instance criminal cases, but they do also have a limited civil jurisdiction.

Criminal jurisdiction

The vast majority of cases heard by magistrates are criminal cases and, in fact, over 95% of all criminal cases are heard in a magistrates' court. The other cases will be heard in the Crown Court, so it is worth mentioning here how criminal cases are allocated to the two courts. The allocation is based on the type of offence, with the three categories of offence being set out in Figure 4.2.

Figure 4.2 The three categories of criminal offences

Category	Description	Examples
Summary offences	More minor offences, so are tried in a Magistrates' Court	◆ Failure to keep company registers ◆ Failure to keep board minutes
Offences triable on indictment only	Serious offences, so are usually tried in the Crown Court	◆ Failure of a commercial organisation to prevent bribery ◆ False accounting
Offences triable either way	Offences that have the potential to be minor or serious. Depending on their severity, they can be tried summarily in a magistrates' court or on indictment in the Crown Court.	◆ Insider dealing ◆ Acting as a director while disqualified ◆ A public company failing to hold an annual general meeting

Defendants convicted of a criminal offence in a magistrates' court can appeal their conviction and/or sentence to the Crown Court (Magistrates' Courts Act 1980, s. 108(1)). If the defendant feels that the magistrates exceeded their jurisdiction or made an error of law, then they can appeal 'by way of case stated' to the High Court (Magistrates' Courts Act 1980, s. 111(1)).

Civil jurisdiction

The civil jurisdiction of the magistrates' court is small and includes (i) the recovery of unpaid council tax and unpaid utility bills; and (ii) Magistrates' Courts can hear appeals from parties relating to local council decisions to grant licences to entertainment or gambling establishments.

2.2 The County Court

The County Court only hears civil cases and is the court where most business disputes will be tried. This is because the bulk of cases heard by the County Court are claims involving contract law and the law of torts (County Courts Act 1984, s. 15), although it also hears cases involving the recovery of land where title is in dispute and certain equity proceedings. Cases are heard by a district or circuit judge, with the latter hearing more complex cases.

A decision of a district judge can be appealed to a circuit judge and a decision of a circuit judge can be appealed to the High Court (Access to Justice Act 1999 (Destination of Appeals) Order 2000, art. 3). However, an appeal may go directly to the Court of Appeal if it raises important points of principle or practice or there is some compelling reason why it should be heard there (Civil Procedure Rules, r. 52.23(1)).

The track system

The County Court and the High Court are the two major first instance civil courts. To try and improve the efficiency of these courts, the Civil Procedure Rules (CPR) established a track system to determine which cases are best allocated to which court. The three tracks are set out in Figure 4.3.

Figure 4.3 The track system

Track	Cases heard
Small claims track (CPR, r. 26.6(1)–(3) and Part 27)	Any claim for £10,000 or less will be allocated to the small claims track and will be heard in the County Court, subject to some exceptions (e.g. personal injury claims, where the claim is worth not less than £10,000, but the damages for personal injuries is over £1,000).
Fast track (CPR, r. 26.6(4)–(5) and Part 28)	A claim will be allocated to the fast track and normally heard in a County Court if: ◆ the small claims track is not the normal track ◆ the value of the claim is not more than £25,000 ◆ the court considers that the trial will last no longer than one day, and ◆ oral evidence will be limited to one expert per party.
Multi-track (CPR, r. 26.6(6) and Part 29)	A case that does not fit into the small claims track or fast track will be allocated to the multi-track. These are normally complex claims and/or claims involving larger amounts, so will normally be heard in the High Court.

Note that, in some cases, statute may expressly provide that certain types of cases must be heard in a particular court (e.g. defamation cases cannot be heard in the County Court (County Courts Act 1984, s. 15(2)(c)).

2.3 The Crown Court

Almost all cases heard in the Crown Court are criminal cases, namely:

◆ offences triable by indictment only (Senior Courts Act 1981, s. 46)

◆ either-way offences that have been sent to the Crown Court for trial (Magistrates' Courts Act 1980, s. 21; Crime and Disorder Act 1998, s. 51)

♦ sentencing defendants who have been convicted of an either way offence by a Magistrates' Court where the magistrates have sent the case to the Crown Court for sentencing, and

♦ appeals from those summarily convicted in a Magistrates' Court (Magistrates' Courts Act 1980, s. 108(1)).

First instance cases heard in a Crown Court can be appealed to the High Court. A defendant convicted in a Magistrates' Court who has his appeal to the Crown Court dismissed may appeal to the Criminal Division of the Court of Appeal (permission to appeal will be required).

Crown Court cases are usually heard by a single judge and a jury of 12 persons, but a jury is not used (i) in appeals; (ii) where the defendant pleads guilty, or (iii) where the case has been sent to the Crown Court for sentence. The prosecution can apply to have a case heard without a jury where there is a danger of jury tampering (Criminal Justice Act 2003, s. 44).

2.4 The High Court of Justice

The High Court consists of three divisions, namely (i) the Chancery Division; (ii) the Queen's Bench Division; and (iii) the Family Division. Each division has a substantial first instance jurisdiction and also an appellate jurisdiction via two judges (or sometimes one) sitting as a 'Divisional Court'.

High Court decisions in civil cases can be appealed to the Civil Division of the Court of Appeal, although it is possible to appeal directly to the Supreme Court if the case involves a point of law of general public importance and

♦ the proceedings entail a decision relating to a matter of national importance or consideration of such a matter; or

♦ the result of the proceedings is so significant that, in the opinion of the judge, a hearing by the Supreme Court is justified; or

♦ the judge is satisfied that the benefits of earlier consideration by the Supreme Court outweigh the benefits of the appeal being considered by the Court of Appeal (Administration of Justice Act 1969, s. 12).

High Court decisions in criminal cases can be appealed to the Supreme Court, providing that the appeal is based on a point of law of general public importance and permission to appeal has been obtained (Administration of Justice Act 1960, s. 1).

As regards businesses, the Family Division is obviously irrelevant, so only the other two divisions will be discussed.

The Chancery Division

The Chancery Division is the senior division of the High Court and its jurisdiction includes cases relating to the sale of land, bankruptcy, the dissolution of partnerships and contentious **probate** (Senior Courts Act 1981, Sch. 1, para. 1). A number of specialist courts and lists also exist within the Chancery Division, including:

probate
The law relating to wills and the dealing of a deceased person's assets.

◆ the Patents Court which hears cases relating to patents and designs;

◆ the Intellectual Property Enterprise Court, which hears higher-value patent cases, and trade mark and copyright disputes; and

◆ the Companies List, which hears certain cases relating to companies, especially insolvent companies.

The Queen's Bench Division

The Queen's Bench Division is the largest division of the High Court, largely due to the breadth of its jurisdiction, which includes:

◆ first instance civil claims, especially in contract and tort;

◆ hearing appeals from the decisions of circuit judges in the County Court;

◆ hearing criminal appeals by way of case stated from a Magistrates' Court;

◆ hearing criminal appeals on points of law from the Crown Court; and

◆ hearing judicial review cases (i.e. cases alleging that courts, or public bodies and persons have acted outside their powers).

The Queen's Bench Division also has its own specialist courts, including:

◆ the Commercial Court, which hears national and international commercial law cases, with particular expertise in international trade cases;

◆ the Technology and Construction Court, which deals with disputes relating to buildings, engineering and surveying; and

◆ the Financial List, which hears complex and high-value (over £50 million) cases involving financial markets.

2.5 The Court of Appeal

The Court of Appeal, as its name suggests, only hears appeals and it has no first instance jurisdiction. It consists of two divisions: the Civil Division and the Criminal Division (Senior Courts Act 1981, s. 3(1)).

The Civil Division

The Civil Division hears the following cases:

◆ appeals from decisions of the High Court;

◆ appeals from decisions of the County Court that raise important points of principle or practice or have some other compelling reason why the Court of Appeal should hear it (CPR, r. 52.23(1));

◆ appeals from decisions of the Upper Tribunal and the Employment Appeal Tribunal (CPR, rr 52.9 and 52.11); and

◆ the Court of Appeal can reopen a case if it is necessary to do so to avoid a real injustice, the circumstances are exceptional, and there is no alternative effective remedy (CPR, r 52.30(1)).

Decisions of the Civil Division can be appealed to the Supreme Court, providing that permission to appeal has been obtained from the Court of Appeal or the Supreme Court.

The Criminal Division

The Criminal Division hears a number of cases, including:

◆ defendants convicted of an indictable offence in the Crown Court can appeal to the Criminal Division (Criminal Appeal Act 1968, s. 1);

◆ prosecutors can apply to the Criminal Division for an order quashing a defendant's acquittal in cases where 'new and compelling' evidence has come to light and it is in the interests of justice for the defendant to be retried (Criminal Justice Act 2003, ss. 75–97);

◆ the Criminal Cases Review Commission can refer convictions to the Criminal Division where the Commission believes that there is 'a real possibility that the conviction, verdict, finding or sentence would not be upheld were the reference to be made' (Criminal Appeal Act 1995, s. 13(1)); and

◆ the Attorney General can refer certain cases to the Criminal Division (e.g. where he considers that the defendant's sentence is unduly lenient, he may apply to the Court, which may then impose a more severe sentence (Criminal Justice Act 1988, s. 36)).

Decisions of the Criminal Division can be appealed to the Supreme Court, providing that the case involves a point of law of general public importance and permission to appeal has been granted either by the Court of Appeal or the Supreme Court.

2.6   The Supreme Court of the United Kingdom

For over 600 years, the highest court in the UK was the Appellate Committee of the House of Lords, but in October 2009, it was replaced by the Supreme Court of the United Kingdom (Constitutional Reform Act 2005, s. 23). While the Court does have an extremely limited first-instance jurisdiction, in practice the only cases it tends to hear are appeals. It can hear appeals from the Court of Appeal, the High Court, the Court of Session (Scotland's highest civil court) and the Northern Irish Court of Appeal and High Court. It can also hear appeals from the Upper Tribunal and the Employment Appeal Tribunal in certain cases.

As the Supreme Court is the UK's final appeal court, its decisions cannot be appealed.

2.7   The Judicial Committee of the Privy Council

The Judicial Committee of the Privy Council acts as the final appeal court for a number of Commonwealth countries (e.g. The Bahamas, Jamaica), and UK overseas territories (e.g. Bermuda, Gibraltar) and Crown dependencies (e.g. Jersey, Guernsey and the Isle of Man). It also hears appeals from certain specialist UK courts (e.g. the Prize Courts, which determine whether vessels have been lawfully captured in times of war) but such cases are extremely rare.

Test Yourself 4.1

1. **Explain the difference between courts with a first instance jurisdiction and appellate courts.**

2. **What are the three categories of criminal offences and how do they differ?**

3. **Identify whether the following statements are true or false and, if false, explain why:**

   ◆ **County Court decisions can only be appealed to the High Court**

   ◆ **the High Court only hears first instance cases**

   ◆ **decisions of the High Court can only be appealed to the Court of Appeal**

   ◆ **decisions of the Court of Appeal can only be appealed to the Supreme Court**

   ◆ **decisions of the Supreme Court cannot be appealed.**

4. **Identify the divisions of the High Court that are most applicable to businesses and explain what types of cases they hear.**

3 Tribunals

Instead of taking a dispute to a court, a claimant may instead apply to have their case heard by a tribunal. Tribunals usually hear cases in panels of three, consisting of a legally qualified chairperson (usually a Tribunal judge) and two laypersons (known as Tribunal members) who are not legally qualified, but have expertise in the relevant subject matter (e.g. in financial cases, the Tribunal members may be accountants). Tribunals hear over 1 million cases per year, which is notably more than the courts. There are several reasons for this:

◆ tribunal cases are often cheaper and decided more quickly than court proceedings, largely because many parties put their case forward themselves and do not need to engage lawyers (a consequence of this is that tribunals tend to be more informal and less intimidating than courts);

◆ tribunals are not subject to the mass of rules that courts are subject to nor are they bound by precedent, meaning that they can operate in a more flexible manner;

◆ it is easier to have a case heard before a tribunal than before a court; and

◆ although many tribunal cases are open to the public, they tend to attract less publicity than court cases.

The UK's tribunal system underwent a significant overhaul in 2007 as a result of the passing of the Tribunals, Courts and Enforcement Act 2007. Most notably, the Act completely reformed the tribunal structure in the UK and provided for a system comprising of three pillars:

1. **First-Tier Tribunal**: The First-Tier Tribunal consists of seven Chambers, each covering a specific area (e.g. the Tax Chamber deals with cases involving tax and MP's expenses). Decisions of the First-Tier Tribunal can be appealed to the Upper Tribunal.

2. **Upper Tribunal**: The Upper Tribunal consists of four Chambers that hear appeals from the corresponding Chamber in the First-Tier Tribunal (e.g. decisions of the Tax Chamber in the First-Tier Tribunal can be appealed to the Tax and Chancery Chamber in the Upper Tribunal). Decisions of the Upper Tribunal can be appealed to the Court of Appeal and, in limited cases, directly to the Supreme Court.

3. **Specialist tribunals**: There are a number of specialist tribunals that are separate from the First-Tier Tribunal and Upper Tribunal, of which the most notable are the Employment Tribunal and the Employment Appeal Tribunal. The Employment Tribunal, unsurprisingly, hears employment law disputes. Decisions of the Employment Tribunal can be appealed to the Employment Appeal Tribunal, whose decisions can be appealed to the Court of Appeal and, in limited cases, directly to the Supreme Court.

Test Yourself 4.2

1. **Explain the composition of a typical tribunal panel.**

2. **Why is it potentially advantageous to have a case heard by a tribunal as opposed to a court?**

3. **Explain the relationship between the First-Tier Tribunal and the Upper Tribunal.**

4. **Can the decisions of the Upper Tribunal be appealed?**

4 Alternative dispute resolution

As discussed at p 39, one of the key purposes of the law is to provide a system for dispute resolution. Commencing proceedings in a court or tribunal is one way to resolve a dispute, but this is expensive, time consuming and will likely destroy the relationship between the parties involved. It is, therefore, unsurprising that a government consultation document stated that '[f]or most people most of the time, litigation in the civil courts, and often in tribunals too, should be the method of dispute resolution of last resort' (Lord Chancellor's Department, *Alternative Dispute Resolution: A Discussion Paper* (1999)). It has been argued that other methods of dispute resolution, collectively known as alternative dispute resolution (ADR), can be preferable for several reasons:

◆   ADR can be cheaper and quicker than commencing proceedings in a court;

◆   as certain forms of ADR focus more on the parties reaching an agreement, it is more likely to preserve the parties' relationship, thereby allowing them to do business again in the future; and

◆ legal proceedings are played out in the public arena and any resulting publicity may have an adverse effect upon a company's reputation and/or share price, or provide the company's competitors with useful information.

The law has come to recognise the value of ADR. For example, the CPR places a duty on the court to effectively manage cases and, as part of this, effective case management can include 'encouraging the parties to use an alternative dispute resolution procedure if the court considers that appropriate and facilitating the use of such a procedure' (CPR, r. 1.4(2)(e)). There are numerous forms of ADR, but the principal types are arbitration, mediation and conciliation.

4.1 Arbitration

The oldest form of ADR, and that most akin to legal proceedings in a court, is **arbitration**. Section 1 of the Arbitration Act 1996 provides that 'the object of arbitration is to obtain the fair resolution of disputes by an impartial tribunal without unnecessary delay or expense'. Arbitration typically involves the parties agreeing to refer their dispute to an impartial third party, known as an 'arbitrator'. Alternatively, if the parties have a contractual relationship, the contract may contain an arbitration clause which provides that, in the event of a dispute, the parties must refer the case to arbitration before commencing legal proceedings.

arbitration
A form of ADR under which the parties refer their dispute to an arbitrator who will impose a legally binding decision upon the parties.

The arbitrator will be an expert in the field in question, but need not be legally qualified. Beyond that, arbitration is similar to legal proceedings in three ways:

◆ both parties will often have lawyers representing them;

◆ the decision of the arbitrator is binding upon the parties and can be enforced by court order (Arbitration Act 1996, s. 66); and

◆ the decision of the arbitrator can be appealed to a court, albeit on more limited grounds than in legal proceedings.

A significant difference is that, unlike court proceedings, arbitration hearings are confidential and are not conducted in public. A notable issue with arbitration is it does involve imposing a decision on the parties. If the parties wish to undertake a more collaborative form of ADR under which they control the outcome, then mediation or conciliation may be preferable.

4.2 Mediation

Mediation involves the parties appointing a mediator, who will then facilitate discussion between the parties in an attempt to reach a voluntary and mutually acceptable resolution. Mediation has some advantages over arbitration:

mediation
A form of ADR under which the parties refer their dispute to a mediator, who will facilitate a dialogue between the parties so that they can resolve the dispute themselves.

◆ it allows the parties to reach a mutually acceptable solution, as opposed to an imposed solution that might be unacceptable to one or both of the parties; and

◆ the parties are more likely to do business or work together in the future if they can reach a mutually acceptable agreement themselves.

However, there is a notable disadvantage. Arbitration will result in a decision being made and is therefore a certain form of dispute resolution. Mediation provides no such guarantee and the parties may be unable to reach an agreement. To remedy this, a hybrid form of ADR called 'med-arb' has been developed which involves referring the dispute to mediation and, if no agreement can be reached, referring the case to an arbitrator for a binding decision.

4.3 Conciliation

conciliation
A form of ADR under which the parties refer their dispute to a conciliator who will lead a dialogue between the parties and help them to resolve their dispute by suggesting solutions.

Conciliation is similar to mediation, in that the parties will appoint a conciliator to help them reach a mutually acceptable solution to their dispute. The difference is that the mediator facilitates dialogue, whereas the conciliator takes a much more active role and will lead the discussion and propose solutions to the dispute. Conciliation does tend to be used in a preventative manner (i.e. to help resolve a dispute as soon as it arises and to prevent it from becoming more substantial). The following provides a notable example of conciliation in practice.

Case Example 4.1 ACAS's Early Conciliation scheme

The Advisory Conciliation and Arbitration Service (ACAS) provides a free Early Conciliation scheme in relation to employment disputes. Under this scheme, a claimant (usually an employee) who is considering making a claim in an employment tribunal must inform ACAS of the claim. ACAS will offer the claimant the opportunity to participate in the Early Conciliation scheme and, if the claimant agrees, ACAS will contact the employee's employer. An ACAS-appointed conciliator will work with both parties to try and resolve the dispute. If a resolution is reached, the parties will sign an ACAS settlement form, which is legally binding and prevents the claimant from making a tribunal claim based on the matter complained of. If a resolution cannot be reached, the claimant may proceed to initiate an employment tribunal claim. However, ACAS states that in 72% of cases the claimant does not proceed with an employment tribunal claim. In an employment setting, where the two parties will probably need to continue working together, the value of such a scheme is considerable.

Test Yourself 4.3

1.   **Explain the potential benefits of using ADR as opposed to commencing proceedings in a court.**

2.   **Explain the differences between arbitration and mediation?**

3.   **How do mediation and conciliation differ?**

5 The judiciary, the law officers and the legal profession

Having discussed the structures that administer the law, we now turn to look at the personnel who work within these structures, beginning with the judiciary.

5.1 The judiciary

For obvious reasons, the judiciary is of key importance to the functioning of the UK's legal system. As discussed at p 68, the judiciary decide cases based upon legal principles, interpret and apply statute law and have a significant law-making function. Figure 4.4 sets out the different types of judge and the courts in which they sit.

Figure 4.4: Judges and the courts in which they sit

Type of judge	Hears cases from which courts
Justices of the Supreme Court	Primarily the Supreme Court and Judicial Committee of the Privy Council, but can occasionally hear cases in the Court of Appeal and the High Court
Lord/Lady Justices of Appeal	Primarily the Court of Appeal, but can also hear cases in the High Court, the County Court, and the Crown Court
High Court judges/ deputy High Court judges	Primarily the High Court, but can also hear cases in the Court of Appeal and the Crown Court
Circuit judges/ deputy circuit judges	Primarily the Crown Court and the County Court, but can also be called upon to hear cases in the Criminal Division of the Court of Appeal
Recorders	Hear cases in the Crown Court and the County Court
District judges/ deputy district judges	Primarily the County Court, but can also hear cases in the High Court and a magistrates' court

There are also a number of specific judicial posts that should be noted, namely:

◆ **Lord Chief Justice**: The Lord Chief Justice is the UK's most senior judge and occupies a number of other roles, including (i) the President of the Courts of England and Wales; (ii) Head of the Judiciary of England and Wales; (iii) the Head of Criminal Justice (unless the Lord Chief Justice appoints someone else to this role); and (iv) President of the Criminal Division of the Court of Appeal.

◆ **President of the Supreme Court**: The President (along with the Deputy President) is responsible for the administrative running of the Supreme Court (e.g. choosing which Justices hear which cases).

◆ **Master of the Rolls**: The Master of the Rolls is the President of the Civil Division of the Court of Appeal and the Head of Civil Justice.

◆ **Heads of Division**: There are three Divisions of the High Court, each of which has a head. The Head of the Chancery Division is called the Chancellor of the High Court, whereas the Heads of the other two Divisions are known as Presidents.

Mention should also be made of the Lord Chancellor. Historically, the Lord Chancellor occupied several senior judicial roles, notably Head of the judiciary, Head of the Chancery Division and President of the Appellate Committee of the House of Lords. The issue was that the Lord Chancellor is also a Cabinet Minister and this created problems regarding separation of powers. Accordingly, the Constitutional Reform Act 2005 provides that the Lord Chancellor is no longer eligible to sit in any court (as a result, we have had several Lord Chancellors who have never been lawyers).

5.2 The law officers and the DPP

There are also several governmental appointees who are involved in the administration of the law, namely the law officers and the Director of Public Prosecutions (DPP).

◆ The law officers (namely the Attorney General and his deputy, the Solicitor General) are the government's chief legal advisers. They are both government ministers, and their principal functions include: (i) superintending certain agencies (namely the Crown Prosecution Service and the Serious Fraud Office); (ii) providing permission to bring certain prosecutions; (iii) representing the government in its important litigation; and (iv) referring unduly lenient sentences to the Court of Appeal.

◆ The DPP, who is appointed by the Attorney General, is the Head of the Crown Prosecution Service. Certain prosecutions (e.g. assisted suicide) can only proceed with the consent of the DPP.

5.3 The legal profession

Unlike many other countries, which have a single legal profession, the UK splits its legal profession into three distinct occupations: solicitors, barristers and legal executives. Mention should also be made of paralegals.

Solicitors

Solicitors are usually the first point of contact for anyone that has a legal issue. The work undertaken by solicitors varies hugely and often depends on the type of business they work for. High-street firms typically consist of a few solicitors who deal with a wide range of legal topics. At the other end of the scale are massive multinational law firms consisting of thousands of lawyers who tend to specialise in corporate and commercial matters. In addition, larger commercial organisations may appoint their own in-house solicitor/General Counsel to deal with any legal disputes.

Solicitors can only advocate in certain courts (known as their '**rights of audience**'), namely a Magistrates' Court, the County Court and, in limited cases, the Crown Court (although solicitors who become solicitor advocates do have rights of audience in higher courts). Where a case is due to be heard in a higher court, the solicitor will usually need to instruct a barrister.

Barristers
The majority of barristers are self-employed. They can work alone, but most barristers form groups known as 'chambers' (barristers are generally prohibited from forming partnerships). Historically, clients could not engage a barrister directly – they had to approach a solicitor and the solicitor would then instruct the barrister. This rule has been partially relaxed and clients can directly approach barristers in certain cases. Barristers, upon qualifying, are known as 'juniors' and most will remain so throughout their careers. Barristers regarded as having outstanding abilities can become Queen's Counsel and will cease to be juniors.

Barristers often undertake the following types of work. They:

◆ represent clients in court (barristers have rights of audience to advocate in any court);

◆ will often provide instructing solicitors and clients with a written opinion on the issues raised in a case, the relevant law and the case's likelihood of success; and

◆ will draft documents for clients, such as contracts, wills, etc.

Legal executives
Legal executives have gained much more recognition in the last 10–15 years, largely due to the Legal Services Act 2007. A fully qualified Chartered legal executive can undertake what are known as 'reserved legal activities'. These include exercising rights of audience in court, conducting litigation, conveyancing, probate activities and the administration of oaths (Legal Services Act 2007, s. 12(1)). Accordingly, legal executives are qualified, fee earners; lawyers who can undertake much of the same work as a solicitor and who can even be appointed as district judges.

Paralegals
Paralegals have not gained the same level of recognition as the other three legal occupations discussed above. A paralegal is someone who conducts legal work but they have not qualified as a solicitor, barrister or legal executive. Anyone can call themselves a paralegal and there are no formal qualifications that must be undertaken, although certain bodies (e.g. the Institute of Paralegals) will provide training and qualifications. As a result, whilst paralegals are often employed by solicitors' firms, companies, charities and other organisations, the work that they undertake is of a lower level than that of qualified lawyers.

rights of audience
The right to advocate proceedings in a particular court.

Test Yourself 4.4

1.   **Identify the six types of judges.**

2.   **What are the law officers and what are their roles?**

3.   **What are the three principal occupations within the legal profession?**

Chapter summary

◆   Courts of first instance hear cases for the first time, whereas appellate courts hear appeals.

◆   There are different appeal routes depending on whether the case involves civil or criminal law.

◆   There are three categories of offences: (i) summary offences; (ii) offences triable on indictment only; and (iii) offences triable either way.

◆   The UK's tribunal system consists of the First-Tier Tribunal, the Upper Tribunal, and certain specialist tribunals.

◆   Decisions of the First-Tier Tribunal can be appealed to the Upper Tribunal. Upper Tribunal decisions can be appealed to the Court of Appeal.

◆   The three principal methods of ADR are arbitration, mediation, and conciliation.

◆   An arbitrator imposes a legally binding decision on the parties, whereas mediators and conciliators will attempt to help the parties resolve the dispute themselves.

◆   There are six different types of judges, they sit in different courts and have different functions.

◆   The law officers are the Attorney General and the Solicitor General.

◆   The legal profession consists of solicitors, barristers and legal executives. Paralegals carry out more minor functions.

Chapter five
Sources of law

CONTENTS

1. Introduction
2. Legislation
3. Case law
4. European Union Law
5. Human rights law

1 Introduction

An understanding of any legal subject can only occur if you understand the various sources of law that make up that subject and the relationship that exists between them. Accordingly, this chapter will discuss the four main sources of law that currently apply in the UK: legislation, case law, European Union law, and human rights law.

2 Legislation

The primary source of domestic law in the UK is **legislation**, which basically refers to laws that derive from Parliament. This section will look at how legislation is created, interpreted and applied, but first it is important to understand the different types of domestic legislation that exist.

legislation
Laws that derive from Parliament.

2.1 Types of legislation

There are two principal types of domestic legislation: (i) Acts of Parliament; and (ii) subordinate legislation. It is important that you understand the difference between them, and how to effectively use them as they often complement one another.

Acts of Parliament
Acts of Parliament (sometimes known as 'primary legislation') constitute the supreme form of domestic law in the UK and cannot be amended or overruled

Act of Parliament
Issued by Parliament, Acts are the supreme form of domestic law in the UK.

by the courts. Acts of Parliament are, unsurprisingly, created by Parliament, which is the supreme law-making body in the UK. Parliament can, in theory, pass any Act that it wishes, except an Act that will bind future Parliaments. To be able to use Acts effectively, it is important to understand the components that make up an Act, as set out in Figure 5.1.

Figure 5.1 The components of an Act

Sections	Acts of Parliament consist of a number of sections. Acts can range from Acts consisting of a few sections (e.g. the UK's shortest Act, the Parliament (Qualification of Women) Act 1918, consists of two short sections) to massive Acts (e.g. the UK's largest Act, the CA 2006, consists of over 1,300 sections).
Subsections	Lengthier sections will usually be divided up into subsections.
Parts	Larger Acts or Acts that deal with multiple topics, will be made up of a number of Parts (e.g. the CA 2006 consists of 47 Parts). Each Part will deal with a distinct topic (e.g. Part 2 of the CA 2006 covers company formation).
Chapters	Larger Parts will often be divided up into Chapters (e.g. Part 15 of the CA 2006, which covers a company's annual accounts and reports, consists of 12 Chapters and spans 94 sections).
Schedules	Some Acts will provide sections that set out the broad legal principles, with more detailed rules being found a series of Schedules at the rear of the Act. For example, the CA 2006 has 16 Schedules which provide more detail on specified sections within the Act.

Subordinate legislation

As discussed at 2.2, creating and passing an Act of Parliament can be a complex business, and Parliament cannot hope to do all its work via the passing of Acts. Accordingly, Parliament will often pass an Act (known as an 'enabling Act') which will set out the broad legal principles, but will then delegate to some other person (e.g. a government Minister) or body (e.g. a local authority) the power to either create more detailed rules or to add, amend or repeal sections of the Act. These delegated functions will be exercised via the passing of **subordinate legislation** (often known as 'secondary' or 'delegated' legislation), of which by far the most important type is the statutory instrument (SI). Whereas Acts consist of sections, SIs consist of regulations.

The value of subordinate legislation is demonstrated by the fact that, in 2017, Parliament passed 35 Acts of Parliament, compared to 1,286 SIs. Some Acts have had a notable number of SIs passed under them (e.g. at the time of writing, 6,151 SIs have been passed under the European Communities Act 1972) resulting in some Acts being considerably different from when they were first passed.

subordinate legislation
Legislation made by a person or body that Parliament has conferred law-making powers upon.

2.2 Creating and passing Acts of Parliament

Most legislative proposals, unsurprisingly, derive from the government. Often, the government will publish a Green Paper that will set out broad legislative proposals for consultation. This is usually followed by a White Paper, which provides more detailed final proposals. This will culminate in a draft piece of legislation, which is known as a **Bill**. There are three broad types of Bill:

1. **Public Bills**: These are Bills that affect the general population. Where a Public Bill is introduced by a government minister, it is known as a government Bill. Where a Public Bill is introduced by a non-ministerial MP, it is known as a Private Members' Bill.

2. **Private Bills**: These are Bills that affect specific persons, groups, organisations, or localities.

3. **Hybrid Bills**: As the name suggests, these are Bills that affect the general population, but will have an increased effect upon specific persons, groups, organisations, or localities.

In order to become an Act, a Bill must pass through Parliament, which consists of the House of Commons, the House of Lords, and the monarch. Bills can be introduced into the House of Commons or House of Lords, but most are introduced into the Commons. There a Bill will undergo the five stages (or less if it is voted down) set out in Figure 5.2.

If a Bill passes through the House of Commons, it will proceed to the House of Lords, where it will go through the same five stages as in Figure 5.2. If the Lords propose any amendments, the Bill will go back to the Commons for consideration (a Bill may pass back and forth between the Commons and Lords multiple times via a process known as 'ping pong'). If the two Houses cannot come to an agreement, the Bill will fail. However, procedures have been put in place by the Parliament Acts of 1911 and 1949 that will not cause a Bill to fail, but instead allows the Lords to delay it by up to one year. After this period has passed, the Bill can proceed without the Lords' consent. This rarely happens – since 1911, only seven Acts have been passed without the Lords' consent.

If the Commons and Lords reach an agreement, the Bill can pass to the monarch for Royal Assent. Once Assent has been granted, the Bill will become an Act of Parliament. However, this does not mean that it comes into force straight away. It is common for parts of the Act to come into force immediately, but other sections are often brought into force later via the passing of a type of subordinate legislation known as a **Commencement Order**. For example, when the CA 2006 was passed on the 8 November 2006, only 29 of its 1,300 sections came into force. Most of the remaining sections were brought into force over the course of the next three years via the passing of eight Commencement Orders (indeed, several sections are still not in force at the time of writing).

Bill
A draft piece of legislation which, if passed by Parliament, becomes an Act of Parliament.

Public Bill
A Bill that affects the general population.

Private Bill
A Bill that affects specific persons, groups, organisations, or localities.

Hybrid Bill
A Bill that affects the general population, but will have an increased effect upon specific persons, groups, organisations, or localities.

Commencement Order
A form of subordinate legislation that brings an Act of Parliament or parts of it, into force on a specified date.

Figure 5.2 The Stages of a Bill

First Reading

The title of the Bill is read out, and an order is made for the Bill to be printed. No vote takes place, and so all Bills will pass the first reading.

↓

Second Reading

The MPs will debate the Bill (although no amendments can be made) and will then vote on whether the Bill should proceed. If the vote passes, it will proceed to the committee stage.

↓

Committee Stage

The Bill will be passed to a committee of MPs, who will scrutinise the Bill and propose amendments.

↓

Report Stage

The committee reports to the House on any amendments made to the Bill. The House will debate these amendments and may add new clauses or make amendments to existing clauses.

↓

Third Reading

The third reading normally takes place immediately following the report stage. Here, further debate may occur, but amendments cannot be made. Following the debate, the House votes on the Bill. If the vote passes, the Bill can proceed to the House of Lords.

2.3 Statutory interpretation

Once a Bill becomes an Act, it may remain on the statute books for decades or even centuries. The effects of the Act will depend on the sections within it, but these will need to be interpreted. Even where a section is detailed, it will likely be the case that ambiguities will arise due to the sometimes imprecise nature of language. Even where the words are clear, it may be unclear how they are to be applied to the facts of a case (especially those facts that were not in the contemplation of Parliament when the Act was passed). The interpretation of statute is one of the key tasks of the judiciary.

The judiciary is assisted in its interpretive function in a number of ways. It may have recourse to certain interpretive aids, including:

◆   **Presumptions**: The courts have created several presumptions to help them interpret legislation (e.g. it is presumed that statute will not affect cases that arose before the statute was passed, unless it states otherwise

(*L'Office Cherifien des Phosphates v Yamishita-Shinnihon Steamship Co Ltd* [1994] 1 AC 486 (HL)).

◆ **Intrinsic aids**: The courts can use aids within the statute itself (e.g. the Preamble, the long title, headings).

◆ **Extrinsic aids**: The courts can use certain material outside the statute, including dictionaries, academic texts, official reports and, in certain cases, the records of Parliamentary debates (known as 'Hansard'). In addition, modern Acts each come with Explanatory Notes, which can be used to interpret the accompanying Act. Finally, the Interpretation Act 1978 provides definitions of terms that commonly appear in statute.

The principal source of aid, however, is found in three rules created by the judges themselves (these are known as the 'canons of interpretation'). Although the rules are supposed to be applied in a particular order (notably the literal rule should be applied first), in practice the courts tend to invoke the rule that best does justice in the case before it. Note that many of the key cases in this area (and some of those discussed below) are not cases involving businesses, but they will demonstrate how the various rules operate.

The literal rule

The literal rule provides that the words of a statute should be given their ordinary, everyday, grammatical meaning or, as Lord Esher stated '[i]f the words of an Act are clear, you must follow them even though they lead to a manifest absurdity' (*R v Judge of the City of London Court* [1892] 1 QB 273 (CA)). One would assume that Parliament would not intend for a statute to lead to an absurdity, but Parliament cannot know the range of facts that the statute will be applied to, and it is possible that the facts of a particular case may result in an absurd result if the literal meaning of the statute is applied, as the following case demonstrates.

Case Law 5.1: *Fisher v Bell* [1961] 1 QB 394 (DC)

FACTS: Bell owned a shop, in the window of which he displayed a flick knife along with a sign stating the price of the knife. Section 1(1) of the Restriction of Offensive Weapons Act 1959 provided that any person who offered for sale a knife of this kind committed a criminal offence. Accordingly, Bell was charged with this offence.

HELD: It was long recognised by the law that a display of goods in a shop window did not amount to an offer to sell the goods (it was the customer who made the offer when he asked to buy the goods). Accordingly, even though s. 1(1) was designed to prevent such knives being sold, the court held that Bell had not offered to sell the knife so he was found not guilty.

Cases such as these led to calls for the creation of an additional rule that could apply where a literal interpretation would be inappropriate; this led to the creation of the golden rule.

The golden rule

The golden rule was created by Lord Wensleydale in *Grey v Pearson* (1857) 6 HL Cas 61, where he stated 'the grammatical and ordinary sense of the words is to be adhered to, unless that would lead to some absurdity … in which case the grammatical and ordinary sense of the words may be modified, so as to avoid that absurdity … but no farther.' As a result, the courts will no longer use the literal rule if its application produces an absurdity, and may instead use the golden rule. The operation of the golden rule is demonstrated in the following case.

Case Law 5.2: *R v Allen* (1872) LR 1 CCR 367

FACTS: Allen married Ann Gutteridge in 1867. In 1871, he purported to marry Harriet Crouch, even though he was still married to Gutteridge. Allen was charged with bigamy, under s. 57 of the Offences Against the Person Act 1861 providing that '[w]hosoever being married shall marry another person during the life of the former husband or wife … shall be guilty of bigamy'. The key words were 'shall marry another person'. Allen argued that, as he was unable to lawfully marry Crouch, he had not married another person and so had not committed bigamy under s. 57.

HELD: Based on a literal interpretation of s. 57, Allen was correct. However, if a literal interpretation was adopted, bigamy under s. 57 could never be proven and it would be rendered worthless. Accordingly, the courts applied the golden rule and stated that the words 'shall marry' shall also include 'go through the form and ceremony of marriage with another person'. Applying this interpretation, Allen was convicted.

Despite the value of the golden rule, it cannot be used whenever the court wishes. It can only be used where a literal interpretation would produce 'an inconsistency or an absurdity or inconvenience so great as to convince the Court that the intention could not have been to use [the words of the statute] in their ordinary signification' (*River Wear Commissioners v Adamson* (1877) 2 App Cas 743 (HL)).

The mischief rule/purposive approach

The mischief rule provides that where legislation was enacted to remedy a particular mischief, the courts will interpret that legislation in a way that remedies that mischief, as the following case demonstrates.

Case Law 5.3: *Royal College of Nursing v DHSS* [1981] AC 800 (HL)

FACTS: In order to combat the rise in 'backstreet abortions', the Abortion Act 1967 was passed, s. 1(1) of which provides that where a pregnancy is terminated by a 'registered medical practitioner', then no criminal offence will be committed. A new form of abortion was introduced which involved a doctor inserting a catheter into the womb and a nurse pumping a chemical into the womb (the doctor was on call, but not present when the chemical was administered). Nurses are not 'registered medical practitioners' so the issue was whether this new procedure breached s. 1(1).

HELD: The majority of the House looked at the mischief that the Act was passed in order to combat, namely unlawful backstreet abortions. The Act was passed to ensure that abortions were carried out in hygienic conditions by staff with the requisite skill. Taking this into account, the House held that the new abortion procedure was not in breach of s. 1(1).

More recently, the courts have tended to adopt a more purposive approach, in recognition of the fact that not all legislation is passed to remedy a mischief and may instead have some other purpose. Accordingly, under this approach, the courts will interpret legislation by reference to the legislation's purpose and context (see e.g. *R (Quintavalle) v Secretary of State for Health* [2003] UKHL 13).

Test Yourself 5.1

1. **What are the two types of legislation?**

2. **Explain the differences between a Public Bill, Private Bill, and Hybrid Bill.**

3. **Explain the process by which a Bill becomes an Act.**

4. **Explain how the three 'canons of interpretation' work?**

3 Case law

Legislation may be the supreme form of UK law but, being a common law country, the bulk of UK law can be found in **case law**. Case law refers to the body of laws that are created by the judges and applied via the doctrine of precedent.

case law
The body of laws that are created by the judges and applied via the doctrine of precedent.

3.1 The doctrine of precedent

The UK's common law system is strongly based on the doctrine of precedent, which simply provides that certain cases are decided based upon principles derived from prior cases. Whether a court is bound by a prior precedent is largely determined by the court hierarchy (discussed below) and the level of precedent that the case provides, of which there are three:

1. **Binding precedent**: Where a precedent is binding, then it must be followed by courts that are bound by that precedent, unless the precedent can be distinguished. For example, the general rule is that precedents established by higher courts must be followed by lower courts.

2. **Persuasive authority**: Certain precedents are not binding and so need not be followed, but they do constitute persuasive authority and may be followed. For example, *obiter dicta* (discussed at 3.3) provides persuasive authority.

3. **No precedent**: Certain cases provide no precedent value at all and need not be followed (e.g. decisions of magistrates' courts and the County Court).

3.2   The court hierarchy

The extent to which a court can establish binding precedent, and must follow binding precedent, depends upon where it sits in the court hierarchy. The general rule is that higher courts can bind lower courts, but some courts are also bound by their own decisions.

The Magistrates' Court and the County Court
The magistrates' courts and the County Court (collectively known as the 'inferior courts') cannot establish binding precedent, nor do their decisions constitute persuasive authority. These courts are bound by the decisions of the High Court (including Divisional Courts), the Court of Appeal, and the Supreme Court/ House of Lords.

The Crown Court
The Crown Court cannot establish binding precedents, but its decisions do constitute persuasive authority. Like the inferior courts, the Crown Court is bound by the decisions of the High Court (including Divisional Courts), the Court of Appeal, and the Supreme Court/House of Lords.

The High Court
Decisions of the High Court are binding on the Crown Court, the County Court, and the magistrates' courts. The High Court cannot bind itself, but it does consider its own decisions to constitute strong persuasive authority and so departs from them rarely. The High Court is bound by decisions of its Divisional Courts, the Court of Appeal, and the Supreme Court/House of Lords

The Divisional Courts
High Court judges can also sit as a Divisional Court (discussed at p 48). Decisions of a Divisional Court bind other Divisional Courts, the High Court, the Crown Court, the County Court, and the magistrates' courts. The Divisional Courts are bound by their own decisions, and those of the Court of Appeal and the Supreme Court/House of Lords.

The Court of Appeal

Decisions of the Court of Appeal bind Divisional Courts, the High Court, the Crown Court, the County Court, and the magistrates' courts. The Court of Appeal is bound by decisions of the Supreme Court/House of Lords, and is also generally bound by its own decisions, subject to some exceptions set out in *Young v Bristol Aeroplane Co Ltd* [1944] KB 718 (CA), including:

◆ if two previous Court of Appeal decisions conflict, the court must choose which one to follow and the other will be overruled;

◆ the court can ignore a prior Court of Appeal decision if it cannot stand with a subsequent decision of the Supreme Court/House of Lords;

◆ a Court of Appeal decision that is mistaken need not be followed by the court (the decision is said to be *per incurium* ('through want of care'). The classic example of a *per incurium* decision is where a court decided a case without referring to a key statute or case.

As criminal law can involve depriving a defendant of his liberty, the Criminal Division does tend to be more flexible than the Civil Division in terms of following its own decisions, and the Criminal Division can refuse to follow a Court of Appeal decision where it feels that the prior decision 'misapplied or misunderstood' the law (*R v Gould* [1968] 2 QB 65 (CA)).

The Supreme Court/House of Lords

Decisions of the Supreme Court/House of Lords bind all the other courts. The Supreme Court is not bound by any other UK court and can overrule its own decisions and those of the House of Lords 'when it appears right to do so' (*Practice Statement (Judicial Precedent)* [1966] 3 All ER 77 (HL)). In practice, the Supreme Court rarely overrules its own decisions or those of the House of Lords.

The Judicial Committee of the Privy Council

The Judicial Committee of the Privy Council occupies a strange position in terms of precedent. Generally, its decisions are not binding on any court, except in relation to certain specialist courts (e.g. the Ecclesiastical Court, which hears disputes on certain religious matters) which we need not concern ourselves with. However, its decisions do constitute persuasive authority and, as the Judicial Committee consists of extremely high-ranking judges, its decisions are regarded as extremely persuasive.

3.3 What aspect of a case is binding?

The court hierarchy determines whether a case constitutes binding precedent, but it does not tell us exactly what aspect of the case is binding. The UK's system of precedent is based on the maxim *stare rationibus decidendis*, which means 'keep to the reasoning of what has been decided previously'. This indicates that it is the reasoning of a case that is binding upon other courts, not the actual decision itself. This reasoning is known as the **ratio decidendi** ('reason for deciding'), but determining the *ratio* of a case is not always straightforward and cases may have multiple *rationes*. It is also important to distinguish between the reasoning and the facts of a case. A *ratio* should be able to apply to a range

ratio decidendi
'Reason for deciding'; the reasons behind a decision of a court, which can be binding on other courts.

of cases involving significantly differing sets of facts, so it is important that the ratio is not too narrow, nor too broad. The following example gives you an idea of how to identify the ratio of a case.

Case Example 5.1

Between 2000 and 2012, John was employed by X-Corp Ltd, a subsidiary of Y-Corp plc. In 2017, John discovered that he had contracted a rare form of cancer and this was caused by him being exposed to certain chemicals whilst working for X-Corp. John should have been given safety equipment to protect him from these chemicals, but was not. John wishes to obtain compensation, but X-Corp was dissolved in 2015. Further, during his period of employment with X-Corp, it had no insurance policy in place that would indemnify John for his loss. John decides to sue Y-Corp and succeeds. Possible *rationes* could include:

◆   **Parent companies are liable for the actions of their subsidiaries**: This *ratio* is far too wide and would render the concept of corporate personality worthless in many cases.

◆   **Parent companies are liable to the employees of dissolved subsidiary companies in cases involving negligent exposure to chemicals**: This *ratio* is far too narrow and could only apply in cases with almost identical facts to those above. Should it only apply to dissolved subsidiaries? Should it only apply to negligent chemical exposure? The answer to these questions is probably no.

◆   **In appropriate circumstances, a parent company may assume a duty of care to protect the health and safety of a subsidiary's employees**: This is a much more sensible *ratio* that could apply to a range of cases with differing facts. It would also allow the law to evolve in terms of what circumstances were deemed appropriate.

obiter dicta
'Statement said by the way'; anything said by a judge in a case that is not part of the *ratio*.

The *ratio* is not the only aspect of a case that has precedent value. A case may also provide persuasive authority in the form of **obiter dicta** ('statements said by the way'), which is essentially anything that is not part of the *ratio*. Examples of *obiter dicta* would be statements of law in dissenting judgments (i.e. those not part of the majority), and the application of law to a hypothetical scenario.

3.4   The law-making role of the judiciary

The traditional constitutionally-accepted role of the judges is to interpret and apply the law, not to create new law. Despite this, it is universally accepted that judges do make new law. There are whole swathes of law that are predominantly judge-made (e.g. the law of agency, the tort of negligence) which needed to be created to deal with prevailing legal issues where no legislative guidance existed. Even where legislation does dominate, the judges still create law via their interpretive function.

The judiciary has now accepted that it does indeed have a law-making role, so the question is how does it exercise that role? In *C (a Minor) v DPP* [1996] AC 1 (HL), Lord Lowry set out five propositions:

1. If the solution is doubtful, the judges should beware of imposing their own remedy

2. Caution should prevail if Parliament has rejected opportunities of clearing up a known difficulty or has legislated, while leaving the difficulty untouched.

3. Disputed matters of social policy are less suitable areas for judicial intervention than purely legal problems.

4. Fundamental legal doctrines should not lightly be set aside.

5. Judges should not make a change unless they can achieve finality and certainty.

From this, it is clear that Lord Lowry indicated that a cautious approach should be adopted by the judges when making new law. Whether the judges have, in all cases, exercised sufficient caution is a matter of debate.

Test Yourself 5.2

1. **Explain the three levels of precedent.**

2. **Identify whether the following statements are true or false, and provide reasons for your answer:**

    ◆ **decisions of the inferior courts are not binding, but provide persuasive authority**

    ◆ **decisions of the Crown Court bind magistrates' courts**

    ◆ **the Divisional Courts are bound by decisions of the High Court**

    ◆ **the Court of Appeal is generally bound by its own decisions**

    ◆ **the Supreme Court is generally bound by its own decisions or those of the House of Lords.**

3. **Explain the terms *ratio decidendi* and *obiter dicta*.**

4 European Union Law

The European Union as we know it today can trace its origins back to 1957, when six countries signed the Treaty of Rome (now known as the Treaty on the Functioning of the European Union (TFEU)), thereby bringing into existence the European Economic Community (EEC). The next few decades would witness massive changes within the EEC, including its evolution into the European Union (EU) in 1992 following the passing of the Treaty on European Union (TEU, commonly known as the Maastricht Treaty). New Member States would join (the UK joined in 1973), leading to the current 28 Member States that make up the EU. However, as is discussed at 4.4, the UK will be leaving the EU in March 2019.

To understand how important that EU is to our legal system, it is necessary to look at how the EU operates, the different laws that it creates and the effect that these laws have upon UK law.

4.1   The EU institutions

The functions of the EU are carried out via seven institutions (TFEY, Art. 13). Two of these institutions, the Court of Auditors and the European Central Bank, are the EU's 'financial' institutions and need not be discussed here. The four 'political' institutions are:

1.   **The European Council**: The European Council consists of the heads of state or government of each Member State, along with the President of the European Council and the President of the European Commission. Given its composition, it is unsurprising that the European Council forms the EU's highest decision-making body and provides the EU with 'the necessary impetus for its development and shall define the general political directions and priorities thereof' (TEU, Art. 15(1)).

2.   **The European Parliament**: The only directly democratically elected body in the EU, the European Parliament consists of 751 Members of the European Parliament, who are elected by the citizens of their respective Member States. The two principal functions of the EU are approval of the EU's budget (along with the Council), and the Parliament is involved in approving almost all EU legislation.

3.   **The Council of the European Union**: The Council of the EU (usually known as 'the Council', not to be confused with the European Council) is the EU's principal decision-making body of the EU and is involved in passing the EU's budget and legislation. The Council consists of a ministerial representative from each Member State, but the representative will differ depending upon which subject is being discussed (e.g. if economic matters are being discussed, the Council will configure into the Economic and Financial Affairs Council and will consist of the economic and finance ministers from the Member States).

4.   **The European Commission**: The European Commission consists of 28 Commissioners (one from each Member State). The Commission has three key roles. First, it 'shall promote the general interest of the Union and take appropriate initiatives to that end' (TEU, Art 17(1)). Second, it is responsible for ensuring that EU law is enforced and, to that end, it is granted extensive powers to investigate and punish breaches of EU law. Third, it is generally the only EU institution that can propose EU legislation.

The remaining institution is the EU's 'legal' institution, namely the Court of Justice of the European Union. Given its importance, it is discussed separately.

The Court of Justice of the European Union

The Court of Justice of the European Union (CJEU) is an umbrella term to describe the two courts of the EU:

1. **The Court of Justice**: Formerly known as the European Court of Justice (ECJ), the Court of Justice (CoJ) is the principal court of the EU and currently consists of 28 judges (one per Member State) and 11 Advocates General. It has jurisdiction to hear numerous cases including cases involving allegations that a Member State has not complied with EU law and cases involving a review of the legality of legislative acts or the acts of EU institutions. It also provides preliminary rulings (discussed below). The CoJ also hears appeals from the General Court.

2. **The General Court**: Formerly known as the Court of First Instance, the General Court was set up to reduce the caseload of the ECJ. It currently consists of at least one judge from each Member State (46 judges at the time of writing). It can hear a wide range of cases including (i) cases brought by persons within the EU against acts of EU institutions, bodies or offices; (ii) actions brought by Member States against the Council or Commission; and (iii) cases seeking compensation for damage caused by EU institutions, bodies or offices.

As noted, once of the key functions of the CoJ is the provision of preliminary rulings. To ensure that EU law is applied consistently, Art 267 of the TFEU empowers domestic courts and tribunals to apply to the CoJ for a preliminary ruling in relation to the interpretation of EU legislation. Once an application for a preliminary ruling has been made, the CoJ will decide whether to accept the request for a ruling. If it does, the domestic proceedings will be suspended and the CoJ will interpret the relevant legislation (note that it will not apply this interpretation to the facts of the case – that is the job of the domestic court that applied for the ruling). Once the CoJ has provided a ruling, the case is referred back to the domestic court, which will decide the case. Note that the preliminary ruling does not compel the domestic court to act in a particular way, but preliminary rulings are almost always followed. If the ruling provides that domestic legislation is incompatible with EU law, the domestic legislation is almost usually changed, as occurred in the following case.

Case Law 5.4: Case C-152/84 *Marshall v Southampton and South-West Hampshire Area Health Authority* [1986] ECR 723

FACTS: Mrs Marshall's employer required employees to retire when social security payments became payable, namely 65 years of age for men and 60 years of age for women. As Marshall was 62, her employer dismissed her and Marshall alleged that this amounted to sex discrimination under the Sex Discrimination Act 1975. However, as the 1975 Act did not apply to cases concerning retirement, Marshall's claim was dismissed by the Court of Appeal. Marshall sought a preliminary ruling.

HELD: The Equal Treatment Directive required that male and female employees be treated equally. Accordingly, the ECJ held that Marshall was subjected to sex discrimination under the Directive and that the relevant provision of the 1975 Act was incompatible with EU law. The 1975 Act was amended shortly after to require employers not to set a retirement age that discriminated on grounds of sex.

4.2   EU legislation

One of the most important functions of the EU is the creation of EU legislation. EU legislation consists of treaty provisions and 'legal acts', of which there are five types, namely regulations, directives, decisions, recommendations, and opinions (TFEU, Art. 288). All six types of EU legislation will be discussed, but first it is important to explain how they impact upon domestic law, and this requires an understanding of the concepts of direct applicability and direct effect:

direct applicability
EU legislation that is directly applicable is automatically incorporated into domestic law as soon as it is passed.

direct effect
EU legislation that can be enforced in a domestic court is said to have direct effect.

◆   **Direct applicability**: EU legislation that is directly applicable is automatically incorporated into domestic law as soon as it is passed (i.e. there is no need for the Member State to implement it). However, directly applicable EU legislation can only be enforced in a Member State if the legislation has direct effect.

◆   **Direct effect**: EU legislation that can be enforced in a domestic court is said to have direct effect, but legislation will only have direct effect if three conditions are met, namely (i) the obligations set out in the legislation must be clear; (ii) the legislation must be unconditional, and; (iii) the legislation must not require the implementation of domestic legislation (Case C26/62 NV *Algemene Transporten Expeditie Onderneming van Gend en Loos v Nederlandse Administratie der Belastigen* [1963] ECR 1). A provision that has direct effect and imposes obligations upon Member States that can be enforced by persons is said to have 'vertical direct effect'. 'Horizontal direct effect' refers to provisions that impose obligations upon persons that can be enforced by other persons.

Each type of EU legislation is discussed more below, but Figure 5.3 provides a useful overview.

Figure 5.3: EU legislation

Legislation	Binding	Directly applicable	Can have direct effect	
			Vertical	Horizontal
Treaty provisions	Yes	Yes	Yes	Yes
Regulations	Yes	Yes	Yes	Yes
Directives	Yes	No	Yes	No
Decisions	Yes	No	Yes	Yes
Recommendations	No	No	No	No
Opinions	No	No	No	No

Treaty provisions

Treaty provision are the highest form of EU law. They are directly applicable and, providing they meet the *van Gend en Loos* conditions noted above, they will also be directly effective (they can be both vertically and horizontally directly effective, unless the wording indicates otherwise). In practice, most treaty provisions provide broad legal statements and so tend not to be directly effective as they lack sufficient clarity.

Regulations

Regulations are used when the EU wishes laws across Member States to be uniform. Accordingly, Regulations are directly applicable (TFEU, Art 288) and, providing they meet the *van Gend en Loos* conditions noted above, they can be both vertically and horizontally directly effective.

Directives

The legal position of directives is more complex. EU Member States have vastly different legal systems, which often require EU legislation to grant Member States flexibility in terms of how they implement EU law. Where such flexibility is required, directives are used. The flexibility of directives can be seen in Art. 288 of the TFEU, which states that a directive 'shall be binding, as to the result to be achieved … but shall leave the national authorities the choice of form and method'. In other words, the directive will set out the broad aim or goal to be achieved, but will let each Member State decide how best to achieve that aim.

A directive will provide the Member States with a period in which the directive's aims must be implemented (usually two years). As directives require implementation, they are not directly applicable and will not meet the *van Gend en Loos* conditions for direct effect. The disadvantage of this is that a Member State may seek to avoid the directive by never implementing it. Accordingly, if a Member State has not implemented the directive by the end of the implementation period, the directive will become directly effective and can be enforced in a domestic court (Case C-41/74 *Van Duyn v Home Office* [1975] 1 CMLR 1). Indeed, this is what occurred in the *Marshall* case discussed at p 71, but in this case, the ECJ established a notable limitation – as directives only impose obligations upon Member States, they only have vertical direct effect, not horizontal direct effect.

Decisions

Decisions can apply to all EU Member States but, unlike the other forms of EU legislation discussed thus far, they can also be addressed to a single Member State, organisation, or person. Decisions are binding only upon those to whom they are addressed (TFEU, Art. 288). Accordingly, decisions are not directly applicable, but providing they meet the *van Gend en Loos* conditions noted above, it can be directly effective against those to whom they are addressed.

Recommendations and opinions

Recommendations and opinions are not legally binding (TFEU, Art 288) so they are not directly applicable or directly effective. They are usually issued by EU institutions to make their views known and to suggest a course of action, but provide no legal obligations upon those to whom they are addressed.

4.3 The supremacy of EU law

Prior to the UK joining the EEC in 1973, it was well established that EU law 'became an integral part of the legal systems of the Member States and which their courts are bound to apply' (Case C-14/64 *Costa v ENEL* [1964] ECR 585). In other words, EU law holds supremacy over the domestic law of Member States. In the UK, this is evident in s. 2(1) of the European Communities Act 1972, which states:

> All such rights, powers, liabilities, obligations and restrictions … created or arising by or under the Treaties, and all such remedies and procedures … provided for by or under the Treaties, as in accordance with the Treaties are without further enactment to be given legal effect or used in the United Kingdom shall be recognised and available in law, and be enforced, allowed and followed accordingly.

From this, it follows that EU Member States are bound to implement EU law and if domestic law is incompatible with EU law, the relevant domestic law must be amended (which is what occurred in *Marshall* discussed at p 71). However, this creates a problem. As discussed at p 59, legislation is the highest form of UK law and the courts must apply it. The question therefore arises what should a court do if it is required to apply a piece of UK legislation that is incompatible with EU law. The answer came in the following landmark case.

Case Law 5.5: *R v Secretary of State for Transport, ex parte Factortame (No 2)* [1991] 1 AC 603 (HL)

FACTS: EU law imposed fishing quotas on each Member State. Factortame, a Spanish company, sought to avoid the Spanish quota by registering its vessels in the UK, fishing in UK waters (thereby adding to the UK quota) and then taking the fish back to Spain. The UK responded by passing the Merchant Shipping Act 1988, which provided that, in order to register a vessel in the UK, title to the vessel had to belong to a UK citizen or company (defined as one with at least 75% of its shareholders and directors being British). A group of Spanish vessels did not meet these requirements, so they commenced proceedings alleging that the 1988 Act breached EU legislation relating to freedom of establishment and prohibition of discrimination. The High Court issued an injunction restraining the government from enforcing the 1988 Act. The House of Lords rescinded the injunction, but referred the case to the ECJ. The ECJ held that domestic courts must enforce any EU legislation that has direct effect (which was the case here).

HELD: The House of Lords renewed the injunction restraining the operation of the 1988 Act (the Spanish fishermen subsequently obtained compensation for their loss). Shortly thereafter, Parliament removed the sections of the 1988 Act that did not comply with EU law.

There is no doubt that the supremacy of EU law has resulted in a loss of sovereignty, but it would appear that, in the UK, EU law will lose it's supremacy due to the UK's decision to withdraw from the EU.

4.4 The UK's withdrawal from the EU

On 23 June 2016, a referendum was held to determine whether or not the UK should remain an EU Member State. Those voting to withdraw from the EU narrowly won the referendum and, on the 29 March 2017, the UK triggered Art. 50 of the TEU and began the formal process of leaving the EU. Accordingly, unless the UK seeks and is granted an extension to the Art. 50 process, the UK will leave the EU by the 29 March 2019. Until that date, EU law will continue to apply in full (and may even apply beyond this date if a transition deal is agreed which requires continued compliance with EU law). The government has also stated that it will also leave the European Economic Area (EEA) and so will not remain part of the single market.

As the process for leaving the EU is ongoing, not much can be said with certainty at this point. The government's European Union (Withdrawal) Bill is currently making its way through Parliament and, if passed in its current state, will have three principal effects:

1. it will repeal the European Communities Act 1972, thereby abolishing the supremacy of EU law over UK law;

2. all EU-derived domestic law will continue to have effect once the UK leaves the EU; and

3. all directly effective EU legislation will form part of domestic law immediately before the UK leaves the EU.

As a result of this, the effect of Brexit upon UK law will likely be minimal in the short term. However, in the medium- to long-term, the effects of Brexit on the UK legal system could be much more significant, especially if Parliament decides to amend or repeal EU-derived laws, many of which are now well established in our legal system. Controversially, the Bill allows government ministers to amend or repeal certain EU-derived laws.

Test Yourself 5.3

1. **Name the seven EU institutions, and identify which institutions could be classed as financial, political, or legal.**

2. **What is a preliminary ruling?**

3. **Explain what is meant by 'direct applicability' and 'direct effect'.**

4. **Name the six types of EU legislation.**

5 Human rights law

One might assume that 'human' rights law would not be applicable to businesses and certainly would not be applicable to non-human persons, such as companies and LLPs. However, this is not the case and, as discussed below, key human rights protections are also provided to businesses. The key source of human rights protection is to be found in the European Convention on Human Rights (ECHR).

5.1 The European Convention on Human Rights

The ECHR was adopted in 1950 and was ratified by the UK in 1951. It consists of 59 Articles, of which Arts. 2–18 are the most important as they contain the various human rights. Additional rights have been added over time by the passing of Protocols. The word 'human' is slightly inaccurate, as some of the rights not only apply to humans, but can also apply to legal persons, such as companies and LLPs. For example, Article 1 of the First Protocol provides that '[e]very natural or legal person is entitled to the peaceful enjoyment of his possessions'. However, not every right in the ECHR is applicable to businesses (e.g. the prohibition of torture in Art. 3 clearly cannot apply to businesses). In addition to Art. 1 of Protocol 1, the key human rights that apply to businesses are the right to a fair trial (Art. 6) and the right to freedom of expression (Art. 10).

It is commonly believed that the ECHR is part of EU law and that EU Member States automatically become signatories or vice versa. This is completely incorrect – the ECHR is not part of the EU and they are completely separate, as demonstrated by the fact that the EU currently has 28 Member States, whereas the ECHR has 47 signatories (although all 28 Member States are signatories to the ECHR). However, a relationship does exist between the EU and the ECHR and the EU is currently in the process of acceding to the ECHR. However, progress has stalled after the CoJ indicated a number of legal difficulties involved in accession. In December 2017, the EU stated that it remains committed to becoming a signatory to the ECHR and is looking at how to overcome the legal difficulties raised.

5.2 The European Court of Human Rights

Cases involving breaches of human rights can be heard at the European Court of Human Rights (ECtHR), which was created in 1959. The ECtHR currently consists of 47 judges (equal to the number of states that have ratified the ECHR). The ECtHR's role is to interpret and apply the ECHR so its decisions form a major part of human rights law. Although the UK ratified the ECHR in 1951, UK citizens were not able to take cases to the ECtHR until 1966. Taking a case to the ECtHR is extremely expensive and, as it has a massive caseload (and a significant backlog of cases), cases can take years to hear. What was needed was a way to enforce the ECHR in a domestic court and this was provided by the Human Rights Act 1998.

5.3 The Human Rights Act 1998

The White Paper that led to the Human Rights Act 1998 (HRA 1998) was entitled 'Bringing Rights Home' and this is what the HRA 1998 does – it allows most of the rights in the ECHR to be enforced in a UK court. UK courts, when determining whether a Convention right has been breached, must take into account judgments of the ECtHR (HRA 1998, s. 2(1)), but need not follow them. However, the Supreme Court has stated that ECtHR decisions should be followed where they have established a clear and constant line of authority, and those decisions have not overlooked some aspect of UK law (*Manchester City Council v Pinnock* [2010] UKSC 45).

Statutory interpretation

On p 63, the 'canons of interpretation' were discussed, but the HRA 1998 introduced a new rule of statutory interpretation, namely that '[s]o far as it is possible to do so, primary legislation and subordinate must be read and given effect in a way which is compatible with the Convention rights' (HRA 1998, s. 3(1)). Section 3(1) is important for two reasons:

1. Section 3 applies to legislation passed before and after the HRA 1998 was passed.

2. The s. 3 rule takes priority over the doctrine of precedent. Accordingly, a court that would be bound to follow a normally binding precedent need not follow that precedent if it feels that the precedent is incompatible with a Convention right.

It is important to note that the s. 3 rule only applies 'so far as it is possible to do so'. In some cases, it will simply not be possible to interpret a piece of legislation in a way that is compatible with Convention rights. What happens next depends on the type of incompatible provision. If the incompatible provision is in a piece of subordinate legislation, then the provision will have no effect, unless primary legislation prevents the removal of the incompatibility (HRA 1998, s. 3(2)(c)). In other cases, the court may issue a declaration of incompatibility.

Declarations of incompatibility

If a court is satisfied that a legislative provision is incompatible with a Convention right, then it may (not must) issue a **declaration of incompatibility** (HRA 1998, s. 4(1)–(4)). A declaration of incompatibility is a declaration stating that the court is of the opinion that a legislative provision is incompatible with a Convention right. Two points should be noted:

1. Magistrates' courts, the County Court, and the Crown Court are not empowered to issue declarations of incompatibility (HRA 1998, s. 4(5)).

2. A declaration of incompatibility does not affect the validity, continuing operation or enforcement of the relevant provision (HRA 1998, s. 4(6)). Accordingly, the court must still apply the law and a declaration does not compel Parliament to change the law. In practice, if a declaration is issued, the law is almost always changed to render it compatible with the Convention.

declaration of incompatibility
A declaration stating that the court is of the opinion that a legislative provision is incompatible with a ECHR right.

A British Bill of Rights

A final point worth noting is that a notable number of MPs (especially Conservative MPs) have expressed dissatisfaction with the ECHR and the HRA 1998, so much so that, following its election victory in 2015, the Conservative Government pledged to repeal the HRA 1998 and replace it with a 'British Bill of Rights'. However, unsurprisingly, following the decision to withdraw from the EU, the government has stated that it does not plan to move forward with its plans until after Brexit.

Test Yourself 5.4

1.   **Explain the relationship between the ECHR and the EU.**

2.   **Are UK courts required to follow the decision of the ECtHR?**

3.   **What does s. 3 of the HRA 1998 provide and why is it important?**

4.   **What is a declaration of incompatibility and what effect does it have?**

Chapter summary

- ◆   The two types of legislation are Acts of Parliament and subordinate legislation.

- ◆   In order to become an Act, a Bill must pass through the House of Commons, the House of Lords, and must receive Royal Assent.

- ◆   Interpreting legislation is a key role of the judges and a range of rules have evolved in relation to how they should interpret legislation.

- ◆   The doctrine of precedent provides that certain courts are bound by the reasoning in prior cases.

- ◆   The general rule is that higher courts bind lower courts, but some courts are also bound by their own decisions.

- ◆   The Court of Justice of the EU consists of the Court of Justice and the General Court.

- ◆   There are six types of EU legislation, namely treaty provisions, Regulations, directives, decisions, recommendations and opinions.

- ◆   EU law is supreme to UK law, but the UK is currently in the process of withdrawing from the EU.

- ◆   Certain rights within the European Convention on Human Rights also apply to legal persons, such as companies and LLPs.

- ◆   Following the passing of the Human Rights Act 1998, cases involving the Convention can be brought in a domestic court.

- ◆   The courts should interpret legislation in a way that is compatible with Convention rights, but if they cannot do so, they may issue a declaration of incompatibility.

Chapter six
Company law and governance framework

CONTENTS

1. Introduction
2. Sources of company law
3. Sources of corporate governance recommendations

1 Introduction

The previous chapter examined sources of law in general. This chapter moves on to look specifically at sources of company law and corporate governance recommendations (these being the areas of law that are most important to company secretaries). While sources of company law and corporate governance recommendations are usually separate, there is an increasingly connected relationship between them. In order to obtain a full understanding of certain topics, it is important to look at both the law and best practice recommendations. The appointment of a director provides a good example of this.

Case Example 6.1

X-Corp plc is a listed company that wishes to appoint a new director to its board. There are a range of laws that will need to be complied with. X-Corp will need to ensure that the proposed new director is eligible to act as a director, as the law provides that certain persons (e.g. minors, X-Corp's auditor) cannot be appointed as a director. The process for appointing a director is a matter for the X-Corp's articles, but case law provides that, if the articles are silent on this, then the power to appoint a director is vested in the company's members. Case law also provides that the members' power to appoint a director must be exercised for the benefit of X-Corp as a whole.

Outside of these laws, the UK Corporate Governance Code also provides numerous recommendations relating to directors' appointments, notably the recommendation that X-Corp should set up a nomination committee. The Code also recommends that the new director's notice or contract period should be set at one year or less, whereas the CA 2006 provides that any guaranteed term of employment over two years requires member approval. Finally, in recent years, increasing focus has been placed on board diversity, so larger companies like X-Corp should bear in mind the gender and ethnic makeup of their boards when considering board appointments.

2 Sources of company law

Companies are legal persons and so owe their existence to the law. The law regulates the activities of companies and those who interact with them. Before these laws can be examined, it is important to understand the various sources of company law that exist. This section discusses these sources, beginning with one of the most important: legislation.

2.1 Legislation

Legislation is the principal source of company law, with Acts of Parliament making up the dominant form of company law legislation. As Lord Halsbury LC stated in *Ooregum Gold Mining Co of India Ltd v Roper* [1892] AC 125 (HL), 'a limited company owes its existence to the Act of Parliament, and it is to the Act of Parliament one must refer to see what are its powers, and within what limits it is free to act'. The Act of Parliament he was referring to is the central Companies Act around which much company law is based.

The Companies Act 2006

The UK system of company law has, since 1856, been built around a central Companies Act, of which there have been many. The current Companies Act, namely the Companies Act 2006 (CA 2006), is reportedly the lengthiest piece of legislation ever passed by Parliament. The Act is divided into 47 Parts, with each Part covering a particular area of company law (e.g. Part 12 sets out the relevant provisions relating to company secretaries). Since the Act's enactment in November 2006, it has been substantially amended and updated by other Acts of Parliament (notably the Enterprise and Regulatory Reform Act 2013 and the Small Business, Enterprise and Employment Act 2015) and subordinate legislation.

Other notable Acts of Parliament

Certain company law topics that were once covered under a Companies Act are now covered by their own Act of Parliament, with notable examples including:

- **Stock Transfer Act 1963**: Establishes rules relating to the transfer of shares.
- **Companies Act 1985**: This Act (which was the predecessor to the CA 2006) has been largely repealed, but some provisions remain in force (namely relating to company investigations).

◆ **Insolvency Act 1986**: The UK's framework for corporate insolvency law can be found in the Insolvency Act 1986, which contains rules on how to wind up a company, as well as providing for a number of mechanisms that seek to rescue financially struggling companies.

◆ **Company Directors' Disqualification Act 1986**: This Act establishes when a director can be disqualified and imposes penalties upon those who act as a director whilst disqualified.

◆ **Criminal Justice Act 1993**: Part V of this Act establishes the rules relating to the criminal offence of insider dealing.

◆ **Financial Services and Markets Act 2000 (FSMA 2000)**: This Act establishes a financial regulator (namely the Financial Conduct Authority (FCA)) and establishes rules designed to regulate financial services and markets.

◆ **Corporate Manslaughter and Corporate Homicide Act 2007**: This Act created the offence of corporate manslaughter.

Subordinate legislation

Subordinate legislation (usually in the form of statutory instruments (SI)) is often overlooked, but it is extremely significant as it has five principal functions.

1. It expands upon the basic rules found within an Act of Parliament. For example, Part 15 of the CA 2006 establishes the broad rules relating to a company's annual reports and accounts, but the detailed rules regarding these reports and accounts are found in the Small Companies and Groups (Accounts and Directors' Report) Regulations 2008 (SI 2008/409) and the Large and Medium-Sized Companies and Groups (Accounts and Reports) Regulations 2008 (SI 2008/410). At the time of writing, over 120 SIs have been passed under the CA 2006, many of which serve to flesh out the Act's provisions.

2. It is used to bring parts of Acts of Parliament into force in the form of Commencement Orders. For example, when the CA 2006 was first enacted, only 29 of its 1,300 sections came into force. The remainder of the Act (absent a few subsections which are still not in force) was brought into force over the next three years via the passing of eight Commencement Orders.

3. It can be used to amend existing legislation including (controversially) amending Acts of Parliament.

4. It is often used to implement EU law (e.g. the Companies (Shareholders' Rights) Regulations 2009 (SI 2009/1632), which implemented the Shareholders' Rights Directive).

5. It can empower certain persons or bodies to create law. For example, the Secretary of State for Business, Energy and Industrial Strategy is empowered by the CA 2006 to make regulations that provide for a model set of articles that companies may use, namely the Companies (Model Articles) Regulations 2008 (SI 2008/3229).

Department for Business, Energy and Industrial Strategy

As noted above, legislation often empowers the Secretary of State for Business, Energy and Industrial Strategy (BEIS) to make law (in the form of subordinate legislation) and to exercise a range of company law powers (e.g. the ability to commence disqualification proceedings). Accordingly, it is worth briefly noting here the role of BEIS. BEIS is the governmental department that, according to its website, is responsible for (amongst other things) 'leading the government's relationship with business'. To that end, it is the government department that is most closely involved in company law and corporate governance reform. For example, at the time of writing, BEIS has engaged in a consultation on company law reform and has published a series of governance reform proposals (see www.gov.uk/government/consultations/corporate-governance-reform).

Rules with legislative backing

Certain rules are not found in legislation, but have legislative backing or are recognised by legislation. Examples of non-legislative rules that are recognised by legislation include:

◆ The FSMA 2000 empowers the Financial Conduct Authority to impose rules (notably the Listing Rules, the Disclosure and Transparency Rules and the Prospectus Rules) on companies who wish to list their shares on a FCA-regulated stock exchange.

◆ The CA 2006 empowers the Takeover Panel to make rules (namely the City Code on Takeovers and Mergers) regulating takeovers, mergers and other transactions that can have an effect upon the ownership of companies.

◆ The Financial Reporting Council is empowered to determine technical standards and other standards on professional ethics and internal quality control of statutory auditors and statutory audit work.

Figure 6.1 provides a table of the key company law pieces of legislation.

2.2 Case law

Despite the breadth and depth of company law legislation, it is not exhaustive and case law still constitutes an extremely important source of company law for four reasons:

1. Certain company law topics are largely creations of case law and have little or no legislative involvement. For example, the rules relating to attribution (i.e. whose actions can be attributed to the company) are entirely judge made.

2. Case-law principles that are well established often become enshrined in legislation. For example, the duties placed upon directors were, historically, case-law-based, but can now be found in ss. 171–77 of the CA 2006.

3. Legislation will often empower the courts to grant remedies and, in the case of criminal offences, impose punishments. The scope and application of these remedies and punishments is often determined via case law.

4. Legislative rules need to be interpreted and applied. In some cases, in order to afford the courts sufficient flexibility, statutory rules will be made

Figure 6.1 Key pieces of company law legislation

Acts of Parliament	Subordinate legislation	Rules with legislative backing
◆ Stock Transfer Act 1963 ◆ Companies Act 1985 ◆ Insolvency Act 1986 ◆ Company Directors Disqualification Act 1986 ◆ Criminal Justice Act 1993 ◆ Financial Services and Markets Act 2000 ◆ Companies Act 2006 ◆ Corporate Manslaughter and Corporate Homicide Act 2007 ◆ Financial Services Act 2012 ◆ Enterprise and Regulatory Reform Act 2013 ◆ Small Business, Enterprise and Employment Act 2015	◆ Uncertificated Securities Regulations 2001 ◆ Companies (Model Articles) Regulations 2008 ◆ Small Companies and Groups (Accounts and Directors' Report) Regulations 2008 ◆ Large and Medium-Sized Companies and Groups (Accounts and Reports) Regulations 2008 ◆ Overseas Companies Regulations 2009 ◆ Company, Limited Liability Partnership and Business (Names and Trading Disclosures) Regulations 2015 ◆ Insolvency (England and Wales) Rules 2016 ◆ Register of People with Significant Control Regulations 2016	◆ City Code on Takeovers and Mergers ◆ Disclosure and Transparency Rules ◆ Listing Rules ◆ Prospectus Rules

purposely broad and vague and the role of applying those rules in specific instances will be left to the courts. For example, the most important member remedy is the unfair prejudice petition, but only three sections of the CA 2006 (namely ss. 994–996) are devoted to this remedy and these sections provide no guidance on the application of the law. Accordingly, the task has been left entirely to the courts and a substantial body of case law has developed. In some instances, as in the following case, the statutory provision may be drafted poorly or unclearly and may need to be interpreted by the court to reveal its full effect.

Case Law 6.1: *Braymist Ltd v Wise Finance Co Ltd* [2002] EWCA Civ 127

FACTS: Sturges entered into a contract on behalf of Braymist Ltd ('Braymist'), under which Braymist would sell a piece of land to Wise Finance Co Ltd ('Wise'). However, at the time that this contract was entered into, Braymist was in the process of being incorporated, and so it did not yet exist. Subsequently, Wise refused to complete the sale and the issue was whether a valid contract existed and, if so, who was it between. Section 36C(1) of the Companies Act 1985 (now replaced by CA 2006, s. 51(1)) provided that if a promoter (which Sturges was) entered into a contract with a third party on behalf of a company at a time when that company had not been formed, then the promoter was personally liable on the contract. From this, it is clear that a contract existed between Sturges and Wise, but it was not clear whether Wise could be held liable on the contract as s. 36C only expressly imposed liability on the promoter.

HELD: Arden LJ stated that it was clearly Parliament's intention that s. 36C resulted in the creation of a contract between the promoter (Sturges) and the third party (Wise). A contract could only take effect if both parties were able to enforce it, so Sturges was able to sue Wise on the contract.

2.3   The constitution of the company

Despite the wealth of company law legislation and case law, companies are afforded the ability to create their own internal rules (namely via the company's constitution) to determine how the company is run. For example, the CA 2006 is largely silent on the processes by which directors' pay is determined, so this is a matter that companies can decide for themselves by placing their own remuneration rules in their articles. In some cases, statute will even allow companies to use their constitution to exclude or modify statutory rules. For example, s. 561 of the CA 2006 grants a company's shareholders rights of pre-emption, which essentially entitles them to the right of first refusal if a new batch of shares are **allotted**. Private companies can, however, insert a provision in their articles completely excluding these pre-emption rights (CA 2006, s. 567).

allotment
Shares are allotted to a person when he acquires the unconditional right to be included in the company's register of members in respect of the shares.

As well as empowering the company and its directors, the constitution can also limit powers. For example, the articles can limit the types of activities that the company, directors or members can engage in. Breach of these limitations can amount to a breach of the **ultra vires** rule, breach of contract, or breach of the directors' duties.

ultra vires
Acting 'beyond one's powers'.

2.4   Contract

An often-ignored source of law, but perhaps the most important from a day-to-day perspective, is contract. Every day, companies enter into contracts with suppliers, directors, shareholders, consumers, clients and many other types of person. These relationships will largely be governed by contract, which allows companies to effectively make their own law. These contracts are governed by general contract law principles, but company law does establish some specific contractual rules. For example, even though the company is a legal person, it cannot write a signature 'on the dotted line' and so special rules have developed regarding how companies enter into contracts.

2.5   European Union law

EU law has had a significant impact upon our company law system. The UK is currently in the process of withdrawing from the EU, so the impact of EU law will predictably be affected by this (as is discussed at p 75). This section looks at the impact EU law has had on our company law system, beginning with the right of establishment.

Right of establishment

One of the key rights contained in the Treaty on the Functioning of the European Union (TFEU) is the right of EU nationals to establish a business anywhere in the EU. Accordingly, Art 49 of the TFEU prohibits restrictions on the freedom of establishment, which includes the right to 'set up and manage undertakings, in particular companies or firms … under the conditions laid down for its own nationals by the law of the country where such establishment is effected …'

A UK company that wishes to establish a presence in another EU Member State (or vice versa) has three broad options:

1. A UK company could simply set up a subsidiary in that Member State, but there may be justifiable reasons for not wanting to do this (e.g. the expense involved, the burden of being subject to that State's legal system).

2. Article 49 provides that prohibitions on restrictions of the right to establishment 'shall also apply to restrictions on the setting-up of agencies, branches or subsidiaries by nationals of any Member State established in the territory of any Member State'. Accordingly, instead of setting up a subsidiary, a UK company could simply set up a branch in another Member State and this branch would not be subject to the full force of that State's law (see, e.g. Case C-212/97 *Centros Ltd v Erhvervs-og Selskabsstryrelsen* [1999] ECR I-1459).

3. A UK company could relocate to another Member State, and will then become subject to the laws of that State.

The harmonisation programme

In order for the right of establishment to be of benefit and to facilitate cross-border company activity, it is also necessary for there to be a degree of harmonisation across the company laws of EU Member States. Accordingly, Art. 50(2)(g) of the TFEU provides that attaining freedom of establishment involves 'coordinating to the necessary extent the safeguards which, for the protection of the interests of members and others, are required by Member States of companies or firms … with a view to making such safeguards equivalent throughout the Union'. To that end, the EU embarked upon a programme that aimed to better harmonise company law across EU Member States.

Article 50(1) of the TFEU states that freedom of establishment shall be attained 'by means of directives' so EU company law harmonisation has been attained by the passing of directives. In theory, directives are useful as they allow Member States considerable flexibility – directives set out the goals or aims of the directive and then allow Member States discretion in terms of how those aims are implemented. In practice, directives are less flexible as many are extremely detailed and some (e.g. the Prospectus Directive) impose 'maximum harmonisation' which means that the directive's minimum standards must be implemented, but the Member State cannot impose more exacting standards.

To date, eleven harmonisation directives have been passed. In 2012, the European Commission recommended that these directives be merged into a single legal instrument and the Commission has adopted a proposal that would merge many of the existing company law directives into a single directive.

The UK's withdrawal from the EU

The general background and effects of the UK's withdrawal from the EU were discussed at p 75. Here, the specific effects upon UK company law will be noted. Despite the significance of EU law, the UK system of company law is predominantly domestic, but there are significant areas of company law that are EU-derived or exist in their current form to comply with EU law, with notable examples including the law relating to:

- cross-border mergers and insolvencies;
- the Listing Regime;
- the regulation and independence of auditors;
- the market abuse regime;
- the capital maintenance regime;
- takeovers;
- shareholders' rights, and;
- corporate transparency.

As noted at p 75, all EU law and EU-derived law will be converted to domestic law on exit day, so the short-term effects of Brexit on our system of company law will likely be minimal. Over the longer term, Parliament may decide that it wishes to reform those areas of company law that it was not able to reform due to having to comply with the EU law, so the longer-term effects of Brexit may be more significant.

passporting
The right of a company registered in a EEA state to do business in another EEA state without obtaining further authorisation.

One concern relating to Brexit is the fact that UK firms may lose their '**passporting**' rights upon the UK leaving the EU. Passporting essentially means that companies engaged in certain areas (notably financial services) that are registered in an EEA state are free to do business in any other EEA state without obtaining further authorisation. Accordingly, a company registered in the UK is free to do business in any other EEA state but, upon the UK leaving the EEA, UK companies will require authorisation to do business there (unless the UK secures some sort of passporting rights as part of the exit agreement). This is of particular concern to companies who provide financial services. London is currently the financial centre of Europe and a number of major financial services companies have stated that they are considering relocating to an EEA state post-Brexit.

2.6 Human rights laws

Despite its title, the European Convention on Human Rights ('ECHR') also applies to legal persons, such as companies. Not all human rights are applicable to companies (e.g. the prohibition of torture) but the ECHR does often specify that certain rights can apply to companies. For example, Art. 1 of the First Protocol of the ECHR states that 'every natural or legal person is entitled to peaceful enjoyment of his possessions'.

Test Yourself 6.1

1. Name the six principal sources of company law.

2. What is the name of the principal piece of company law legislation; identify five other pieces of important company law legislation.

3. Why is case law an important source of company law?

4. Why is contract an important source of company law?

3 Sources of corporate governance recommendations

The UK's corporate governance system is not dominated by sources of law, but instead by a series of reports and codes, which establish guidance and best practice recommendations. Corporate Governance is 'the system by which companies are directed and controlled' (Cadbury Report, 1992).

3.1 Codes

The UK was one of the first countries in the world to establish a corporate governance code (Cadbury Code 1992). Today, the UK's corporate governance system is dominated by two governance codes, namely:

◆ the UK Corporate Governance Code, which is primarily aimed at companies and directors; and

◆ the UK Stewardship Code, which is aimed at certain large shareholders, known as institutional investors.'

The UK Corporate Governance Code

The principal code is the UK Corporate Governance Code, which was first published in 2010 (although this was an updated renamed version of the Combined Code on Corporate Governance, first published in 1998). The Code was updated in 2012, 2014 and 2016, with the 2016 Code being in force at the time of writing. However, the Financial Reporting Council (FRC) has published a proposed revised Code. This is expected in mid-2018 and will come into effect on 1 January 2019. This proposed revised Code is notably shorter than the 2016 Code and is a complete restructure.

Stop and Think 6.1

The FRC is of the opinion that the Code will only command widespread acceptance if it is concise, so the proposed revised Code 'shortens and 'sharpens' the existing Code, reducing it from 23 pages to 13 pages. Do you think the Code's reduction is beneficial, or do you think the lack of detail may prove to be a detriment?

The 2016 Code provides a series of best practice recommendations in five broad areas:

leadership, effectiveness, accountability, remuneration and relations with shareholders (the five sections of the proposed revised Code are structured differently). The FRC has stated that:

> A regulatory framework that aims to improve standards of corporate governance is more likely to succeed if it recognises that governance should support, not constrain, the entrepreneurial leadership of the company, while ensuring risk is properly managed. This requires a degree of flexibility in the way companies adopt and adapt governance practices … To be effective it needs to be implemented in a way that fits the culture and organisation of the individual company. This can vary enormously from company to company depending on factors such as size, ownership structure and the complexity of its activities.

The FRC clearly believes that the Code must be flexible, so it operates on a **'comply or explain'** basis. As a result, companies do not need to comply with the Code's recommendations (unless it mirrors a legal obligation), but **listed companies** must include within their annual report:

comply or explain
The obligation placed upon listed companies to state in their annual reports how they have applied the UK Corporate Governance Codec and explain any areas of non-compliance.

listed company
A company whose shares are admitted for listing on the official list (i.e. can be traded on certain stock exchanges).

- a statement as to whether the company has complied with all the relevant provisions of the Code; or
- a statement identifying which provisions were not complied with, the period within which they were not complied with, and the reasons for non-compliance (Listing Rules, LR 9.8.6(6)).

This approach means that companies can comply with the Code where they think it correct to do so, but can also depart from it if there are good reasons for doing so.

Premium Listing
A company whose shares have a Premium Listing is subject to additional rules and is expected to meet the highest standards of regulation and governance.

One criticism of the Code is its scope. The Code states that it applies to companies with a **Premium Listing**, although the proposed revised Code does state that other listed or unlisted companies may wish to adopt it in whole or in part. The result is that the UK's corporate governance system does largely focus on the UK's largest publicly listed companies and tends to ignore smaller companies. The collapse of BHS Ltd and the subsequent revelations of poor governance in the company led to an increased recognition that governance is not only relevant to listed companies. As a result, as part of its Corporate Governance Review, the government has invited the FRC, the Institute of Directors, and other interested bodies to develop a voluntary set of principles for larger private companies (BEIS, 'Corporate Governance Reform: The Government Response to the Green Paper Consultation' (2017)). In January 2018, an industry group was set up by the government to draw up these principles.

Stop and Think 6.2

The government's recognition that governance is not only important to larger companies is welcome, but should it simply be focusing on larger private companies? What about unlisted public companies? Another issue for debate is whether a new Code should be created or whether the UK Corporate Governance Code should be expanded in scope to cover a broader range of companies. What do you think?

The UK Stewardship Code

The UK Corporate Governance Code is primarily aimed at companies and directors, but shareholders also play an important role in promoting good governance. The 2009 Walker Review noted that, during the financial crisis, large **institutional investors** (e.g. insurance companies, pension funds and banks) were slow to act and exercised insufficient oversight over the companies in which they held they held shares. Accordingly, the Walker Review recommended that a Stewardship Code be created which would provide best practice guidance and recommendations to institutional investors. The UK Stewardship Code was published in 2010 and was updated in 2012. It has not been updated since, but the FRC intends to consult on an update in the middle of 2018.

> **Institutional investors**
> Powerful shareholders such as banks, pension funds, and insurance companies that invest significant sums in the stock market on their own behalf and on behalf of their customers/clients.

The Stewardship Code consists of seven broad principles and accompanying guidance. The UK Stewardship Code, like the UK Corporate Governance Code, operates on a 'comply or explain' basis, so investors may choose not to comply. However, certain investors and fund managers (notably those authorised by the Financial Conduct Authority) must comply with the Stewardship Code or explain their reasons for non-compliance.

3.2 Reports

The Codes are complemented and influenced by a series of reports. In 1992, the first major UK report on corporate governance was published, namely The Report of the Committee on the Financial Aspects of Corporate Governance (better known as the Cadbury Report). This report laid the foundations of the UK's corporate governance system and, since then, numerous reports have been published on a wide range of governance issues, including:

- the Greenbury Report (1995) on directors' remuneration;
- the Turnbull Report (1999) on internal control;
- the Smith Report (2003) on audit committees;
- the Higgs Report (2003) on the role and effectiveness of non-executive directors;
- the Walker Review (2009) on the governance of UK banks during the financial crisis;

◆ Lord Davies' Women on Boards reports (2011-2016) on gender diversity in the boardroom (the Hampton-Alexander Review has taken over from Lord Davies); and

◆ the Parker Review (2017) into ethnic diversity in the boardroom.

These reports often establish recommendations or best practice guidance which, if commanding enough acceptance, often find their way into the corporate governance codes discussed at 3.1.

Test Yourself 6.2

1. **Name the two principal corporate governance codes that operate in the UK?**

2. **Explain how the 'comply or explain' approach operates.**

3. **What type of company does the UK Corporate Governance Code apply to?**

Chapter summary

◆ The sources of company law are legislation, case law, the constitution of the company, contract law, EU law and human rights law.

◆ Legislation is the principal source of company law, with the Companies Act 2006 being the dominant piece of company law legislation.

◆ Case law is important because (i) certain areas of law are created by case law; (ii) case law principles may end up in legislation; (iii) case law sets out the operation and scope of statutory remedies and punishments; and (iv) case law provides the interpretation of statutory rules.

◆ Many rules by which a company is run are created by the company itself via its constitution (notably its articles of association).

◆ EU law has had a significant effect on the UK system of company law, but the UK has decided to withdraw from the EU.

◆ The sources of corporate governance recommendations are codes and reports.

◆ The two key corporate governance codes are the UK Corporate Governance Code and the UK Stewardship Code.

◆ Both codes operate on a 'comply or explain' basis, meaning specified persons must comply with the Code's recommendations or explain their reasons for non-compliance.

Chapter seven
Law and business

CONTENTS

1. Introduction
2. Contract law
3. The law of torts
4. Employment law
5. Commercial law
6. Consumer law
7. Environmental law
8. Intellectual property law
9. Cyber-security and data protection
10. Competition law

1 Introduction

The previous chapter looked at sources of company law and corporate governance recommendations and, while these two areas are arguably the most important areas of law for a company secretary, there are a number of other areas of law that are applicable to businesses. This chapter will highlight nine other legal topics that can apply to businesses but, as each topic is a major topic in its own right, this chapter will only provide a brief overview of each topic, why the topic is important to businesses and the main sources of law.

2 Contract law

As noted on p 84, on a day-to-day basis, contract law is one of the most important legal topics. Almost all commercial and consumer dealings are undertaken via contract and businesses may enter into hundreds or thousands of contracts, ranging from contracts with employees, contracts with suppliers, contracts to sell shares, contracts to borrow money etc. The advantage of contracts is that they allow the parties to effectively create their own law via the agreed terms in the contract. However, whilst contractual flexibility is important, a framework is needed within which contracts can be regulated – this is the role of contract law. Contract law puts rules in place that help clarify certain issues, such as:

◆   It is important that the parties know whether a contract has been created and when the contract comes into existence. Contract law therefore provides for several ingredients that must be present for a contract to exist and, once those ingredients are present, a valid contract comes into existence.

◆   Powerful parties may seek to impose unfair or onerous terms on weaker parties. Contract law therefore provides protection to certain parties by regulating the use of certain terms (e.g. the Unfair Contract Terms Act 1977 and the Consumer Rights Act 2015 stringently regulates the use of exclusion and limitation clauses).

◆   Contract law provides that certain events may terminate a contract (or allow a party to terminate if they so choose) and also sets out the consequences of termination.

◆   Contract law provides remedies (e.g. damages, injunctions, specific performance) to parties who have suffered loss due to the other party not performing their contractual obligations, or performing them in an unsatisfactory manner.

Contract law is largely a common law subject and many areas are almost completely judge-made (e.g. the rules relating to the formation of a contract). However, over the last 40 years or so, legislation has come to play a more significant role, especially in relation to consumer contracts, where businesses may seek to use their bargaining power to force unfair terms upon consumers.

3   The law of torts

tort
A form of civil wrong, with examples including negligence, nuisance and defamation.

The word '**tort**' derives from the Latin *tortus*, meaning 'twisted' or 'wrong' and therefore a tort is a particular form of civil wrong (although some torts, such as libel, can also result in criminal liability). It is important to note that not all civil wrongs are torts – torts are only one form of civil liability, with breach of contract being the other notable area of civil liability.

The law of torts consists of a series of these torts, with many of them being applicable to businesses, including:

◆   The principal tort is the tort of negligence, under which liability can be imposed on persons who engage in certain negligent acts or omissions. Examples include a business that sells a defective or dangerous product (although some might argue that product liability is a separate tort), or a professional who provides a negligent service (e.g. an auditor who conducts a negligent audit by failing to spot irregularities or falsehoods in the accounts).

◆   Persons who unlawfully interfere with other people's goods may have committed the tort of wrongful interference with goods.

- The tort of occupiers' liability provides that liability can be imposed on occupiers of premises who fail to take adequate care of persons upon those premises (e.g. a business which fails to adequately protect the safety of customers in its stores).

- The tort of nuisance can result in liability being imposed on those whose land or property (including the use of land or property) causes loss to others (e.g. fumes or waste from a factory that causes damage to nearby property).

- The tort of **defamation** imposes liability on persons who make untrue and harmful statements about others (e.g. a shareholder falsely states that a director is stealing from the company).

  defamation
  A collective term for the torts of libel and slander.

- A group of torts (often known as the 'economic torts') aim to protect businesses against unlawful interference with contract, trade or business. For example, the tort of passing off imposes liability on those who try to trade off the business or goodwill of others (e.g. by using a specific product name belonging to another, or by manufacturing goods that imitate the appearance of another manufacturer's goods).

The law of torts also provides additional rules relating to who can be liable for the commission of a tort. In the business context, the key rule here is the doctrine of vicarious liability, which provides that certain persons can be liable for the tortious acts of others (e.g. an employer can be vicariously liable for the negligent acts of his employees whilst in the course of their employment).

The law of torts, like contract law, is largely judge-made, but with statutory inroads in relation to certain torts. Notable examples include the Consumer Protection Act 1987 (which establishes the legal framework in cases involving defective products) and the Defamation Act 2013 (which reforms the common law defamation rules and places others on a statutory footing).

4 Employment law

Despite its name, employment law is not merely concerned with the relationship between employers and employees, but also with persons who are not employees, but are classified as 'workers.' This is an important distinction as certain rights (e.g. the right to sue for unfair dismissal) only apply to employees, whereas other rights (e.g. the right to the national minimum wage) also apply to workers. The increase in those working under 'the gig economy' has made the matter even more complicated.

Case Example 7.1

The contracts of those who provide work for certain business (e.g. Uber, Deliveroo) state that the provider of the service is an independent contractor and is not regarded as an employee or a worker. The consequence of this is that the persons who provide work for these businesses lack many of the rights provided to employees and workers.

In recent years, a number of cases have arisen in which gig economy contractors have asserted that, in substance, they are employees or workers and so should have access to the relevant employment rights. In many of these cases (notably *Uber BV v Aslam* (unreported 10 November 2017, EAT) although an appeal to the Supreme Court will take place in 2018), the court or tribunal has held that the claimants are indeed employees or workers and so are entitled to the relevant employment rights.

Other key employment law topics include:

◆ what employment rights are provided to employees and workers;
◆ health and safety in the workplace;
◆ the prevention of discrimination in the workplace;
◆ providing a remedy to those who are unfairly or wrongfully dismissed;
◆ rights provided to employees following a business transfer; and
◆ rights relating to collective action (e.g. strikes).

Employment law is a mixture of statute and case law. Many key employment rights are provided for either under the Employment Rights Act 1996 (arguably the most important employment law statute) or under some other more specific piece of legislation (e.g. the right to a minimum wage is provided for under the National Minimum Wage Act 1998). It should also be noted that many employment law cases are not heard in a court, but are instead heard by employment tribunals, with appeals being made to the Employment Appeal Tribunal.

5 Commercial law

Commercial law concerns the body of laws that seek to regulate and facilitate the commercial dealings of businesses. Although commercial law is usually taught as a distinct topic, it is often regarded as an umbrella term for a collection of topics, of which the most notable are:

◆ **Domestic sale of goods**: many businesses sell goods and commercial law establishes detailed rules regarding what 'goods' are, what types of sale contracts exist, when the goods are transferred to the buyer, rules regarding payment and delivery of goods, implied terms and remedies afforded to the buyer or seller if the other party fails to uphold their obligations.

◆ **International sale of goods**: The sale of goods from a business based in one country to a business or person based in another country involves a number of difficulties not encountered in a purely domestic sale. Accordingly, specific rules exist regarding the international sale of goods.

◆ **The law of agency**: Businesses will often engage other persons (known as agents) to undertake some act on the business's behalf (e.g. the directors are agents of the company). The law of **agency** establishes rules regarding when an agency relationship is created, what acts the agent is authorised to undertake, the relationship between the parties in an agency relationship and how a relationship of agency can be terminated.

agency
A relationship under which one person (the principal) appoints another person (the agent) to undertake some act on the principal's behalf.

Commercial law overlaps significantly with other legal topics, notably contract law (as most businesses transact via contract) and consumer law (as many businesses deal with consumers). Commercial law is a mixture of statute and case law. Some topics (e.g. the law of agency) are dominated by case law with very little statutory involvement. Other topics (e.g. the domestic sale of goods) are based around a statutory framework. As regards international topics (e.g. the international sale of goods) there are also a number of international treaties and agreements that are of significant importance.

6 Consumer law

Many businesses derive either the majority, or all of their income from transacting with consumers, so adhering to consumer law requirements is of paramount importance. The principal aim of consumer law is to protect consumers and it does this in a number of ways, including:

◆ establishing standards that providers of goods and services must meet (e.g. ss. 9–11 of the Consumer Rights Act 2015 imply terms into consumer contracts providing that goods must be of satisfactory quality, fit for the purpose and as described);

◆ providing consumers with a remedy (e.g. damages, right to repair/replacement/rejection of goods) if goods and services fail to meet the required standards or are in breach of contract;

◆ prohibiting anti-consumer trade practices (e.g. aggressive trade practices, such as making persistent and unwanted phone calls to consumers to persuade them to purchase goods or services);

◆ establishing a system of licensing or authorisation, so that only licensed/authorised persons can provide certain services (e.g. businesses that wish to provide certain forms of credit to consumers must obtain authorisation from the Financial Conduct Authority);

◆ requiring providers of goods and services to provide specified information regarding those goods and services (e.g. providers of package holidays must provide in their brochures specified information, such as the destination and means of travel, type of accommodation and which meals are included in the package); and

◆ providing consumers with cancellation rights in certain cases (e.g. in a number of consumer contracts (e.g. those for goods purchased at a distance), consumers are provided with a 'cooling-off' period, during which they are allowed to cancel the contract without penalty).

In certain areas (e.g. the domestic sale of goods), there is a significant overlap between commercial law and consumer law. Consumer law also overlaps strongly with contract law (as most consumer transactions are conducted via contract) and the law of torts (e.g. if a product is defective, the torts of negligence or product liability might be relevant).

The framework of many areas of consumer law is set out in legislation (e.g. the framework for consumer credit is set out in the Consumer Credit Act 1974), with case law applying and interpreting the relevant statutory rules. However, certain areas of consumer law are not predominantly regulated by statute or case law, but are regulated by independent regulators based on rules they create. For example, the Committee for Advertising Practice writes the various Advertising Codes that regulate advertisements and these are enforced by the Advertising Standards Authority.

7 Environmental law

The dominant purpose of environmental law is the protection of the environment and, as the activities of businesses can clearly impact the environment, it is an area of law that has acquired increased importance for businesses over the last 30 years. Prominent environmental law topics include:

- regulating activities that can affect air and water quality;
- measures designed to combat climate change;
- requiring businesses that engage in certain activities to obtain an environmental permit;
- rules regarding the disposal of waste;
- the decontamination of contaminated land; and
- conservation of plants, wildlife and habitats.

Environmental law tends to be relatively self-contained and does not significantly overlap with the other areas of law discussed in this chapter, with the exception of the law of torts as certain torts (e.g. nuisance) can clearly be environmental-based. Company law does contain some references to environmental protection, namely (i) when complying with the duty to promote the success of the company (CA 2006, s 172), directors must take into account the impact of the company's operations on the environment and (ii) quoted companies must state in their strategic report the amount of greenhouse gases that they produce.

Given that protection of the environment is a worldwide issue, it is unsurprising that international law plays a major role in protecting the environment. A notable example of this is the United Nations Framework Convention on Climate Change, which aims to combat climate change by stabilising greenhouse gas emissions. 197 countries have ratified the Convention to date which has led to several major environmental initiatives being passed, notably the Kyoto Protocol and the Paris Agreement. EU law has also played a major role, with a notable amount of EU environmental legislation being passed in the last 20 years. This has resulted in the UK environmental law framework being predominantly statutory, with numerous pieces of legislation covering the various areas of environmental law (e.g. the Wildlife and Countryside Act 1981, the Environmental Protection Act 1990, the Climate Change Act 2008).

8 Intellectual property law

Businesses will want to prevent others from stealing or copying (i) the names or designs of their products or brands; (ii) their inventions; and (iii) certain other outputs, items or images. These are collectively known as 'intellectual property' (IP) and a business's IP can be a genuine and high-value business asset that can help a business stand out from its competitors. Enabling businesses to protect their IP, where appropriate, is the principal goal of IP law and it does this in a number of ways, including:

◈ **Patents**: Businesses that are engaged in developing new technologies will wish to protect any innovative technological inventions they develop. This can be done by applying for a patent over such inventions, the effect of which is to prevent others from making, using or selling the patented invention without the patent holder's consent for a period of 20 years (the patent can be renewed).

◈ **Copyright**: In a business context, copyright tends to arise in relation to businesses that produce some form of creative output (e.g. films, sound recordings, broadcasts). Such businesses can obtain a copyright over their output for a certain period, which basically means that certain activities (e.g. copying or distributing the output) are prohibited without the copyright holder's consent.

◈ **Designs rights**: Businesses that produce goods may wish to prevent others from copying the design (e.g. the shape or appearance) of that product. This can be done by obtaining a design right over the product, the effect of which is to prevent others from copying the product's design for up to 15 or 25 years (depending on the type of design right obtained).

◈ **Trade marks**: A business will wish to protect certain items, such as the name of a product, or a company name or logo. This can be done by obtaining a trade mark over the item in question, the effect of which is to prevent others from utilising the trade mark (e.g. by placing it on goods or services sold) without the trade mark holder's authorisation.

It should be noted that these are not mutually exclusive and a combination of IP rights can be obtained in relation to a single product (e.g. the name of a product may be trade marked, whilst a new technological component within it may be patented). Should an IP right be breached, the IP holder will be entitled to a remedy (e.g. damages, recovery of profits, injunction).

The framework for most areas of IP law is found in UK legislation (e.g. the framework for patents is found in the Patents Act 1977). Certain areas of IP law (notably trade marks and design rights) have been almost fully codified by EU law, with the result that there is a high degree of harmonisation of IP law across the EU and numerous pieces of UK legislation have been passed to implement EU law (e.g. the Trade Marks Act 1994 was passed to implement the 1989 Trade Marks Directive).

9 Cyber-security and data protection

Many of the legal topics discussed in this chapter have existed for centuries, but cyber-security and data protection are more recent areas of business interest, largely due to the massive increase in the number of online connected devices and the amount of data that businesses store online.

A governmental report in 2017 stated that 46% of UK businesses were subjected to some form of cyber attack in the previous year. The scale and number of cyber attacks is growing each year. Common forms of cyber attack include:

◆   fraudulent e-mails, especially phishing e-mails (e-mails that contain a link which, if clicked, can result in the victim's data being stolen);

◆   infecting computer systems with viruses and malware, which can disrupt the business's systems or steal data;

◆   ransomware (a malicious piece of software that blocks access to the victim's data or threatens to publish it, unless a ransom is paid); and

◆   denial of service attacks, under which attackers send large amounts of data to a company's network, so that the network is disrupted.

Given the increasing threat posed by cyber attacks, it is vital that companies take cyber-security seriously, with the National Cyber Security Centre stating that this involves:

◆   identifying, assessing and understanding security risks;

◆   having security policies and processes in place;

◆   being clear about who or what has authorisation to interact with the business's systems;

◆   ensuring that data stored or transmitted electronically is protected from attack;

◆   businesses should have policies in place to deal with disruption caused by cyber attacks;

◆   relevant staff should have the training, information and skills they need to support the business's security systems;

◆   the security systems should be monitored to determine their continued effectiveness; and

◆   businesses should have an Incident Response Plan, which includes reporting on the cyber attack, with the following infamous example demonstrating how not to respond to an attack.

Case Example 7.2

In October 2016, hackers accessed Uber's computer systems and downloaded personal details (e.g. names, e-mail addresses, mobile phone numbers) of 57 million customers and drivers from around the world. The company decided to conceal the data breach and paid the hackers

$100,000 to destroy the data and keep the breach a secret (although it had no guarantee that the hackers did destroy the data). In November 2017, Uber's CEO disclosed details of the hack, leading to numerous civil and criminal proceedings being commenced against the company. Around the world, government agencies (including the UK's National Cyber Security Centre, the National Crime Agency and the Information Commissioner's Office) opened an investigation into the attack and Uber's cover up. Uber's Chief Security Officer was later fired, but the damage had been done – Uber's reputation was severely damaged and its market value decreased significantly.

Given the increased importance of cyber-security and data protection, it is unsurprising that this area has seen a lot of legislative activity in recent years and this is due to continue. Much of this activity is at EU level, with two notable developments being:

1. The EU General Data Protection Regulation came into force in May 2018 and seeks to harmonise data protection laws across the EU by setting out the legal framework for data protection law. At the time of writing, the Data Protection Bill is making its way through Parliament and will establish a new data protection system in the UK that largely mirrors that found in the Regulation.

2. The Directive on Security of Network and Information Systems has to be implemented by May 2018 and places obligations (i) upon Member States to put a national framework in place to promote the security of network and information systems; and (ii) upon businesses that provide essential services to take appropriate and proportionate security measures to manage risks in their network and information systems.

10 Competition law

It is widely accepted that competition amongst businesses produces numerous benefits, including a wider choice of products, lower prices, better quality products and increased efficiency. Conversely, monopolies can result in opposite effects (e.g. reduced choice, higher prices, etc.). At its broadest level, competition law seeks to maximise competition both to benefit consumers and to prohibit certain anti-competitive practices. Key competition law topics include:

◆ prohibiting businesses from engaging in activity that can prevent, restrict or distort competition;

◆ preventing businesses from abusing their dominant position in the marketplace;

◆ prohibiting **cartel** activity;

◆ determining whether proposed mergers or takeovers will adversely affect competition in the marketplace and blocking those that will; and

◆ empowering certain bodies to investigate competition concerns in the marketplace and impose solutions.

cartel
Where a person agrees with one or more other persons to engage in certain activities designed to adversely affect competition (e.g. price-fixing or limiting the supply of goods).

There is a very close relationship between EU competition law and UK competition law, in the sense that the UK's system of competition law is closely modelled on that of the EU (namely that the Chapter I and II prohibitions found in the Competition Act 1998 are very similar to Arts 101 and 102 of the TFEU). The UK competition law framework is largely set out in statute, notably the Competition Act 1998 and the Enterprise Act 2002. Responsibility for investigating and enforcing UK competition law is placed not just on the courts, but on a series of bodies that are known as the competition authorities, of which the most noteworthy is the Competition and Markets Authority (CMA). The CMA's roles include:

- investigating breaches of EU and UK competition law;
- conducting marker studies and investigations into markets where a lack of competition could be adversely affecting consumers;
- prosecuting those who engage in cartel activity; and
- investigating mergers that could affect competition, with the following recent example demonstrating this.

Case Example 7.3

21st Century Fox Inc (a US company) owned 39% of the shares in Sky plc and wished to take it over. The matter was referred to the CMA by the government and, in January 2018, it issued a provisional decision in which it stated that it would not be in the public interest for the takeover to proceed because it would give the Murdoch Family Trust (which controls Fox and, via News Corp, several news providers in the UK) too much control over news providers in the UK. However, the CMA also stated that prohibiting the takeover was only one solution and that other options did exist (e.g. if News Corp divested its shares in Sky News). In June 2018, the CMA published a report in which it stated that the takeover would result in public interest concerns and, to allay these concerns, it recommended that Sky should divest Sky News to another purchaser (notably Disney). The Secretary of State accepted this report and the CMA's recommendations. At the time of writing, Fox has undertaken to divest Sky News to Disney and the Secretary of State has stated that the undertakings remedy the public interest concerns he had. Accordingly, the takeover will now likely proceed.

Test Yourself 7.1

1. **Provide six examples of a tort.**

2. **Identify six employment law topics.**

3. **What is commercial law and what other legal topics does it overlap with?**

4. What are the four principal methods of protecting a business's intellectual property?

5. What tasks are undertaken by the Competition and Markets Authority?

Chapter summary

◆ Contract law establishes rules regarding when a contract is created, what terms may be used, what will cause the termination of a contract and the remedies for breach of contract.

◆ A tort is a form of civil wrong, examples of which include negligence, nuisance and defamation.

◆ Increasingly, employment law not only focuses on the rights and obligations of employees, but also on persons who are workers.

◆ The principal commercial law topics are domestic sale of goods, international sale of goods and the law of agency.

◆ Many topics within consumer law are based around a central statute (e.g. the Consumer Credit Act 1974).

◆ As the protection of the environment is a worldwide issue, many key pieces of environmental legislation derive from international sources.

◆ Businesses can protect their intellectual property via the use of patents, copyright, design rights and trade marks.

◆ In recent years, cyber attacks have increased notably and so cyber security and data protection have become extremely prominent topics of late, with a number of key EU pieces of legislation recently coming into force.

◆ The aim of competition law is to maximise competition in order to benefit consumers.

Part three

Principles of company compliance and administration

Overview

This Part examines the historical origins of modern company law and important differences and separation between ownership and management. The three chapters will review corporate structures, the incorporation process and key constitutional documents, the roles of directors and members and the obligations on companies for transparency and the provision of information on their structure and financial status.

Chapter 8 gives an overview of the evolution of modern company law, examines the structure of UK companies and takes a brief look at the differences with two other main international structures. The chapter reviews the incorporation process, share capital structures and the importance of the Articles of Association and their interaction with the legislation and the obligation to place certain information on the public record.

Chapter 9 provides an in-depth review of the obligation on companies to maintain various registers of their members and directors, the requirement to file details of any changes in those registers and their constitution with the Registrar of Companies. The chapter also outlines the need for companies to properly identify themselves in communications, data protection considerations of the information that companies generally hold together with a look at document retention policies.

Chapter 10 examines the key differences between directors and members and the different legislation regime for decision making and the convening and holding of meetings of the members and of the directors.

Learning outcomes

At the end of this part, you will be able to:

- Understand the concepts of corporate persona and limited liability and the differences between ownership and management

- Consider the choices available and most appropriate company type to choose when incorporating a new company depending upon the purpose for which the company is required

- Demonstrate knowledge of the obligation on companies to identify themselves in their communications with members, suppliers and customers in their hard copy or electronic communications, websites and property signage

- Identify the interaction of data protection requirements with the obligation to maintain registers of members and directors and the need to ensure privacy of certain information whilst allowing public access to others and the conflicting obligations not to retain personal data unnecessarily and the need to maintain business records.

- Demonstrate a clear understanding of the differences between members and directors and the different regimes for the conduct of meetings of directors and members

- Appreciate the at times conflicting duties placed upon directors to consider the needs of differing groups interacting with the business under their control

Chapter eight
How companies are structured

CONTENTS

1 Introduction

This chapter looks at the historical background and the development of the concepts of limited liability and separate corporate persona and an overview of the different business vehicles available and the types of **company** that can be incorporated.

There will be a review of the relationship between the corporate entity, its managers and owners and the roles of the **directors** and **members**.

Finally the chapter will cover the ongoing administrative obligations of companies following their **incorporation**.

2 Historical background

2.1 Limited liability and separate legal personality

Prior to 1844 companies were established by Royal Charter or Act of Parliament but due to the costs involved had limited take up. Consequently most businesses were unincorporated associations with sometimes many hundreds of members. At this time neither companies nor unincorporated association benefited from **limited liability** for their members. For unincorporated associations all contracts and property assets had to be held in the name of the

company
An association of persons which, on incorporation, becomes a legal entity entirely separate from the individuals comprising its membership. In the Companies Act 2006, 'company' is restricted to companies registered under that Act or previous Companies Acts.

director
An officer of the company responsible for determining policy, supervising the management of the company's business and exercising the powers of the company. Directors must generally carry out these functions collectively as a board.

members
A subscriber to the memorandum of association and any other person who agrees to be a member and whose name is entered in the register of members.

incorporation
See registration.

limited company
The most common form of company, in which the liability of members for the debts of the company is limited – either to the amount of share capital for which they have applied (a company limited by shares) or to a specific amount guaranteed in the event of a winding up (a company limited by guarantee).

registration
Process by which companies are created by filing (or registering) several specified documents at Companies House.

partnership
A business run by two or more persons where the owners share ownership (partners) and have unlimited liability for the business's debts.

members. This made it very costly and complex to sue businesses due to the need to join in all the members.

The concept of incorporating a separate legal entity to set out, principally for administration reasons, the rights and duties of investors and managers was established in 1844 under the Joint Stock Companies Act 1844. Incorporation gave the company legal personality and perpetual succession of ownership of assets separate from its investors via a simple **registration** process.

The Limited Liability Act 1855 made it possible for investors to limit their liability for the debts of the companies they invested in. If the shares are fully paid on issue there is no further liability to pay any additional funds. If the shares are issued as either nil or partly paid then the liability is limited to the amount agreed to be paid for those shares when they were originally issued and cannot be subsequently increased.

These two features of separate legal identity and limited liability were combined in the first modern company law act, the Joint Stock Companies Act 1856, which has been modified and added to over the years culminating in the Companies Act 2006.

A company is an artificial construct having its own legal identity separate from its owners and managers.

There are a number of different forms of trading entity including sole traders, **partnerships** and incorporated companies. This chapter concentrates on companies incorporated under the Companies Act 2006 or previous Companies Acts. Although there had been many different Companies Acts, the 2006 Act was the first unified Act applying equally to England & Wales, Scotland and Northern Ireland. Previously, for certain provisions, there were different sections applicable to England & Wales or Scottish companies while for Northern Ireland-registered companies, the regulations were contained in a separate Order.

In addition to companies incorporated under the Companies Act 2006 it is also possible to incorporate companies under other UK Acts including the Limited Liability Partnerships Act 2001, the Charities Act 2011 and the Co-operative and Community Benefit Societies Act 2014. It remains possible, although very rare, to incorporate a company by Act of Parliament.

The UK corporate model has a unitary board structure with separation of management and ownership with the owners electing directors to manage the company on their behalf. This contrasts with the 'German' model which uses a two-tier board structure. Under the two-tier system, shareholders and employee representatives elect a supervisory board who, in turn, appoint a management board to undertake the day-to-day management of the company. Under the 'Japanese' model, the company's principal bankers take a much more hands on approach not only by taking up ownership of shares, but also providing assistance to the supervisory board. This supervisory board has members elected or seconded from the bank and by shareholders and the board ratifies decisions of the company president, who consults with the executive management.

Figure 8.1: Japanese Corporate Model

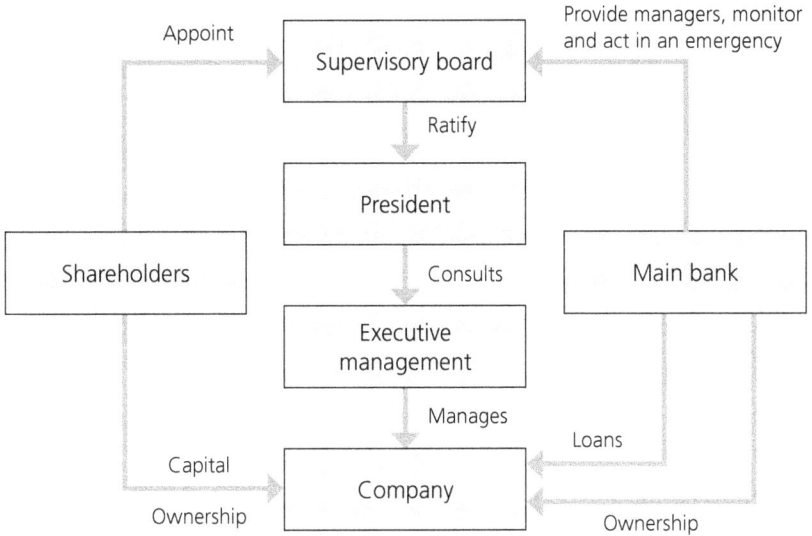

Anglo American Corporate Model

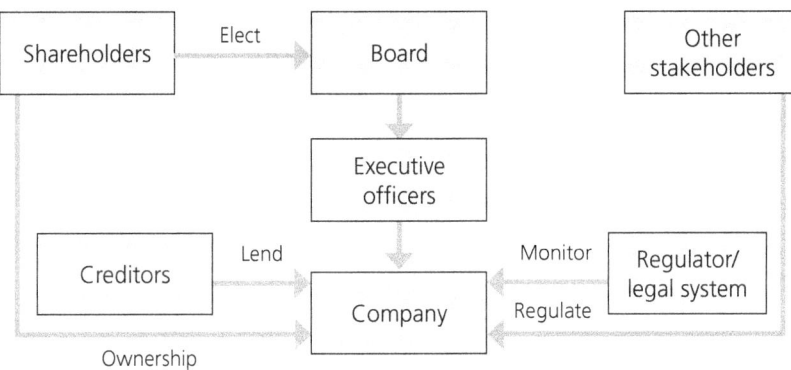

German Corporate Model

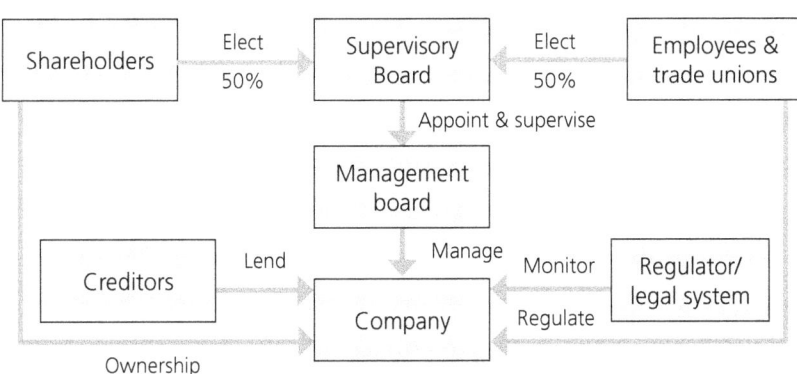

Stop and think 8.1

Company secretaries need to be aware that not all businesses that they interact with will be incorporated companies but will also include LLPs, partnerships, sole traders and associations. The type of structure will inevitably influence each organisation and in particular their attitude to risk appetite, payment terms, transaction transparency and speed of decision making. For international trading an appreciation of the differing corporate structures, board management structures and the roles of directors with similar job titles will assist greatly.

Test Yourself 8.1

1. What was the main method of creating an incorporated business prior to the Joint Stock Companies Act 1844?

2. What two key aspects were introduced by the Joint Stock Companies Act 1844?

3. When was company law unified across England, Wales, Scotland and Northern Ireland?

3 Company structure

3.1 Types of company

private company
A company that is not a public company.

public company (plc)
A company which meets specified requirements as to its minimum share capital and which is registered as a public company. Only public companies can offer shares and debentures to the public.

guarantee
A formal agreement under which a guarantor undertakes to meet the contractual obligations of one person to another in the event of default. A company limited by guarantee is one in which the liability of the members is limited to a specified amount in a winding up.

Under the Companies Act 2006 there are four types of company that can be incorporated:

- **Private company** limited by shares;
- **Public company** limited by shares;
- Private company limited by **guarantee**;
- Private unlimited company, with or without shares.

Companies may be incorporated under the Companies Act to undertake any activity, provided that activity is legal.

Private companies limited by shares are effectively the default form of corporate vehicle used by the majority of trading businesses.

Private companies limited by guarantee are primarily used for non-profit organisations that require legal personality. Many companies that are or wish to be, registered as a charity will be formed as a company limited by guarantee although other forms of charitable company are now possible. Such non-profit organisations can include clubs and membership organisations, residential property management companies and sports associations, unless these non-profit organisations are to hold property they could alternatively operate via an unincorporated association.

Private unlimited companies are now quite rare, although they do provide a formal structure to manage the relationship between managers and investors together with perpetual succession of title. In addition, disclosure of financial information is not required but needs to be balanced against the potential requirement to fund any deficiency of funds in the event of an insolvent **liquidation**. If the company does not have a share **capital** the **Articles** (the Articles) or a separate agreement will need to set out the ownership structure and rights.

A public company is mandatory if shares are to be offered for sale to the public. Public companies offer greater protection to their members and require greater financial disclosure and a mandatory **audit** of their **financial statements**. Although a public company must be established if shares are to be issued to the public, it is not mandatory for shares in public companies to be issued to the public and many public companies exist which in every other aspect are private companies. In some cases, a public company vehicle was used as a marketing ploy to make the company appear bigger and more important than if it were just another private company. Due to the increasing compliance obligations and costs, the majority of public companies are now publicly owned companies with their shares admitted to trading on a regulated market, such as the London Stock Exchange. Such companies are also subject to the more onerous disclosure requirements contained in the UK Corporate Governance Code.

Private companies far outnumber public companies and at 30 September 2017 of the 3.9 million registered companies in the UK only 6,194 were public companies.

liquidation
The process under which a company ceases to trade and realises its assets for distribution to creditors and then shareholders. The term 'winding up' is synonymous.

capital
The money or money's worth used by a company to finance its business. *See also* working capital.

articles of association
The constitutional document setting out the internal regulations of the company. Unless modified or excluded, the specimen articles in the relevant version of Table A/model articles have effect.

audit
The independent examination of, and expression of opinion on, the company's accounts. All persons or firms offering audit services must be registered auditors and belong to one of the recognised accountancy bodies.

Stop and Think 8.2

As a company secretary you may well be called upon to advise directors on the best type of company to incorporate for a new business venture or group division. While unlimited and companies limited by guarantee will have fewer uses, especially in a commercial setting, understanding the key differences between public and private is essential. For instance being able to advise on the relative merits of utilising a public company vehicle even where external funding is not required but where the positive marketing aspects need to be balanced against the increased administrative, and in particular accounting, requirements.

Take a look round any High Street and you will see many examples of private companies, public unlisted companies and public listed companies. Consider why each company type might have been chosen in each case.

financial statements
The term adopted by the joint accountancy bodies to signify balance sheet, profit and loss accounts, statements of source and application of funds, notes and other statement which collectively are intended to give a true and fair view of financial position and profit or loss.

3.2 Registered address

All companies must have a registered office in the country of their registration. Although this is often the head office address, some companies use the address of one of their professional advisers as their registered office.

Wherever the registered office is located, the name of the entity must be displayed on the outside of the building. Where a number of companies use the same address, this may be displayed electronically on a scrolling display in the reception area/lobby.

Companies that are dormant or use the residential address of a director as their registered office are not required to display the company name externally on the building.

The registered office is the legal address of the company and the address where all official letters and other documents required to be served on the company must be delivered.

Copies of the company's statutory registers and other documents such as directors' service **contracts**, contracts to re-purchase shares and minutes of meetings of the members must be kept available for inspection either at the registered office or, if it has one, at a Single Alternative Inspection Location (SAIL address).

3.3 Ownership

Members

Companies are owned by their members, who either at the time the company is formed or subsequently will contribute working capital in exchange for ownership rights. As noted earlier, more than 99% of companies are private companies limited by shares. Each **share** represents a proportion of the ownership of the company. The exact proportion will vary from company to company depending upon the total number of shares that have been issued. In a small private company one share might represent 100% of the issued shares whilst in a substantial listed public company, with hundreds of millions of shares issued, each share represents a very small percentage of the issued shares.

Due to the dominance of private companies limited by shares, the terms members and **shareholders** have become interchangeable when describing owners of companies.

All companies limited by shares must have at least one member and there is no maximum. A company limited by guarantee and unlimited companies must have at least two members.

There are two elements to becoming a member of a company. First, the person must consent to becoming a member, which usually also includes specific agreement to being bound by the memorandum and the Articles and secondly, by having their details entered in the company's register of members.

contract
An agreement between two or more legal persons creating a legally enforceable obligation between them.

share
A unit of ownership of the company, representing a fraction of the share capital and usually conferring rights to participate in distributions. There may be several kinds of shares each carrying different rights. Shares are issued at a fixed nominal value, although the company may actually receive a larger amount, the excess representing share premium. Members may not be required to subscribe the full amount immediately, in which case the shares are partly paid. The members then await calls, which require them to pay further amounts until the shares are fully paid.

shareholder
A member holding shares of a company with a share capital. The most common form of company member.

Share allotment

The process by which a company sells its own shares is referred to as share **allotment** or share issue. Prior to the Companies Act 2006 coming into effect, companies had a pool of shares available for issue, known as the authorised **share capital**, which was set out in the Memorandum of Association and this pool would be 'topped up' as required by **resolution** of the shareholders. The 2006 Act, however, abolished the concept of authorised share capital and there is now no maximum number of shares that can be issued, subject to any restrictions in the Articles.

In order to allot any new shares, the directors require authority to issue them to either be contained in the Articles or by resolution of the members. The Articles of private companies following either **Table A** or the **Model Articles** (see Chapter 9) give the directors full authority to issue new shares, subject only to observing the rights of pre-emption. Pre-emption rights on the allotment of new shares gives protection to existing members by giving them the right to acquire new shares being offered by the company, in proportion to the number of shares already held, before those shares may be issued to any non-members Directors of Companies with bespoke Articles, and public companies, will typically only be authorised to issue shares up to a maximum stated number often limited to no more than one third of the existing issued capital of which up to only 5% may be issued without observing the rights of pre-emption.

Existing members' rights are, however, protected by rights of pre-emption, set out in the Articles. Care is needed, however, as these rights can vary or be removed entirely from the Articles either by them never being adopted on incorporation or by resolution of the shareholders at any time.

Where there are rights of pre-emption, the Articles will set out the process by which existing shareholders must be offered any new shares in proportion to their existing holding before they may be offered to anyone else. Typically the rights of pre-emption will set out: a timetable for the offering of shares pro-rated to existing shareholdings; the process for application to take up those rights, whether in full or in part; and the eligibility to acquire excess rights, if required. If an existing shareholder does not take up their rights in full or in part their percentage holding will be diluted once the new shares are issued.

Public companies with shares traded on a stock exchange will usually seek a partial waiver of the pre-emption rights, so as to allow modest share issues without the need for a lengthy and expensive formal share offer process.

Transfer and transmission of shares

A share transfer is the process by which a shareholder can **transfer** ownership of shares they hold to another person. The directors authorise the transfer of shares and must ensure that any rights of pre-emption contained in the Articles are observed or waived and that the transfer form itself is properly executed, is 'stamped' if required and is accompanied by a share certificate for at least the number of shares being transferred. Although rarely found in public company articles and not contained in the model articles, many private companies, especially those with investors not actively involved in the running of the

allotment
The issue of shares.

share capital
The capital of a company contributed or to be contributed by members. Nominal capital represents the nominal value of the shares issued and excludes any premium paid.

resolution
A decision at a meeting reached by a majority of members voting.

Table A
The specimen articles of association for a company limited by shares incorporated under former Companies Acts. Unless specifically modified or excluded, the version of Table A in force at the time of a company's incorporation automatically applies to the company.

model Articles
The specimen articles of association for a company limited by shares incorporated under the Companies Act 2006. Unless specifically modified or excluded, the version of the Model Articles in force at the time of a company's incorporation automatically applies to the company.

transfer
Process where ownership of shares passes from one person to another usually by way of a sale.

business, have pre-emption rights on transfer. These are used to give existing members the right to acquire any existing shares being offered for sale before those shares are sold to a non-member.

Stamping is the process under which share transfers are taxed (at a stamp duty rate of 0.5% of the consideration) on the transfer of UK shares, where the consideration exceeds £1,000. There are a number of exemptions where stamp duty is not payable with the main one being if the shares relate to a 'Growth' company whose shares are traded otherwise than on a regulated exchange. The main market for such shares is the Alternative Investment Market (AIM) of the London Stock Exchange.

Although rare for public companies, some private company Articles will contain pre-emption rights on the transfer of shares which require any shares being offered for transfer to be offered to the remaining shareholders pro rata to their existing holdings. Pre-emption rights on the transfer of shares for a listed or publicly traded company is not possible as the shares must be freely transferable.

Transmission of shares is a share transfer by operation of law, typically when a member dies or the shares form part of a divorce settlement. In these circumstances the transfer of ownership is documented using a letter of request rather than a stock transfer form.

Stop and Think 8.3

Although the members are the owners of a company unless they are also the directors they have no day to day management involvement. Accordingly, the Articles of Association contain a number of provisions protecting the members. Consider how the interaction of the requirement for directors to be authorised by the members to issue new shares and the members' rights of pre-emption on the allotment of new shares affords protection to the members from their holding being diluted. What other rights to protect members holdings might the Articles of Association contain?

3.4 The role of directors in managing the company

Appointment and cessation of office
Directors are appointed to exercise the powers and authority of the company subject to any restrictions set out in the company's Articles.

natural directors
Companies are required to have at least one natural director, by which is meant a human being rather than a corporate entity.

The first directors are those persons set out in the incorporation document IN01. All companies must have at least one **natural person** as a director, who must be at least 16 years old. Additional directors may be appointed, subject to any maximum number set out in the Articles. A private company only needs one director and a public company must have at least two.

All directors must consent to act. Until 2016 the appointment forms AP01 and AP02 contained a consent statement that the appointee had to sign but this was dropped following the implementation of the company law provisions contained in the Small Business, Enterprise and Employment Act 2015. In its place is a statement that the appointee has consented. It is recommended that companies obtain explicit written consent from all prospective directors, as appointees are now able to challenge their appointment which will be struck out if consent cannot be demonstrated.

There is no upper age limit on the appointment of natural directors or their continuing to hold office. **Corporate directors** are still permitted although there are proposals to introduce a general prohibition on the appointment of corporate directors subject to a number of permitted circumstances.

corporate director
A corporate entity that is appointed as a director of another company. Quite common within groups of companies.

Generally, for a private company, the appointment of a director continues until they resign, are removed from office or incapacitated through illness or death. Directors of all companies may be removed by a simple majority of shareholders and any provisions in a company's articles to increase the required majority or purport to appoint directors for long or permanent terms of office are void.

Directors of public companies will typically be required to stand down and offer themselves for re-election on a rotating three-year basis. Directors of companies subject to the **UK Corporate Governance Code** are recommended to offer themselves for re-election annually.

UK Corporate Governance Code
The code on corporate governance that applies to UK listed companies. It is a voluntary code rather than a legal requirement.

Authority
As noted above, directors, by default, have full power to exercise the company's authority and powers subject to any restrictions set out in the articles. Such restrictions might include an upper borrowing limit, a cap on the number of new shares that can be issued, restrictions on the transfer of shares or the ability of the company to buy back its own issued shares. Any such restrictions may be varied, waived or cancelled only by **special resolution** of the shareholders requiring a 75% majority in favour.

special resolution
A resolution required either by the Companies Act or a company's articles which must be carried by at least 75% of the members voting at a general meeting. Such resolutions tend to be required where the proposal would change the nature of the relationship between a company and its members, such as an amendment to the articles.

In addition to any general restrictions in the articles the board as a whole may have restrictions imposed by shareholders' or investment agreements or commercial agreements such as banking covenants. Individual director's authority may be further restricted by their **service contract** or board policies such as banking mandates, matters reserved for the board or internal authority/signing mandates.

service contract
A director's contract of employment.

Duties, responsibilities and accountability
Until the Companies Act came into force the duties of directors were not set out in legislation but were to be found in the directors' services contracts, board policies and historic case law. The Companies Act 2006 however codified seven duties derived from existing case law:

- to act within their powers (s. 171)
- to promote the success of the company (s. 172)
- to exercise independent judgement (s. 173)
- to exercise reasonable care, skill and diligence(s. 174)
- to avoid conflicts of interest (s. 175)
- not to accept benefits from third parties (s. 176)
- to declare interests in any proposed transaction or arrangement (s. 177).

Directors carry personal liability for their action or inaction in managing the affairs of the company. Where a company fails and a liquidator or administrator is appointed to protect the interests of creditors, one of their tasks is to review the behaviour of the directors to consider whether action against them is appropriate and to consider if disqualification from their being involved in the management of companies in the future should be sought.

Stop and Think 8.4

Directors manage companies on behalf of their members and, especially where they are not also members themselves, owe them a duty of care to operate the company properly and fairly.

The Companies Act sets out seven key duties of directors which are supported and expanded upon by the body of common law established over the years.

Consider which of these duties might have been breached in the recent corporate scandals or failures of BHS, Royal Bank of Scotland Group and the Tesco accounting irregularities.

company secretary
An officer of the company with a number of statutory duties, such as to sign the confirmation statement and accompanying documents, and usually charged with a range of duties relating to the company's statutory books and records, filing requirements, etc. Under the Companies Act 2006, private companies are no longer required to appoint a company secretary.

officer
Includes a director, manager or (where appointed) the secretary of a company. Not everyone with the title of manager is sufficiently senior to be regarded as an officer, who must have a level of supervisory control which reflects the general policy of the company. Also includes the company's auditor.

3.5 Company secretary

All public companies are required to appoint a **company secretary**. Following a change to the legislation made by the CA 2006, this position is now optional for private companies. It is important to note, however, that while appointment may be optional, the tasks frequently delegated to the company secretary will fall to another, typically a director or senior executive, to undertake. Unlike directors, there are no specific duties set out in the Companies Act, although the company secretary, as an **officer** of the company, does share responsibility with the directors for ensuring relevant documents, forms and resolutions are filed at Companies House within the stipulated filing periods.

Although there are no statutory duties it is generally accepted that the role of the company secretary can be divided into three categories:

The board
The company secretary should ensure that proper board procedures are in place and are adhered to and that all relevant papers are circulated to board members in advance of meetings. They should also provide practical support and guidance, particularly to non-executive directors (NEDs) and monitor and guide the company's corporate governance policies.

The company
The company secretary should ensure the company's compliance with relevant legislation and codes of conduct specific to the company's business activities. The company secretary will often provide a central source of information to the board and senior executives.

The members

The company secretary is often the primary point of contact for members and institutions, particularly in matters related to corporate and environmental governance.

3.6 Persons with significant control

Introduced in 2016 by the Small Business Enterprise and Employment Act 2015 (SBEE 2015) the register of **persons with significant control** (PSC) was the UK's response to the G7 commitment to combat terrorism, organised crime and money laundering by requiring most companies to maintain a register of those people exercising control over IT. Control is usually demonstrated by ownership. However, it may be exercised as a result of agreements etc. The PSC may be very different to the register of members since ownership may be held through one or more layers of trusts or nominees.

On introduction, the legislation only required companies to update their PSC filings at Companies House on an annual basis, with the confirmation statement. However, in order to meet the requirements of the Market Abuse Regulations adopted across the European Union (EU) in 2017, the reach of the PSC regime was both broadened to bring more corporate entities into scope, require any changes to the information to be notified to the company within 14 days and for the company to provide notice of those changes to the **Registrar of Companies** within 14 days.

The PSC register is intended to contain details of natural people with control and in group situations it is necessary to follow the chain of ownership until the ultimate person with control is identified.

There are a limited number of exemptions – the principal one being that listed companies need not comply since details of those holding or controlling 3% of more of a **listed company's** shares are already required to disclose that information.

The obligation relates to UK-registered corporate entities, so for groups headed by an overseas entity, ownership may be disclosed by reference to the top UK registrable legal entity (RLE).

Person with Significant Control (PSC)
An individual owning or exercising control over 25% or more of a company's equity shares or voting rights.

registrar of companies
The official responsible for maintaining the company records filed under the requirements of the Companies Act.

listed company
A company whose shares are listed by the Financial Services Authority on the Official List of the UK and admitted for trading on the London Stock Exchange or NEX Listed markets.

Stop and Think 8.5

Introduced as part of the fight against organised crime and terrorist financing the PSC legislation requires all companies to disclose those with ultimate control over them. For many companies, this information will replicate the information shown in the register of members. However, for others, there has been a need to establish ultimate ownership in instances where shares are held by nominees or on family trusts.

Consider what legitimate reasons beneficial owners might have for holding shares through nominees and trusts.

Figure 8.2 summarises the disclosure obligations:

Figure 8.2: PSC disclosure obligations

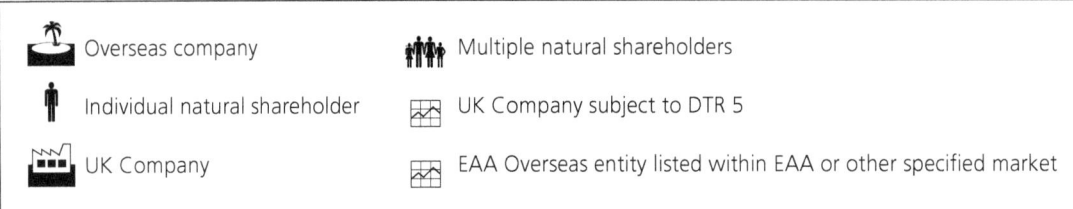

Example 1

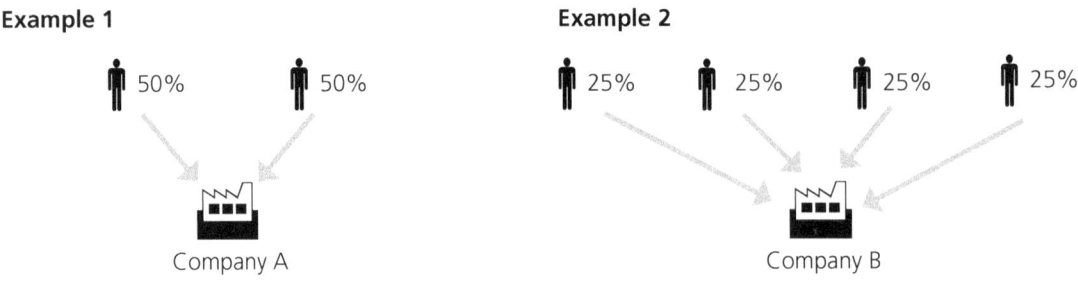

Example 3

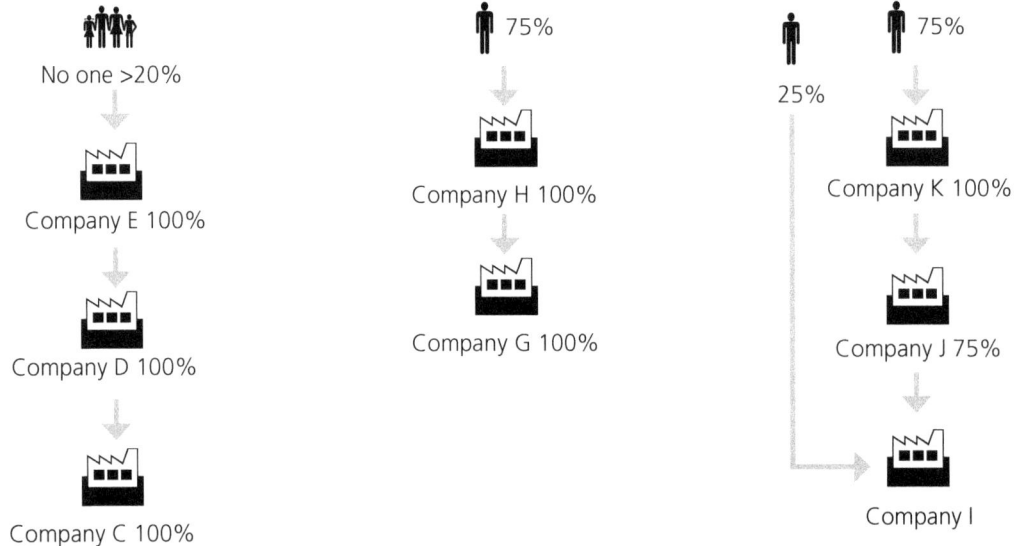

Example 4

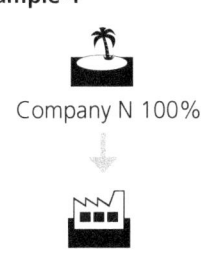

Company N 100%

Company M 100%

Company L

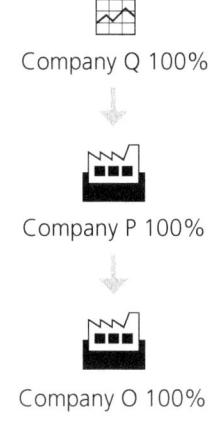

Company Q 100%

Company P 100%

Company O 100%

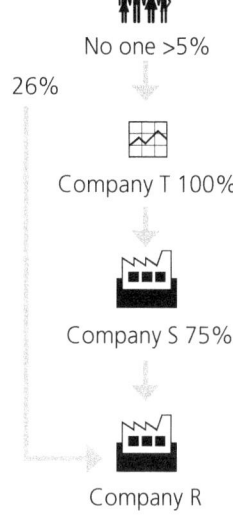

No one >5%

26%

Company T 100%

Company S 75%

Company R

Company L has no PSCs but an RLE –

Company M Company M has no PSC and no RLE

Company N is not required to maintain a PSC register as an unlisted overseas company

Company O has no PSCs but an RLE – Company P

Company P has no PSC but an RLE – Company Q

Company Q is not required to have a PSC register as a Listed company

Company R has a PSC and an RLE – Company S

Company S has no PSC but an RLE – Company T

Company T is not required to have a PSC register

Example 5

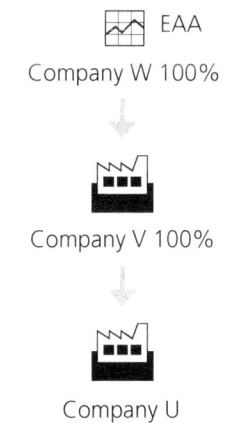

EAA

Company W 100%

Company V 100%

Company U

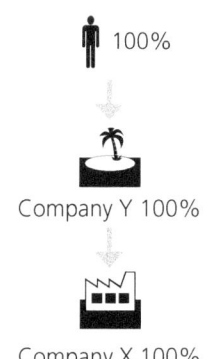

100%

Company Y 100%

Company X 100%

Company U has no PSCs but an RLE – Company V

Company V has no PSC but an RLE company W which is Listed in the EU

Company W is not required to maintain a PSC register as an overseas company

Company X has a PSC and no RLE due to the look through of ownership of overseas ownership where the overseas company is not Listed in the EAA

Test Yourself 8.2

1. What are the four types of UK company that can be incorporated?
2. Which of these four types of company is the most popular?
3. What are the seven codified duties of directors?
4. Which three categories of work does the role of a company secretary usually comprise?

4 Incorporation process

When forming a new company, there are number of key questions to consider. As discussed in section 3.1, there many types of company and each will be suited to a particular set of circumstances. The main criteria being:

◆ Is a separate corporate personality required?
◆ Are profits to be taxed in the hands of the company or the owners?
◆ Are the roles of management and ownership separate?
◆ Is charitable status to be sought?
◆ Ownership structure.
◆ Privacy of financial information.

Table 8.1 sets out the more common company types most appropriate to each scenario.

Table 8.1: Types of trading entity

Factors to consider	Plc	Ltd	Unltd	Guarantee	LLP	Unincorporated
Set up to make a profit	✓	✓	✓		✓	✓
Not for profit				✓		
Liability of members to be limited	✓	✓		✓	✓	
Liability of members to be unlimited			✓			✓
Financial information to remain confidential			✓			✓
Financial information to be public	✓	✓		✓	✓	
Profits to be assessed for tax on owners					✓	✓
Profits to be assessed for tax on trading vehicle	✓	✓	✓	✓		
Shares to be offered to the public >100 persons	✓					
Shares to be offered to a defined restricted membership		✓	✓	✓	✓	✓

Once the type of proposed corporate vehicle has been agreed upon, the next stage is usually to agree on company name. There are a number of strict rules governing the name to be used by a company set out in the Company, Limited Liability Partnership and Business Names (Sensitive Words and Expressions) Regulations 2014. Company names must be made up of specified characters or numbers, punctuation characters and a limited range of symbols. The full list can be found in Sch. 1 to the Company, Limited Liability Partnership and Business (Names and Trading Disclosures) Regulations 2015 (SI 2015/17)**.**

These restricted use words are known as 'sensitive words'.

For example, a name including the words 'Royal', 'government' or 'chartered' which imply pre-eminence requires approval whereas a name including words such as 'bank', 'audit' or 'investment' which are associated with regulated activities requires consent from the relevant regulator or governing body.

When choosing a company name, in addition to the restrictions under the Companies Act, care must also be taken to ensure that the name is not already protected as a registered trademark or a registered internet domain name.

Stop and Think 8.6

Nothing better identifies a company than its name and companies will spend considerable amounts to create their unique brand and to protect it from being used by others. When choosing a company name it is important not only to check the register of company names but also registered trade marks and website addresses. Just because a name has not previously been registered at Companies House does not mean that no one else is already using it.

Doing your research prior to registering the name will pay dividends in the long run and help prevent potential legal action for passing off or breach of trade mark.

4.1 The company formation process

The process of incorporating a company is known as incorporation, registration or **formation**. The vast majority of companies are now incorporated directly with Companies House using their online registration portal. Such companies are incorporated by default with the model articles relevant to the type of company being incorporated (see section 6 below). Companies with bespoke share capital structures or specially drafted clauses in their articles will most often be incorporated by a third-party registration **agent**, lawyer or accountant.

formation
See registration.

Form IN01 and the memorandum and articles should be submitted to Companies House together with the registration fee payable. The fee varies depending on the method of delivery to Companies House. Incorporation using the online portal carries a fee of £13, incorporation using a third-party software product is £15 and a paper-based form is £40.

agent
Someone who is authorised to carry out business transactions on behalf of another (the principal), who is thereby bound by such actions.

certificate of incorporation
A certificate issued by the Registrar of Companies on receipt of specified constitutional and other documents of the company. The company assumes its identity as a legal person on the date of incorporation shown on the certificate.

The details on the form will be checked and, provided there are no problems, a **certificate of incorporation** noting the registered name, registered number, date of incorporation and type of company will be issued, executed on behalf of the Registrar of Companies.

Once incorporated a private company can commence trading activities immediately, whereas a public company must demonstrate that it meets the authorised minimum share capital requirement and apply for a certificate to commence business and borrow, more commonly known as a trading certificate. Application is made using form SH50.

Test Yourself 8.3

1. **Which type of company would be best suited for the following businesses:**

    (a) A high street shop

    (b) An animal charity

    (c) A company proposing to raise working capital on the London Stock Exchange

2. **Are there any restrictions on the name a company can adopt?**

3. **What is form IN01 used for?**

ordinary shares
The most common form of share in a company, giving holders the right to share in the company's profits in proportion to their holdings and the right to vote at general meetings (although non-voting ordinary shares are occasionally encountered).

dividends
The distribution of a portion of the company's assets (usually cash) to its members.

redeemable shares
Shares which are issued as redeemable may be bought back by the company at a future date.

call
A formal notice issued by a company requiring shareholders to pay all or part of the amounts unpaid on partly paid issued shares.

5 Share capital structures

All public and most private companies are limited by shares. Their articles will set out the rights attaching to those shares and, in particular, between different classes of shares. If a company has more than one class of shares, while it is important for the articles to distinguish between them, there are no rules setting out how the share classes should be named. By convention, in most cases, the default class, having 'ordinary' rights, will be called **ordinary shares** and shares with preferential rights to **dividends** or capital and shares which are redeemable or convertible will most often be called preference shares, **redeemable shares** or convertible shares.

Under the model articles shares which are nil or partly paid should have distinguishing numbers. Bespoke articles usually omit this requirement and the directors can also elect to drop it. Whether or not shares carry distinguishing numbers, share certificates must make it clear when shares are nil or partly paid so that, in the event of a sale, the purchaser is clear about the extent of any liability for future **calls**.

5.1 Different types of shares and rights attached to them

As noted above, shares in the same company can have different rights. In theory any right attaching to shares can be enhanced or restricted but, in practice, the variable rights fall into the following categories:

- ◈ Rights to vote
- ◈ Rights to profit
- ◈ Rights to capital
- ◈ Rights to manage.

Ordinary shares

In almost all cases where a company only has one class of shares, those shares have full rights to vote, participate in profit **distribution** or **return of capital**, make changes to the constitution, composition of the board of directors and generally to exercise all the powers and authority vested in the members by the company's articles or the Companies Act. As discussed above although there are no specific naming rules, by convention such shares are usually called ordinary shares.

Preference shares

As the name suggests these shares carry a preferential right to one or more of the variable rights of voting, profit, capital or management. Most often **preference shares** are issued by companies seeking to raise additional working capital, either generally or for a specific purpose, without diluting control. As a result, most preference shares have no right to vote but carry a preferential right to profit by way of a fixed preferential right to dividends and a preferential right to a return of capital. Such rights are preferential as compared to the ordinary shares.

Rights to a preferential dividend may be expressed in terms where the dividend is only due in years when the company makes sufficient profit or may be due regardless of the level of profit and the amount is carried forward in those years where it cannot be paid until such time as the company makes sufficient profit. This type of dividend right is commonly called a 'cumulative right to dividend'.

Redeemable shares

Such shares carry the right to be purchased by the company subject to the availability of **distributable reserves**. Shares may be redeemed at fixed dates or at any time at the option of the shareholder, the company or both.

The redemption price may be at the same amount as the issue price or at a premium and can be for a fixed amount or calculated by reference to balance sheet value or retained profit. Some preference share redemption calculation will include overall caps or ratchet mechanisms.

distribution
The transfer of some or all a company's assets (usually cash) to its members, generally by way of dividend or on a winding up.

return of capital
An amount paid back to members being a repayment of the principal originally invested. A return of capital will occur if shares are redeemed or otherwise purchased by the issuing company.

preference shares
Shares carrying the right to payment of a fixed dividend out of profits before the payment of an ordinary dividend or the preferential return of capital or both.

distributable reserves
Profit retained by a company which may be distributed to its members.

Stop and Think 8.7

The three most common rights to enhance or restrict are the rights to dividends, return of investment and rights to vote. As a company secretary you might find yourself tasked with drafting bespoke articles of a new class of shares. Understanding the advantages and disadvantages for a company and existing members of raising funds via a share issue rather than by loan finance will considerably assist in this process.

5.2   Protection for existing shareholders

The articles may contain provisions safeguarding the existing shareholders from additional share allotments without their consent and/or pre-emption provisions requiring any new shares to be offered to existing shareholders in proportion to their holdings prior to being offered more widely.

The pre-emption provisions may be excluded in full or in part. Listed companies will typically authorise directors to issue additional shares on a non pre-emptive cash basis for up to an additional 5% together with an additional 5% in connection with an acquisition or specified capital investment. In addition, those limits are often expressed in terms of annual limits together with a rolling three-year aggregate limit. Guidance in the use of pre-emption waivers is issued by the Pre-emption Group which represents the interests of listed issuers, investors and intermediaries and is published via the FRC website.

Many private companies will adopt pre-emption rights on transfer so that existing shareholders are given the opportunity to purchase shares from another shareholder wishing to dispose of shares before they are offered externally.

Typically seen in private companies where external investors have put in seed or working capital but have no management involvement, there may also be so-called 'tag along' or 'drag along' rights. These give protection to existing shareholders where a major shareholder or group of shareholders obtains a buyer for their shares; the minority holders can oblige the purchaser to acquire their shares on the same terms. By contrast, the 'drag along' rights give the purchaser of a majority holding the right to acquire the minority's shareholdings on the same terms.

5.3   Share administration

As noted earlier, one of the key elements of becoming a member of a company is being entered in the register of members. For the majority of companies, where there is little movement in the membership, this is not going to present any significant issues. However, for companies with actively traded shares this can be burdensome and, in almost all cases where a company's shares are publicly traded, management of the register of members is outsourced to specialist share registrars.

Updating the register of members

Companies must update their register of members with details of any new share allotments or transfers of shares and issue any new shares certificates resulting from the changes within two months of the date of registration.

The register of members must contain the full name and address of each member, the date their membership commenced, date and number of shares acquired or disposed of, whether the shares are fully or partly paid (if partly paid, the amounts still due) and, where relevant, the date of cessation of membership.

Share transfers and transmissions

Share transfer is the process of transferring ownership of a share from an existing member to a new member or members. Transfer of ownership is a two-stage process. Beneficial ownership passes once a **stock transfer form** is signed and the consideration for the shares is paid. Legal title, however, only passes once the detail of the new shareholder(s) is entered in the register of members which can be a few days or weeks after beneficial ownership changes. In this interim period the seller of the shares holds the registered title on trust for the purchaser(s).

stock transfer form
Document used to transfer ownership of shares from one person (transferor) to another (transferee).

Subject to the observance of any rights of pre-emption on the transfer of shares contained in the company's articles, it is a relatively straightforward process to transfer shares. The seller of the shares must complete and sign a stock transfer form and pass this to the purchaser together with a share certificate(s) for at least the number of shares being sold in exchange for receipt of the agreed purchase price. The purchaser should arrange for stamp duty to be paid where the purchase price exceeds £1,000 unless the transfer qualifies for any exemption from stamp duty. Subject to any exemption, stamp duty is payable at the rate of 0.5% of the purchase price.

Once stamped, the stock transfer form and share certificate(s) should be forwarded to the company for registration and issue of a share certificate in the name of the purchaser and any balance certificate, if required, in the name of the seller.

Transmission of shares is an almost identical process but reflects a transfer by operation of law (e.g. following the death of a shareholder where the shares pass to the executor or beneficiaries of the deceased member's will). In these cases, the process is the same, although the transfer form is usually substituted by a Letter for Request and stamp duty is not payable.

Issuing a replacement share certificate

A shareholder might lose or damage their share certificate. In these circumstances they can request that a replacement be issued. Where the certificate has become damaged it can be returned for cancellation. However, where the certificate has been lost the process is more difficult as share certificates are **prima facie** evidence of title. This means that the share certificate is sufficient evidence of title unless evidence is produced to show that not to be correct. At common law, a company may be stopped from denying statements in a share certificate against someone who has relied on the statement. This, combined with the ability to sell the shares and receive the sales proceeds before the transfer is lodged with the company, creates the opportunity for fraud. To protect both the shareholder and the company, it is often necessary for the shareholder to complete an indemnity form and, in many cases, especially for publicly traded shares, for an insurance indemnity to be purchased in case the old certificate comes to light at a future date.

prima facie
On the face of it, at first sight.

Sometimes a shareholder will request that their holding is split over a number of certificates and this is perfectly acceptable.

Death of a member

The process to register the death of a member can, unfortunately, be rather slow due to the probate process. For the company, the process is divided into three parts.

First, the death of the member should be notified to the company – usually by a family member or a solicitor dealing with the deceased's estate. It is obviously important to verify the details and notification should include an original or certified copy of the death certificate. The date of death should be noted in the register of members, any dividend mandates cancelled and the death certificate returned.

When a person dies, only their executor or personal representative has the authority to deal with their estate, including disposing or transferring shares. This authority exists only when the Grant of Probate or Personal Representative is given. The Grant of Probate may take some time, especially if the will is disputed or if there is no will. Where shares are held in joint names, the registration automatically passes to the remaining joint holders.

Once probate has been issued, the original or a copy should be forwarded to the company for registration. The executor can elect for the shares to be registered in their own name pending distribution to the beneficiaries or they can be transferred to the beneficiaries immediately.

Communicating with members

For the majority of private companies, communicating with their members in hard copy via the postal system does not present any logistical issues. However, some public companies have hundreds of thousands of members and a few count their members in millions. Having such large numbers of members brings with it logistical problems when printing and despatching large volumes of mail, together with the not insignificant associated costs.

To assist such companies, provisions were included (now contained within the Companies Act) to allow companies, by consent, to communicate with their members using electronic means. Initially, members were required to give positive consent to receive communications electronically but in 2000 this was changed to deemed consent. Companies must still seek members consent, but any that do not respond are deemed to have consented. Although members may opt to receive any communication via e-mail it is more typical for documents to be available on the company's website with notification being sent electronically or by post to each member.

All companies, public and private, can take advantage of electronic communication provided their articles do not specifically require hard copy communication. The requisite authority was added to the model articles by the legislation, including those companies already incorporated, but any companies with bespoke articles will need to ensure they provide suitable authority.

Test Yourself 8.4

1   What four broad categories do shareholder rights comprise?

2   What rights protect existing shareholders from their holding being diluted?

3   Which rights might a majority shareholder wish to incorporate in the Articles to ensure they can sell the company to a third party?

4   Which document provides authority for an executor to deal with the shares of a deceased shareholder?

6 Constitutional documents

As noted above, when a company is first incorporated one of the documents that must be registered is the memorandum and the articles. Although routinely referred to as one document these are, in fact, separate: the **memorandum of association** and the articles of association. However, they are most often printed and even bound as one document.

memorandum of association
A constitutional document setting out details of the subscribers on incorporation.

6.1 Memorandum of association

As part of the general update and modernisation of the Companies Act legislation the CA 2006 greatly simplified the content of the memorandum of association and it now only includes the subscriber clause. It is through this clause that the subscribers make a statement that they wish to form a company under the Companies Act, agree to become the first members and, if the company is to be limited by shares, agree to take at least one share.

Under the previous Companies Acts, the memorandum of association included additional clauses such as type of company, the company name, authorised share capital and the objects for which the company was incorporated. For older companies these clauses are now deemed to form part of the articles and for companies incorporated under the CA 2006 there is no requirement to state a company's objects as all companies have full authority to undertake any lawful purpose (CA 2006, s. 7(2)).

Once the company has been incorporated it is not possible to alter the memorandum of association.

6.2 Articles of association

The articles contain the regulations governing the relationship primarily between the company and its members, between members and members' rights to appoint and remove directors. There are some provisions relating to how directors regulate directors' meetings although, in general, directors are free to organise their meetings as they see fit.

The articles form a contract between each member and the company which is why new members acquiring shares must also agree to become members and to agree to be bound by them.

As discussed below it is possible to designate some clauses as 'entrenched', which means they can only be amended if authorised by the articles. This might include a greater majority than that required for a special resolution. When filing a copy of the resolution amending an entrenched article, a certificate of compliance with the articles must be lodged.

Except for entrenched articles, the clauses within them may be amended by the members by approving a special resolution. If the variation affects any share **class rights** the consent of that class is also required. It is not possible to change the rights attaching to a particular class of shares without giving the holders of those shares the opportunity to vote on the changes. This applies even if, at a **general meeting**, the class in question has no voting rights.

Although the content of the articles is for each company to decide upon, they generally follow a similar format, set out below.

class rights
Where a company has more than one class of shares, the rights attached to those different classes of shares.

general meeting
Any general meeting of the company's members that is not an annual general meeting.

Share capital

◆   The company's capacity to allot additional shares, ability to make calls on partly or nil-paid shares together with any forfeiture rights in the case of non-payment.

◆   If the company has more than one class of shares, details of the differing rights attached to each class. As noted above, these rights are usually divided into right to vote, right to income/dividend and right to return of capital. There may also be detailed conversion rights and redemption rights in addition to any general return of capital rights.

◆   Although the Companies Act contains general pre-emption provisions on the allotment of new shares, these rights are often replaced by more expansive and detailed rights set out in the articles.

◆   Rights of pre-emption on the transfer of shares together with the so-called 'tag' and 'drag' rights discussed in section 5.2 above.

Directors

◆   Directors' general authority to exercise the company's powers.

◆   Restrictions, if any, on the maximum or minimum number of directors.

◆   Quorum for meetings of directors.

◆   Any restrictions on who can be appointed.

◆   Detail of the appointment and removal process for directors. As noted above, the articles cannot restrict the members' absolute right set out in s.168 to remove directors by ordinary resolution.

◆   **Retirement by rotation** provisions – usually only applicable to public companies.

◆   Provisions relating to conflicts of interest, disclosure and voting rights.

retirement by rotation
The annual standing down of directors (usually one third) for re-election by members at an annual general meeting.

Meetings

Detailed provisions for the convening and holding of and voting at general meetings. Such provisions will include details on who can convene a meeting, notice periods, details of what constitutes clear days' notice (see Chapter 10), who can propose resolutions, selecting the chairman, procedure for lodging proxies and procedure for calling poll votes.

Communication

Methods of giving notice and any variation to the default notice periods for convening general meetings

6.3 Shareholder's agreements

For companies with a small number of shareholders providing working capital, and most often not involved in day-to-day management, there may also be an investment or shareholder's agreement. Although very often containing provisions on the same matters as the articles, these provisions will give greater control to those shareholders who are party to the agreement.

A shareholder's agreement might include some or all of the following:

◆ right to approve any changes in company name, banking arrangements, the articles and senior employees;

◆ right to appoint or change a director together with agreement to support the appointment of other parties nominees and not to vote in favour of their removal;

◆ provisions relating to the convening, quorum and voting at directors meetings;

◆ **pre-emption rights** on transfers and permitted transfers – usually intra-group transfers or those to close relatives are permitted;

◆ pre-emption rights on allotment and 'drag and tag along' rights. These will very often contain a ratchet mechanism or complex valuation process in the event of a company sale or flotation, especially where the shareholders have provided working/development capital.

◆ Rights to dividends or return of capital.

pre-emption rights
Preferential right of existing members to purchase new shares to be issued or existing shares being offered for sale by way of transfer by an existing member.

In general, the clauses in a shareholder's agreement can be included in the articles. However, unlike the articles which are a public document, a shareholder's agreement is private. The only exception to this is if the agreement is referred to in the articles. If so, a copy of the agreement should also be placed in the company's file at Companies House.

Test Yourself 8.5

1 **What is the constitutional document called?**

2 **What other document might contain additional rights and protections for shareholders?**

7 Ongoing obligations

It is important that decisions of both directors and members are properly taken to ensure that there can be no challenge to the validity of any action or change.

Day-to-day management decisions are often delegated to an executive committee of executive directors and senior managers. However, strategic decisions and certain approvals are reserved to the board and constitutional changes reserved to the members.

Where management is delegated to an executive committee it is important to ensure that there is a proper record of the matters delegated. This is most often achieved by the board approving terms of reference for the committees together with a schedule of matters reserved to the board.

7.1 Meetings

Directors' meetings

Unlike members meetings, the Companies Act is silent on detailed provisions for the convening, holding and running of directors' meetings. It is for the directors themselves to regulate their own affairs according to their own needs.

Any director or the company secretary under the direction of a director may convene a directors' meeting. There is no mandatory minimum notice period provided reasonable notice is given.

Whatever notice is given there should be sufficient time for the directors to consider any papers circulated with the notice to give the subject matter appropriate consideration.

The quorum for meetings will be set out in the articles and most often the quorum is set at two directors. The quorum must be maintained throughout the meeting to continue to conduct valid business.

Directors' meetings tend to be less structured than members meetings. Typically, the chairman will introduce each section followed, if necessary, by a presentation or summary from the relevant executive director, a discussion followed by a decision.

It is the directors' obligation to ensure that appropriate minutes of all meetings of the directors are made and kept.

For further information on directors' meetings, see Chapter 10.

Members' meetings

By contrast the convening and conduct of members meetings is tightly regulated. In general, members meetings can only be convened by resolution of the board of directors and any notice of meeting will be stated as being issued on behalf of the board. Where the company has a company secretary, issuing notices of members meetings is usually delegated to them.

In exceptional circumstances, the members themselves may convene a meeting.

The Companies Act sets out minimum notice periods for differing types of meeting and company types as set out in Table 8.2.

Table 8.2: Notice periods for members' meetings

◆ Annual general meeting of a public company	21 days
◆ General meeting of a public company	14 days
◆ General meeting of a private company	14 days
◆ Notice to company of intention to put resolution	28 days
◆ General meeting of a traded company that is not an AGM, where electronic proxy voting is available and a resolution permitting notice of not less than 14 days has been passed at either the previous AGM or a subsequent general meeting	14 days

Members may agree to shorter notice, however the majority required to do so means that this option is only available to companies with modest or small numbers of members. To hold the AGM of a public company on short notice requires all the members to agree.

Like a directors' meeting, a quorum of members must be present to open the meeting and be maintained to validly conduct business. The default quorum for members meetings is two members present in person or by a representative on their behalf – a **proxy**.

It is an obligation of the directors to ensure that minutes of members meetings are made and kept. For more information on members meetings, see Chapter 10.

Many resolutions of the members must be notified to Companies House. In general, these are any ordinary resolutions that change the constitution or share capital of the company and all special resolutions. Types of ordinary resolution include resolutions authorising the directors to issue additional shares.

proxy
A person authorised by a member to vote on his behalf at a general meeting. A proxy need not also be a member of the company.

Stop and Think 8.8

Completely understanding the procedures for the convening and holding of both directors and members meetings is an essential part of the company secretary's role. Familiarity with the requirements will assist with the usual day-to-day tasks of setting the timing of meetings and circulating agendas, notices and accompanying documents ahead of the meeting and dealing with any potential conflicts of interest.

These requirements are, however, essential in times of dispute where in-depth knowledge of the requirements for notices and the quorum for meetings can prove instrumental in ensuring that there can be no question about the legality of any decisions taken or conversely minimising any disruption from protestors or disgruntled members.

Many private companies are formed by a pair of entrepreneurs coming together to undertake a particular venture. However, should these two fall out, knowledge of the processes for holding and convening meetings may assist in breaking any deadlock situation or ensuring that the deadlock continues such that the parties settle their dispute rather than see the company fail.

confirmation statement
A form filed each year with the Registrar of Companies, confirming that specified information about the company's directors, secretary, registered office, shareholders, share capital, notified to Companies House is correct or that any changes to the information are being notified at the same time as the confirmation statement. Replaced the annual return from 1 July 2016.

annual accounts, annual report and accounts
The accounts which are prepared to fulfil the directors' duty to present audited accounts to members in respect of each financial year. Annual accounts of limited companies must be filed with the Registrar of Companies.

administration order
Court order to appoint an administrator to manage the affairs of a company in financial difficulty.

charge
A means by which a company offers its assets as security for a debt. A charge is a general term that includes, but is not limited to, a mortgage. A fixed charge relates to a specific asset or assets. A floating charge relates to whatever assets of a specified class are in the company's possession at the time the charge crystallises (if it does so).

7.2 Filing requirements

During their life, companies are required to file information with a number of bodies on a regular or semi-regular basis. The exact range of filings to be made varies depending upon the type of company, whether it is listed, the trade the company undertakes and its size.

Set out below are a number of the more common ongoing filing obligations but the list is by no means exhaustive:

Companies House – annual filings

* **Annual report** and accounts
* **Confirmation statement**

Companies House – ad hoc filings

* Appointment and termination of appointment of officers
* Changes to the articles
* Changes of name or re-registration of type of company
* Allotment, cancellation, redemption, conversion etc. of shares
* Changes to PSC register
* Commencement of liquidation, **administration** and winding up
* Registration of **charges**

HMRC – annual filings

* Corporation tax

HMRC periodic and ad hoc filings

* VAT
* PAYE
* Stamp duty

Listed and traded companies

* DTR notifications of trades
* PDMR and PCA notifications of trades
* Announcement of results and interim financial statements
* Trading updates

General disclosures

◆ Payment practices disclosure

◆ Gender pay gap disclosure

Insurance

Although not a filing requirement, companies with employees are required to obtain employee liability insurance and are recommended to obtain other types of insurance in respect of their general trading, product, employee and security risks.

Test Yourself 8.6

1. **Who can convene a meeting of the directors and what notice period is required?**

2. **What type of members' resolutions must be filed at Companies House?**

Chapter summary

◆ A company is an artificial construct having its own legal identity separate from its owners and managers.

◆ Board structures differ between countries, with the most common being the unitary and two-tier structures.

◆ The four different types of company that can be incorporated are a private company limited by shares, a public company limited by shares, a private company limited by guarantee and a private unlimited company, with or without shares. The most popular type of company out of these is the private company limited by shares.

◆ It is important to separate management (the directors) and ownership (the members) of a company.

◆ Directors are required to carry out their duties according to legislation set out in the Companies Act 2006.

◆ The company secretary's main duties are concerned with supporting the board, the company and the members.

◆ Companies are required to disclosure details of persons with significant control within the company.

◆ The incorporation process may differ according to the corporate vehicle chosen for the company.

◆ Different types of shares (ordinary, preference and redeemable) have different rights attached to them.

◆ The register of members needs to be managed and maintained.

◆ The main constitutional documents of a company are the memorandum of association and the articles of association.

◆ Ongoing obligations placed on companies include obligation to hold meetings and information filing requirements.

Chapter nine

Records management, filing requirements and document retention

CONTENTS

1. Introduction
2. Statutory registers
3. Companies House
4. Company identification
5. Data protection considerations

1. Introduction

This chapter looks at the obligations placed on companies to maintain transparency as to the identity of their directors, members, controllers and capital structure. As noted in the previous chapter, incorporated companies have their own separate legal identity from their owners – the members. Unlike natural persons, who can trade in their own capacity without the requirement to place any documents on the public record, companies must place on record details of their constituting documents, their offices and details about their members and any capital subscribed.

There will be a review of the information required to be disclosed on the incorporation of companies and the processes to record and update both the company's own record but also those kept by the Registrar of Companies. This information is filed with the incorporation documents but must be updated either when it changes or annually. In addition, companies are obliged to publish their financial statements on an annual basis. The requirement to disclose information is sometimes referred to as the price of limited liability.

2. Statutory registers

In addition to publishing information regularly, companies must also maintain registers of this and other information and documents which must be both available for inspection at the registered office or single alternative inspection location (SAIL) and be able to be copied so that copies may be provided upon request.

Companies are required by the Companies Act to keep the following registers and books:

◆ Register of members – ss. 114 and 128D

◆ Register of directors – s. 162

◆ Register of directors' residential addresses – s. 165

◆ Directors service contracts – s. 228

◆ Directors' indemnities – s. 237

◆ Books containing minutes of directors' meetings, resolutions in writing of directors and decisions of a sole director – s. 248

◆ Register of secretaries – s. 275

◆ Books containing minutes of company meetings, resolutions in writing of members and resolutions of a sole member – s. 355

◆ Accounting records – s. 386

◆ Contracts for purchase of own shares – s. 702

◆ Documents for purchase of own shares out of capital – s. 720

◆ Register of **debenture** holders, if any – s. 743

◆ Register of people with significant control – ss. 790M and 790Z

◆ Report to members of investigation by public company into interests in its shares – s. 805

◆ Register of interests in voting shares disclosed to a public company – s. 808

◆ Register of charges – s. 859Q.

debenture
A written acknowledgement of a debt owed by a company, often – but not necessarily – secured. It is common practice for a debenture to be created by a trust deed by which company property is mortgaged to trustees for the debenture holders, as security for the payment of interest and capital.

Other legislation also requires companies to keep documents and records including:

◆ Certificates of employer's liability insurance – Employers' Liability (Compulsory Insurance Act 1969.

◆ Accidents in the workplace – Reporting of Injuries, Diseases and Dangerous Occurrences Regulations 2013, Health and Safety at Work etc. Act 1974.

◆ PAYE, VAT and corporation tax records – Income Tax Act 2007, Corporation Tax Act 2009, Value Added Tax Act 1994.

◆ Complaint handling records – certain FCA regulated firms – Dispute resolution rules 1.3.

2.1 Main registers

The main statutory registers that companies are required to keep include:

Register of directors
The register of directors must contain for each current and former director:

◆   Name and former name – Former names need not be disclosed if not used in business or not used in the previous 20 years. Maiden names need not be disclosed.

◆   Service address. This can be an office or residential address. An office address is recommended to mitigate against identity theft. The address in the register of directors, which must be available for public inspection should be the same as on the central register maintained at Companies House. In the case of a corporate appointment the address should be the registered or principal office.

◆   Country of residency. For a corporate appointment this is the country of registration and registration reference (in the case of an EAA registered company) or the legal form, law by which governed and the register on which the registration is entered, if any.

◆   Nationality.

◆   Business occupation, if any.

◆   Date of birth.

◆   Date of appointment.

◆   Date of termination of appointment, if relevant.

Register of directors' usual residential addresses
As a fraud prevention measure, the publicly available directors' register contains details of a director's service address. While this can be the director's usual residential address it is now more commonly the registered or head office address. The company must, however, also maintain a register of the usual residential address of each director, and any changes in it. This register is not available for inspection (see section 2.6 below).

Register of secretaries
Where the company has appointed a company secretary, their details must be entered in the register of secretaries. The content of this register is very similar to the register of directors, with the exception that the nationality and occupation are not required. Company secretaries register a service address but there is no requirement for a separate register or disclosure of their usual residential address.

Register of debenture holders
Even where a company has issued debentures, there is no obligation to maintain a register, but this is convenient. Where a register is kept it must comply with the requirements set out in CA 2006, ss. 743–748. These requirements broadly mirror the rights to request a copy of the register of members and the obligation of the company to ensure that the request is made for a proper purpose (see section 2.6 below).

PSC register
Introduced in 2016 by the Small Business, Enterprise and Employment Act 2015, the majority of companies are now required to maintain a register of people

with significant control (a PSC) – the PSC register. This is intended to be a register of the natural person(s) who ultimately control the company, rather than a register of members which records the identity of the registered members rather than beneficial ownership.

A PSC is anyone in the company who meets at least one of the conditions set out in the Register of People with Significant Control Regulations 2016 (SI 339/2016). Some companies will have no PSCs while others may have several. Most companies will have one PSC reflecting that the majority of companies have a sole shareholder.

A PSC is a person who either:

◆   holds, directly or indirectly, more than 25% of the shares;

◆   holds, directly or indirectly, more than 25% of the voting rights;

◆   holds the right, directly or indirectly, to appoint or remove a majority of directors;

◆   otherwise has the right to exercise or actually exercises, significant influence or control over the company;

◆   has the right to exercise, or actually exercises, significant influence or control over the activities of a trust or firm which is not a legal person, the trustees or members of which would satisfy any of the four conditions above.

Accordingly, where a company has a corporate shareholder it is necessary to move up the chain of ownership until the ultimate owner is identified. The identity of all individuals exercising control over 25% or more of the ownership or voting rights of the company or the right to appoint directors must be disclosed.

Other than a company that is exempt, all companies must have a PSC register and it can never be blank. Where there is no PSC, that fact must be recorded. Where the company has identified a potential PSC or is seeking clarity for a group entity, then those details must be recorded. There is a comprehensive schedule detailing the permitted statements that may be made depending on the stage of the enquiries into establishing the identity of PSCs.

Although in general, it is details of individual ownership that must be recorded in the PSC register two other types of entity are permitted. Accordingly, there are three types of ownership structure whose details must be entered into a company's PSC register. The categories are individual, registrable relevant legal entity (RLE) and other registrable person.

The information to be registered about each category of ownership is as follows:

◆   For an individual person the following must be recorded:
   –   the date the individual became a registrable person
   –   full name
   –   country/state of residence
   –   nationality

- – service address
- – usual residential address (this is not shown on the public record)
- – date of birth (only the month and year is shown on the public record)
- – the nature of their control over the company.
- ◆ For a registrable relevant legal entity (RLE) (such as a company):
  - – the date that they became a registrable RLE
  - – corporate name
  - – address
  - – legal form of the corporate body
  - – governing law under which the RLE was registered
  - – place of registration (if applicable)
    - • registration number (if applicable)
    - • the nature of their control over the company
- ◆ For another registrable person (such as a corporation sole or local authority):
  - – date on which they became a registrable person in relation to the company in question
  - – name
  - – principal office
  - – the legal form of the person
  - – law by which they are governed
  - – the nature of their control over the company.

Listed companies, but not their subsidiaries, are exempt from the requirement to keep a PSC register as they and their shareholders are already under an obligation to disclose interests in shares in excess of 3%.

Register of replies to disclosure requests

Public companies have authority under the Act and usually expanded upon in their Articles to require members to disclose information on the beneficial owner of the shares and whether they or the beneficial owner are a member of a 'concert party' relating to the shares (s. 793).

Where a company makes a s.793 enquiry, they must keep a register containing the date of the request and any information disclosed. The register kept pursuant to s. 808, often referred to as 'the s. 808 register' must be kept at the registered office or the SAIL address.

Register of transfers

Many bound statutory register books and electronic statutory register applications make provision for a register of transfers. Although a useful register to maintain it is not a statutory requirement. Companies keeping such a register must ensure that the data kept follows data protection legislation as any protections available for data kept on a statutory register will not apply.

Register of allotments

Many bound statutory register books and electronic statutory register applications make provision for a register of allotment. Although a useful register to maintain it is not a statutory requirement. Companies keeping such a register must ensure that the data kept follows data protection legislation as any protections available for data kept on a statutory register will not apply.

Register of members

All companies must maintain records of their members and any changes in the information. The precise information will vary slightly depending on the type of company and category of membership but in general the register of members will contain: full name and address of each member, date of becoming a member, any acquisition or disposal of shares and date of cessation of membership.

Register of mortgages and charges

Prior to 3 April 2013 companies had to keep full details of all charges against their assets. The amended procedure is that the mortgage registers is maintained on the central register kept at Companies House and there is no requirement for companies to keep their own register of charges. There is a requirement to keep the historic register updated with details of any changes to those charges.

Copies of charges (and any amendments) and instruments creating a charge must be made available for inspection at either company's registered office or its SAIL address (ss. 859P and Q)

Minute books

Minutes of members' meetings, which must be available for inspection, must be kept at the registered office. There are no provisions concerning the availability or location where minutes of meetings of the directors must be kept.

There are no rules concerning the format of minute books and it is up to each company to set its own preference which will often be determined by the size of the board, the regularity of meetings and the regulatory environment that the company operates in.

Historically they were kept in bound books, either handwritten or with typed sheets of paper pasted into the bound book. It is now as common for these to be hard copy minutes filed folders or files.

Some companies also maintain an index at the back of the minute book giving reference to the items covered by the minutes. The company secretary must decide whether the time spent in indexing the minutes will serve any useful purpose.

Minutes of general meetings should be kept separate from board minutes since members have a right to inspect the minutes of general meetings but not of board meetings (s. 358).

Stop and Think 9.1

One of the key tasks usually delegated by the directors to their company secretary is keeping and maintaining the company's statutory books. It is for each company secretary to decide the format in which they wish to keep the statutory books, whether manually or electronically and, if electronically, whether in a word processing or spreadsheet program or using a bespoke entity management software application.

2.2 Obligation to maintain statutory registers

In house
Until 30 June 2016 all companies had to keep their own statutory registers, ensure that they were kept up to date and were available for inspection at either the registered office or SAIL address.

Due to the logistics involved in maintaining a large share register and the need to synchronise the register with the electronic settlement system, **CREST**, companies with shares traded on a public market in almost all cases appoint an external share registrar to maintain their register of members. As a result, the viewing facility available at the share registry will have to be the company's SAIL address and the remaining statutory registers must be available for inspection at the registered office.

CREST
Operated by Euroclear UK & Ireland Limited, CREST is the major UK securities settlement system for UK equities, government bonds and a range of other securities providing simultaneous and irrevocable transfer of cash and securities for all sterling and euro payments and real-time settlement.

Use of central registry
Introduced by SBEE 2015 from 30 June 2016 private companies can elect to hold five of the statutory registers on the central register maintained by the Registrar of Companies at Companies House. This facility, although available to all private companies, is principally a deregulating measure intended for use by those single-member sole-director companies where there are few, if any, changes to the registered information during the life of the company.

The registers that may be kept on the central register are:

◆ Register of directors
◆ Register of directors' usual residential addresses
◆ Register of secretaries
◆ PSC Register
◆ Register of members.

The main disadvantage of taking advantage of this facility is that the private residential addresses of the directors and shareholders are available on the public record. The government announced in early 2018 that it would introduce legislation to allow persons to apply to have this residential address information suppressed on the public record. Individuals must opt in to take advantage of the suppression and provide a service address.

Companies wishing to take advantage of this option opt in to the service by giving notice to the Registrar in respect of each register they wish to hold on the statutory register. From the time of the election there is no need for the company to update the historical registrars it kept until such time it opts out. If a company opts out of keeping the registers on the central register it simply files notice and then takes responsibility for maintaining the registers itself. There is no requirement to re-create the records relating to the period the registers were held on the central register as those records will remain on the central register as a permanent part of the statutory registers of the company.

Third-party service provider

Many companies, large or small, private or public, use a third-party service provider to maintain their statutory registers and minute books and provide inspection facilities on their behalf in addition to any other services they might provide. While such service provision is entirely acceptable, the company directors remain liable to ensure compliance with the relevant legislation and should ensure suitable oversight is in place. This will routinely be delegated to the company secretary, where appointed.

Stop and Think 9.2

Although intended for use by small private companies with often only a sole director and shareholder any private company can elect to hold some of their statutory records on the central register maintained by Companies House. As company secretary you may have the choice of using the central register or holding those records in-house.

2.3   Where the registers must be kept

The statutory records and related documents must be kept either at the registered office or SAIL address.

There are requirements about the place where various statutory records are kept and where they may be inspected.

As an alternative to the registered office address companies can choose to keep and make available for inspection some or all the records and registers at a SAIL address.

The options available to a company for where to keep these registers and records are:

Table 9.1: Where statutory registers may be kept

Record	Registered office	SAIL Address	Central Registry (private companies only)
Register of members	✓	✓	✓
Historic register of members	✓	✓	
Register of Directors	✓	✓	✓
Register of Secretaries	✓	✓	✓
Register of directors' residential address	✓	✓	✓
Register of charges	✓	✓	
Register of interests in voting shares	✓	✓	
Register of debenture holders	✓	✓	
PSC Register	✓	✓	✓
Historic PSC register	✓	✓	
Company minutes and resolutions	✓		
Directors minutes and resolutions	✓		
Accounting records			
Directors' service contracts	✓	✓	
Directors' indemnities	✓	✓	
Contracts for purchase of own shares	✓	✓	
Documents re purchases of shares out of capital	✓	✓	
Report into ownership of own shares	✓	✓	

2.4 Format of the statutory registers

There is no prescribed format in the Companies Act and the statutory records may be kept in hard copy or soft copy. Where hard copy is used, this can be in the form of pre-printed 'statutory books' with manual entries or registers created using a word processing application and then printed out. Provided the registers contain the prescribed information the format is of no consequence.

There are several statutory book and company secretarial software applications available which can be used to store statutory register information. However, companies can commission their own bespoke applications or a word processing or spreadsheet application to maintain the registers. The commercial applications tend to be favoured by groups as changes of address for one director can be easily replicated across all group companies and the necessary statutory forms generated or filed directly from the application.

Whatever form the statutory records take they must be secure, confidential and any none prescribed information must comply with data protection requirements.

The statutory registers must be capable of being made available for inspection and for copies to be taken (see section 2.7 below).

2.5 Updating the statutory registers

The Companies Act sets out prescribed timescales for updating the various statutory registers with any changes together with any relevant notification to the Registrar of Companies. These timescales are set out below:

Table 9.2: Period allowed to update register following notification of change

Register of Directors	14 days (s. 167)
Directors residential addresses	14 days (s. 167)
Register of Secretaries	14 days (s. 275)
Register of Members entry of allotments or transfers	2 months (ss. 554, 769 and 771)
Register of Charges – satisfaction of historic charge	As required
Register of People with Significant Control	14 days (s. 790M)
Register of debenture holders	2 months (ss. 554, 769 and 771)

2.6 Inspection of statutory registers and who can request copies

The Act stipulates not only where the statutory registers must be held but also contains provisions regarding their inspection. Inspection of all the registers is free to members and in the case of the historic register of charges, free to creditors. Anyone else may be required to pay a fee.

The register of directors' residential addresses is not available for public inspection.

Requests to inspect the register of members or the PSC register must be accompanied by a statement identifying the person requesting the information and the purpose for which they require the information. If the company does not believe that the request is being made for a proper purpose, application may be made to the court for a direction either to supply the information or to order the company not to comply with the request. Any application to the court must be made within five days of the request being made. Due to the short timescale and costs involved in making an application to the court this is seldom used. All the registers must be kept at and be available for inspection either at the registered office or SAIL address.

The following registers and documents must be available for inspection:

◆ register of members (s. 114);

◆ register of directors (s. 162);

◆ directors' service contracts (s. 228);

◆ directors' indemnities (s. 237);

◆ register of secretaries (s. 275);

◆ records of resolutions, etc. (s. 358);

◆ contracts relating to purchase of own shares (s. 702);

◆ documents relating to redemption or purchase of own shares out of capital by private company (s. 720);

◆ register of debenture holders (s. 743);

◆ register of people with significant control, excluding usual residential address information (s. 790N)

◆ report to members of outcome of investigation by public company into interests in its shares (s. 805);

◆ register of interests in shares disclosed to public company (s. 809);

◆ instruments creating charges and register of charges: England and Wales (s. 877);

◆ instruments creating charges and register of charges: Scotland (s. 892).

The statutory registers and other documents of a public company must be available for inspection for at least two hours between 9.00 a.m. and 5.00 p.m. on business days.

The registers and other documents of a private company must be available for inspection for at least two hours between 9.00 a.m. and 3.00 p.m. on business days and the company must be given two days' notice of inspection where such request is made during the notice period of a members' meeting or during the circulation period of a written resolution and 10 days' notice at all other times.

2.7 Fees in respect of inspection of registers by non-members

The fee relates to the inspection of the registers of members, register of interests in shares and register of debenture holders. It is £3.50 per hour or part thereof during which the register(s) is/are inspected.

2.8   Fees for provision of copies of entries in registers and copies of reports

The fees for copies of the registers of: members, register of interests in shares and register of debenture holders are:

- £1.00 for the first five entries
- £30.00 for the next 95 entries or part thereof
- £30.00 for the next 900 entries or part thereof
- £30.00 for the next 99,000 entries or part thereof
- £30.00 for the remainder of the entries in the register.

Fees for provision of copies of trust deeds, service contracts and minutes is 10 pence per 500 words or part thereof.

Stop and Think 9.3

Although both members and non-members have the right to attend the registered office or SAIL address and request to inspect the statutory registers, in practice this is very rare. The main exception is requests to inspect or be provided with copies of the register of members or the s. 808 register of listed companies.

As company secretary any such requests will be brought to your attention either to deal with or alternatively, if a service provider maintains the records, to confirm that the purpose for which the information is required is a proper one.

The company secretary should ensure that appropriate procedures are established and documented to ensure that any request is dealt with in accordance with the legislation.

Test Yourself 9.1

1.   Which are the main statutory registers relating to individuals?

2.   Where can the statutory registers be kept?

3.   Who has the right to inspect the statutory registers?

3. Companies House

3.1   Reasons why companies are required to file documents with Companies House

On incorporation, companies record details of their constitution, officers, members and address. Suppliers, customers, business partners as well as potential investors and employees will use this information to assess the financial strength and potential of the business. As noted in Chapter 8, in exchange for limited liability of their members, companies must disclose financial information.

Accordingly, companies are obliged to ensure that the information recorded at Companies House and available to the public remains up to date.

In addition to notifying details of any changes companies must file an annual statement of this information in the form of a confirmation statement (s. 853A). The confirmation statement replaced the annual return.

Duty to notify any changes to the Registrar of Companies

The Act sets out details of which events must be notified to Companies House, together with the allowed period for giving the notification and the penalty for non-compliance.

Broadly, all changes to the information in the statutory registers, to the company's constitution and certain financial information, require disclosure.

3.2 Regular filing requirements

Annual report and accounts

All companies, whether trading or **dormant,** must file financial statements in respect of every financial period including the period between incorporation and commencement of trading activities.

dormant company
A company which has not traded or has ceased trading and has no accounting transactions that need to be entered in its financial records.

The format and content of the accounts will vary hugely depending on the size and type of the company, whether or not its shares are traded and which accounting standards it follows.

CA 2006 lays down a default format and content for private companies together with several disclosure exemptions for micro, small and medium-sized companies as well as additional disclosures and requirements for public and traded companies. On top of this there are additional disclosures for traded companies under the Disclosure Guidance and Transparency Rules and the UK Corporate Governance Code.

Table 9.3: Content of individual accounts prepared in accordance with s. 396

	Dormant	Micro	Small	Medium	Large	Plc	Quoted
Balance sheet	A	A	A	✓	✓	✓	✓
Notes to the accounts	A	A	A	A	✓	✓	✓
Profit & loss account		A	A	A	✓	✓	✓
Audit report (if audited)		✓	✓	✓	✓	✓	✓
Directors' report			A	✓	✓	✓	✓
Strategic report				A	✓	✓	✓
Corporate governance statement					✓	✓	✓

Remuneration report								✓
UK Corporate governance code and DTR disclosures								✓

Key
✓ = required
A = abridged information may be disclosed

Confirmation statements – Form CS01

All companies have an obligation under s. 853A to prepare and file a confirmation statement at least once in any 12-month period commencing on the date of incorporation of the company.

The confirmation statement replaced the annual return and is intended to offer an easier and more efficient way for companies to check and confirm the information held at Companies House, especially where there are no changes to that information from year to year.

As noted above, a confirmation statement must be delivered with the information as at a date not more than 12 months since the previous confirmation statement or the date of incorporation and must be filed within the period of 14 days from the made up date. There is a filing fee payable on filing the confirmation statement. If, however, a company files any additional confirmation statements within 12 months following a fee paid confirmation statement then there is no additional fee payable.

The confirmation statement must confirm that any changes to specified relevant events have either already been delivered to Companies House or are being delivered with the confirmation statement. The confirmation statement cannot be used to notify any changes. These relevant events are changes to:

◆   Registered office
◆   Appointment, termination or change to details of directors (including residential address)
◆   Appointment, termination or change to details of company secretary
◆   Change to location of statutory registers
◆   PSC register.

In addition to any relevant event changes, companies must also provide details of any changes to the following:

◆   SIC code
◆   Statement of capital
◆   Trading status of shares
◆   Shareholder information.

The shareholder information required depends upon the trading status of the company's shares. A company with shares traded on a public market need only provide the names and shares held in respect of their largest shareholders. Companies with non-traded shares must provide the name and number of shares held by each shareholder at the date of the confirmation statement and the number and date of transfer of any shares during the period since the previous confirmation statement. Where there have been no changes this information may be omitted.

The statement of capital information is required where there has been any change in the statement of capital information. Accordingly, a company with three classes of shares would need to provide details on all three classes even if the change only related to one.

The statement of capital contains the following information:

- Total number of issued shares
- Aggregate nominal value of issued shares
- Aggregate amounts unpaid on the nominal and (separately) any **share premium** on issued shares
- For each share class
  - Narrative summary of the rights attaching to the class
  - Total number of issued shares of that class
  - Aggregate nominal value of issued shares of that class.

share premium
The excess of the price at which shares are issued above their nominal value.

Changes in PSC information – Forms PSC01–PSC09
Whenever the information in the PSC register is updated the company is under an obligation to update the register within 14 days and must provide Companies House with details of those changes within 14 days of the register being updated.

Changes in officers – Forms AP01– AP04, CH01– CH04, TM01 and TM02
Whenever a director or company secretary is appointed, their appointment is terminated or their registered details change, notice must be given to Companies House. In the case of an appointment or termination, notice must be given within 14 days of the event and in the case of a change of details within 14 days of being notified of the change.

Change of registered office – Form AD01
If a company needs to change its registered office the change only takes effect once the form giving notice of the change has been accepted by Companies House. It should also be noted that documents may be validly served at the old address for up to seven days after the change has been registered.

Change of accounting reference date – Form AA01
Changes to a company's year end only take effect once the form has been accepted and registered by Companies House. Unlike most of other notifications given to Companies House, when the financial year end is changed Companies House issues a letter confirming the change and the new deadline for filing the accounts for the first new year end.

Changes to share capital – Forms SH01–SH19

Notice of allotments, redemptions, cancellations, conversion and other changes to shares must be made to Companies House within 28 days of the date of the relevant change.

Changes to constitution – Copy of resolution, Forms CC01–CC06, NE01–NE06

Copies of all special resolutions and specified ordinary resolutions must be filed at Companies House usually within 15 days of the date of approval of the resolution. Where the resolution amends the articles of association, an amended copy of the articles must also be filed.

The filing period can be longer for certain resolutions where there is a right for dissenting minorities to object.

Mortgages and charges – Forms MR01–MR10

Notice of the creation of security for loans, financing facilities, overdrafts etc, also known as charges, must be registered within 21 days of the date of creation of the charge. If the charge is not registered within this 21-day period, it is not valid. For this reason, it is usually the recipient of the charge, the bank or other lending institution, who registers the charge.

Although giving notice that a charge has been satisfied, in full or in part, is not mandatory most companies will wish to do so to keep their financial records up to date so that the presence of the charge does not deter or stop any future loan applications. Charges rarely give notice of satisfaction and these are more frequently filed by the company itself.

Liquidation/administration/receivership – Form RM01, RM02 and LQ01

Notice of the appointment of a liquidator, **administrator** or receiver should be given as soon as possible and no later than 14 days after appointment so that those doing business with the company are aware of its financial position and to provide protection for the directors against fraudulent trading from that point. Filing of the notice is usually made by the appointee.

3.3 Presenter information and fees

All forms and copy resolutions are required to be signed on behalf of the company to which they relate to confirm their authenticity. The signature may be that of a director, company secretary or authorised signatory.

Where the notification is filed electronically, these will be authenticated either by an authorised signatory providing personal information (e.g. first three letters of parent's name, place of birth or eye colour) or alternatively the documents are authenticated by being submitted by an approved presenter.

Where the actual forms or documents are submitted by a third party, such as the company's accountant, legal adviser or service provider, it is useful to provide presenter information as otherwise any queries will be directed to the company's registered office. This can cause delays in responding to the query which might

administrator
A person appointed by the court to manage a company in financial difficulties to protect creditors and, if possible, avoid liquidation. The administrator has the power to remove and appoint directors. A person who administers the estate of a deceased person in the absence of any executors.

cause a filing deadline to be missed and in the case of accounts filing incur a late filing penalty.

Certain documents incur a filing fee including incorporation documents, confirmation statements, changes of name or registration and registration of charges. Fees for forms filed online can be paid by debit/credit card. Regular submitters should set up an account with Companies House which can be used for documents filed online and those filed via software.

Stop and Think 9.4

As a core duty of company secretaries it is essential that you understand which forms are required for any particular event, information required and the filing period for those forms.

As almost all forms can now be filed online at Companies House it is seldom necessary to hold stocks of forms in readiness for use. There should, however, be a clear process to establish who is responsible for the preparation and checking of forms, obtaining the necessary signatures and finally filing them.

In addition to obtaining an acknowledgement of receipt from Companies House it is good practice to check the company's filing history after a few days to ensure the documents have been placed on file.

3.4 Format of filings

To ensure documents filed with Companies House are readily accessible, CA 2006, s. 1068 allows the registrar to issue rules on the format and means of delivery of all documents required to be submitted to companies.

Hard copy
Copies of all statutory forms are available free of charge from Companies House and may be requested by post, telephone or via the Companies House website.

In the past, Companies House insisted that all hard copy forms filed bore an original signature. However, following a review and after seeking counsel's opinion, this policy was changed. Companies House has determined that it is acceptable for a person to authorise others to apply their signature to documents. There is a presumption that the use of an automated signature will be subject to internal controls. Accordingly, forms and documents will not be rejected simply because they do not have, or appear not to have, original signatures.

This does not extend to allowing submission of documents by fax, due to issues relating to document quality.

In addition to rejecting documents that are incorrectly completed, not dated correctly or not signed, Companies House now regularly rejects documents that cannot, or cannot easily, be read or cannot be captured electronically in a useable sized format and legible when reproduced. Documents that are handwritten, printed in and/or on coloured paper and documents with shading or graphics are at most risk of being rejected as 'illegible' (ss. 1068 and 1072).

Ideally, documents should be printed or typed on white A4 paper.

Electronic filing

For many years Companies House has promoted and encouraged the use of electronic filing. In addition to the advantages for companies themselves, use of electronic filing aids quicker, efficient, more cost effective and often automated processing by Companies House and these savings are passed on in the form of lower electronic filing fees.

Companies can file their statutory forms electronically either by using the Companies House WebFiling service or by Software filing using an approved third-party software package or by developing their own bespoke in-house software solution.

There is no registration fee for using either WebFiling or Software filing.

Web filing

Companies House has now made almost all forms available for completion and submission online. Where there is a fee, this is reduced where the forms are submitted electronically. Registering to use the WebFiling service is very simple. It requires the online registration of a username and password and then requesting an authentication code for the company/ies for which WebFiling is to be used. The authentication code is posted to the company's registered office address so this will need to be set up in advance. The authentication code acts as the confirmation signature on the forms.

Electronic filing has several advantages for companies over paper-based filing including:

◆ quicker
◆ cheaper
◆ rejection rates are lower due to in-built checks, pre-population of data;
◆ automatic confirmation of filing; and
◆ security.

To improve security further users of the WebFiling and Software filing services can opt in to receive e-mail reminders for submission of annual accounts and confirmation statement and can opt in to the **PRO**tected **O**nline **F**iling service (PROOF). PROOF combats corporate identity theft by making changes of registered office or director changes only notifiable using either WebFiling or Software filing.

Software filing

Software filing enables software solutions to be developed, often in association with entity management applications, to allow companies and service providers to file Companies House forms, resolutions and documents electronically following an approved message structure issued by the Registrar.

Stop and Think 9.5

The choice of paper filing, web filing or software filing will most often be determined according to a combination of the cost of any software application, the benefit from being able to bulk file any changes, number of companies in the group and any additional features such as structure charting or board portal.

3.5 Penalties for late submissions

As noted below, failure to file documents on time, if at all, is an offence for which those responsible can be prosecuted, although the Registrar generally favours the carrot rather than the stick to promote increase rates of compliance. However, the late filing of financial statements is one set of documents for which there is an automatic penalty. The amount of the fine is calculated according to a sliding scale depending on the type of company and lateness of the filing as shown below.

Table 9.4: Late filing penalties

	Private companies	Public companies
Up to one month late	£150	£750
Up to three months late	£375	£1,500
Up to six months late	£750	£3,000
More than six months late	£1,500	£7,500

The penalty is doubled if your accounts are late two years in a row.

The registrar can also fine a company for failure to file an amended copy of its articles of association. This penalty regime was introduced to encourage filing of amended articles of association and is not an automatic penalty. It arises where a company files a resolution amending its articles but then fails to file a copy of the amended articles as required by CA 2006, s. 26. The registrar can issue a notice requiring the filing of an amended copy of the articles of association. If the company fails to comply with that notice within a period of 28 days a £400 fine can be imposed.

3.6 Consequences for failure to file documents

Failure to file documents and returns required under the Act is an offence for which responsible directors and company secretaries can be prosecuted. Although prosecutions are relatively rare, this is most often for failure to file financial statements or confirmation statements. This is primarily due to almost all other filings being event driven, so the Registrar will have no knowledge of a filing being late until the documents are filed.

It is very rare for a prosecution to be made after a document has been filed unless the filing takes place after the summons has been served.

If the directors fail to file the accounts or the confirmation statement and do not respond to the reminders issued by Companies House there is a very real risk that the registrar will take action to dissolve the company. The registrar can use powers set out in CA 2006, s. 1000 to strike off companies if there is reasonable cause to believe it is not carrying on in business or in operation.

A director's track record on filings may, however, be considered if action is being taken to disqualify a director as evidence of unfitness to be a director or if the company's affairs are being investigated.

Test Yourself 9.2

1. **What options are available to file information at Companies House electronically?**

2. **Are there any penalties for filing documents late?**

3. **Which documents must be filed every year?**

4 Company identification

4.1 Legal requirements for stationery

The company's full name as registered, place of registration, registered number and registered office must be shown on all business letters, e-mail and other documents, as specified in the Companies (Trading Disclosures) Regulations 2008 (SI 2008/495), including publications, cheques, orders for goods and services on behalf of the company, invoices and receipts.

It is not necessary to show the amount of the share capital on business letters, but if this is done, the reference must be to the paid-up share capital.

The names of directors do not need to be shown on business letters, but if it is desired to do so, the names of all the directors must be stated, not just one. However, it would still be in order for a letter to be signed by a director with that title under their signature without showing the names of all the directors on the paper (reg. 8 of the Companies (Trading Disclosures) Regulations 2008 (SI 2008/495)).

If it is intended that directors of the company should have headed paper stating their office, it is essential that care is taken not to breach the provisions. Although it is acceptable to show that the letter is from the 'Office of the Chairman', it would not be acceptable to state from the 'Office of Mr J Smith,

Director', unless the names of the other directors were also shown. It is not necessary for the names to appear with equal prominence, merely that they are all legible.

If the company has its registered office in Wales and uses the Welsh equivalent of 'Limited', or 'public limited company' in its name ('cyfyngedig' and 'cwmni cyfyngedig cyhoeddus', respectively), the fact that the company is limited must be stated in English on its stationery, bill heads and other official documents. It must also be included in a notice displayed at every place of business of the company.

4.2 Offices

The company's name must be displayed outside every office or place of business. Place of business includes a share transfer or share registration office.

If the company has its registered office in Wales and uses the Welsh equivalent of 'Limited', or 'public limited company' in its name ('cyfyngedig' and 'cwmni cyfyngedig cyhoeddus', respectively), the fact that the company is limited must be stated in English in a notice displayed at every place of business of the company.

4.3 Website

The company's full name as registered, place of registration, registered number and registered office must be shown on the company's website, if it has one, as specified in the Companies (Trading Disclosures) Regulations 2008 (SI 2008/495).

In addition, the website must disclose the VAT number if the company is registered for VAT, regardless of whether or not it is used to sell goods or services.

4.4 Business names

If a company carries on business under a name which is not its registered corporate name, it must comply with the provisions of CA 2006, ss. 1192–1207.

Although the controls on 'same' or 'too like' names do not apply in relation to business names, names implying connection with central or local government or containing certain words and expressions may be used only with the written approval of the Secretary of State (ss. 1193 and 1194).

A company may use its business name on business letters, e-mails, invoices etc. but, as noted above, the registered name and other statutory disclosures must be made. Typically, the statutory information is contained in a footnote to the letter.

Branded corporate signage on buildings is perfectly acceptable provided the registered name is also displayed. Typically, this is by way of a plaque near the entrance to the building.

Stop and Think 9.6

Unlike the register of company names there is no central register of business names. As a result companies should always check registered trademarks, web addresses and simply general internet searches to check the availability of a name whether for a registered company name or just as a business name.

Care must also be taken as there are many type of scam which appear to offer registration on a business names register for an often inflated fee. There is no central business names register.

Test Yourself 9.3

1. What company information must be shown on company letterheads?

2. Can a company display just its branded business name on its properties and website?

5 Data protection considerations

5.1 Suppression of individuals' residential address data

Directors and company secretaries are no longer required to provide their private residential addresses for inclusion in the public register and accordingly it is longer necessary to make an application to suppress that information. However, that is currently not the case for those companies that elect to hold their register of directors' usual residential address on the central register. Following a rise in the instances of identity theft against company directors the government announced in February 2018 that legislation will be passed to allow such directors to apply to have their residential address information suppressed on the central register.

Provision of a service address does not suppress residential address information previously provided and an application will need to be made to Companies House to have the address information redacted from the public record.

Residential address information will also be included in the PSC registers and application to the court is required to enable an individual to have information about their address suppressed.

5.2 Data protection registration regime

Registers which must be made available for public inspection under the requirements of the Companies Acts are exempt from the provisions of the General Data Protection Regime (GDPR) introduced with effect from 25

May 2018, provided that the information in the registers only includes that information which is specified in the Companies Acts and no non-statutory information is also available.

Notification under GDPR is required if additional non-statutory information is kept with the statutory records. Where such additional non-statutory information is held it is important to be able to exclude that information from any inspection by a member or a third party. For example, to facilitate payment of dividends by bank transfer companies will need to keep details of members' bank accounts and that information must not be made available to anyone inspecting the records or who requests a copy of the register.

5.3 Retention of documents

The company secretary is often responsible for exercising control over the company's policy regarding the filing and retention of documents. The period for which documents should be retained depends on the nature of the document.

Case law has demonstrated the necessity for companies to have an effective document retention policy that is relevant to their business, is adhered to by all parts of the business and that if litigation is anticipated, prompt action is taken to ensure documents are not destroyed either deliberately or in accordance with the normal operation of the policy.

Set out below are suggested retention periods for common documents.

Table 9.5: Suggested document retention periods

Statutory records	
Certificate of incorporation	Original to be kept permanently
Certificate to commence business	Original to be kept permanently (public company)
Articles of association	Original to be kept permanently
Seal book/register	Original to be kept permanently
Registers other than register of members	Original to be kept permanently
Register of members	Current members permanently Former members 10 years
Meeting records	
Minutes of general and class meetings, written resolutions	Originals to be kept permanently for meetings held prior to 1 October 2007 Ten years after meeting for meetings held after 1 October 2007

Table 9.5: Suggested document retention periods *continued*

Directors' minutes	Originals to be kept permanently for meetings held prior to 1 October 2007
	Ten years after meeting for meetings held after 1 October 2007
Circulars to shareholders including notices of meetings	Master copy to be kept permanently
Accounting and financial records	
Annual report and accounts	Signed copy to be kept permanently (a stock of spare copies should be maintained for up to five years to meet casual requests)
Accounting records required by the Companies Acts	Six years for a public company
	Three years for a private company
Taxation returns and records, Internal financial reports, Statements and instructions to banks and Customs and Excise returns	Six years
Tax returns	Permanently
Expense accounts	Seven years
Share registration documents	Refer to articles, but typical periods are:
Forms for application of shares, and transfer, renounceable letters of acceptance and allotment, renounceable share certificates, request for designation or re-designation of accounts, letters	Ten years from date of registration
Powers of Attorney and Indemnity for lost certificates	Ten years after cessation of membership to which power relates
Dividend and interest bank Mandate	Two years after registration forms
Cancelled share or stock certificates,	One year after cancellation
changes of address	Two years
Any contract or Memorandum to purchase the company's own shares	Ten years
Report of an interest in voting shares	Six years for investigations requisitioned by members
Register of interest in shares when	Six years company ceases to be a public company
Property records	
Deeds of title, Patent and trademark records	Permanently

Table 9.5: Suggested document retention periods *continued*

Leases	Twelve years after lease has terminated
Agreements with architects,	Six years after contract completion builders, etc.
HR records	
Staff personnel records	Seven years after employment ceases
Patent agreements with staff	Twenty years after employment ceases
Applications for jobs	Up to twelve months
Payroll records, Medical records, Accident books	Twelve years
Employment agreements	Permanently
Time cards and piecework records	Two years
Salary registers, Wages records, Industrial training records	Six years
Pension records	
Trustees and rules (pension schemes), Trustees' minute book, Pension fund annual accounts and Inland Revenue approvals, Investment records, Actuarial valuation records, Contribution records	Permanently
Records of ex-pensioners	Six years after cessation of benefit Pension scheme investment policies
Insurance records	
Group health policies, Group personal accident policies	Twelve years after final cessation of benefit
Public liability policies, Product liability policies, Employers' liability policies	Permanently
	Permanently
	Permanently
Sundry insurance policies	Three years after lapse
Claims correspondence, Accident reports and relevant correspondence	Three years after settlement
Insurance schedules	Ten years
Other records	
Vehicle registration records, MOT records	Two years after disposal of vehicle certificates and vehicle maintenance

Certificates and other documents of title	Permanently or until investment disposed of
Trust deeds	Originals to be kept permanently
Contracts with customers, suppliers or agents, Licensing agreements, Rental and hire purchase agreements, Indemnities and guarantees	Six years after expiry

Stop and Think 9.7

Data protection legislation companies must not only ensure that any data they keep is appropriate and relevant to their services but also that they do not keep any data longer than is necessary. Unfortunately there is no guidance on what constitutes an appropriate retention period.

As a useful default position it has been suggested that the period during which any claims can be brought against the company would be an appropriate retention period, which is six years in most cases.

Test Yourself 9.4

1. **Why should companies not include non-mandatory information on company registers such as bank details on the register of members to facilitate dividend payments?**

2. **Can individuals keep their residential address private and not disclosed on public registers?**

Chapter summary

◆ Companies have an obligation to keep and update registers of officers, members and persons with significant control.

◆ Certain registers can be kept on the central register maintained at Companies House. Registers can also be kept in house and a third party provider can be engaged to maintain registers on a company's behalf.

◆ Registers must kept by the company at the registered office or SAIL single (alternative inspection location) address.

◆ Companies have an obligation to allow inspection and copying of the registers.

◆ Companies are required to keep public information about the company at Companies House up to date.

◆ Companies face penalties for late or no filing of required documents and notifications.

◆ Companies are required to identify the company on company correspondence, e-mails, websites, documents and property.

◆ Companies must comply with data protection legislation regarding the storage and retention of information, registers and other documents over long periods.

Chapter ten
Meetings

CONTENTS

1. Introduction

This chapter looks at meetings of directors and members. As previously discussed, although there is a general framework for the convening and holding of directors' meetings the detail of how each board operates is very much for each board and chair to decide for themselves. Members' meeting are tightly regulated by the Companies Act 2006, together with a number of optional elements contained within the articles of association.

As ever, the motto for the company secretary when arranging for meetings is to consult and familiarise themselves with the articles of association especially in group situations where subsidiaries may not have articles of association or slightly different notice periods or quorum might apply across the subsidiaries. This is increasingly relevant as older company articles will include provisions from Table A to the Companies Act 1985 which are different in a number of key areas to the provisions in the Model Articles for companies incorporated under the Companies Act 2006.

2. Overview of meetings

Approval of resolutions of the members of private companies may be sought by the written resolution process or by holding a general meeting. For the majority of private companies, which only have a few members, the written resolution process is likely to be used in the majority of cases, as holding a members' meeting is a much more time-consuming process.

Use of written resolutions is now the default mechanism for most resolutions of the members of private companies. With the abolition of the requirement to hold an **annual general meeting** there are very few instances where a meeting of the members of a private company is necessary.

2.1 What is a meeting

In order to constitute a valid members' meeting, a minimum notice period must be given to all members entitled to attend the meeting. The notice must contain, as a minimum: the name of the company; the place, date and time of the meeting; details of the business to be considered; any special resolutions must be identified; and details on the members' rights to appoint proxies. At the meeting itself, there must be a quorum of members present in person or by proxy and that quorum must be maintained for any decisions reached to be valid. If the meeting is to be the annual general meeting the notice must identify the meeting as such.

The same basic principles apply to a meeting of the directors, but the requirements are much less prescriptive. For example, only reasonable notice need be given which can vary from meeting to meeting and only general details of the subject matter need be given.

The persons taking part in the meeting do not need to be in the same place and may participate by audio visual communications provided all parties are able to hear what is being said and are able to take part and contribute to the meeting, ask questions and lodge their vote.

2.2 Purpose of different meetings

Companies with more than one director and especially where there are directors who are not employed full time and involved with the company on a day-to-day basis will usually have a regular series of meetings, usually called board meetings, to discuss strategic and management issues. The directors collectively have authority to exercise the powers of the company subject to any restrictions in the articles of association. Where there is more than one director there must be a mechanism to record decisions on how to exercise that authority for any specific purpose.

Companies with a combination of executive and non-executive directors will usually delegate executive authority to the executive directors and will agree the corporate strategy and monitor performance against that strategy.

> **Annual general meeting (AGM)**
> A general meeting of the company's members, which must be held in each calendar year within 15 months of the previous AGM. Under Companies Act 2006, private companies are (generally) no longer required to hold AGMs, although the requirement remains for public companies.

Stop and Think 10.1

In order for decisions at meetings to be valid, the meeting must be properly convened and a quorum present. Consider the situation of a company with two directors, one holding 15% of the shares, the other with 85%, quorum for meetings of both directors and members is two and where the chairman has a casting vote.

If the two directors fall out, consider how the minority shareholder might be able to frustrate the majority shareholder from removing the minority shareholder as a director.

Consider how having different model articles or versions of Table A can provide different possibilities for both sides.

2.3 Limits on authority

Directors have general authority to exercise all the powers of the company in the day-to-day management of the company. This power may be subject to restrictions and caps set up in the articles, an individual director's service agreement, board schedules of matters reserved to the board generally and any shareholder or investors agreement.

Shareholders consent to changes of the company's constitution or to relax any restriction limiting the directors' authority in the articles, but should not involve themselves in day-to-day management decisions.

Accordingly, members' consent to permit the directors to allot more shares might be required but the members could not recommend the purchase of new machinery. Directors would have general authority to recruit additional employees but might require members' authority to sell off the company's existing business to redirect it in a new direction (e.g. previously carrying out a trade as a builder to becoming a recruitment agency).

The Companies Act 2006 fundamentally changed the basis of directors' powers. Previously directors' authority was explicit and required authority in the memorandum for general trading objects and the articles for specific corporate authorities including the issue and purchase of own shares. Those authorities were often expressed in terms of providing authority up to a specified level, such as the allotment of up to an additional 50,000 shares. Under the Companies Act 2006, companies have unfettered powers and directors can exercise those powers without recourse to shareholders. Any previous authorities contained in the articles, such as to issue shares, now serve as a restriction on the directors' general authority.

2.4 Types of meeting

Directors will hold formal meetings, possibly at regular intervals for larger boards or on a more ad hoc basis for smaller boards typically consisting only of executive directors. In addition to board meetings, directors may also hold separate management or executive committee meetings. Publicly traded companies typically constitute standing committees to which certain tasks and oversight are delegated including committees for audit, risk, remuneration, nomination and disclosures.

Members' meetings are usually restricted to an annual meeting to receive the report and accounts and to renew various general authorities and will hold ad hoc general meetings only when required. It may also be necessary to hold a class meeting (see section 3.1 below).

Stop and Think 10.2

As company secretary you might be asked to brief your directors on their powers and authority compared to that of the members. What key points would you draw attention to? Many companies and in particular listed companies establish a number of standing board committees with delegated authority. Why are there not committees of shareholders established too?

2.5 Reaching decisions without a meeting

With a few exceptions, the members of a private company may pass any resolution that could be put to a general meeting by written resolution. The exceptions are:

* removal of a director under s. 168
* removal of an auditor under s. 510.

Written resolutions may be proposed by the directors using the procedure set out in s. 291 or by the members using the procedure set out in ss. 292–295 (s. 288).

A copy of the proposed written resolution must be sent by post or electronic means to all members entitled to attend and vote at a general meeting (s. 289).

A member signifies their agreement to a written resolution by returning to the company a document in hard copy or electronically, identifying the resolution and signifying their consent (s. 296).

A written resolution is approved when the requisite majority of members have signified their agreement, votes being calculated according to the number of shares held by each member (ss. 284 and 296).

If agreement has not been given within 28 days from the date the resolution was circulated, it is deemed to have lapsed and any consent given after that date has no effect (s. 297).

Copies of written resolutions circulated to members must also be sent to the company's auditor if it has one (s. 502(1)).

2.6 Shareholder requisitions

Meetings
Directors must convene a general meeting if requested to do so by any member or members holding between them at least 5%, in nominal value, of the **paid-up** issued share capital of the company or, if the company does not have share capital, 5% of the voting rights.

paid-up capital
Refers to the amounts paid up on any issued shares.

The requisition must state the objects of the meeting and must be authenticated by all the requisitionists.

If the directors do not issue a notice to convene the meeting within 21 days, the requisitionists may convene the meeting themselves, provided they call it for a date not more than three months later. The directors are deemed not to have convened the meeting if they issue a notice convening a meeting for a date more than 28 days after the date of that notice. Any reasonable expenses incurred by the requisitionists in issuing a notice must be repaid by the company, which can retain the money out of the fees payable to the directors (ss. 304 and 305).

Resolutions

Members of a public company may also put forward resolutions to be included in the next annual general meeting notice (s. 338).

For the resolution to be considered it must be proposed by holder[s] holding between them at least 5% of total voting rights or by not less than 100 members. In addition, the notice proposing the resolution must be received by the company at least six weeks prior to the date of the meeting or, if earlier, the date of issue of the notice. Companies do not need to accede to a request to propose a resolution that is defamatory or vexatious or that has no effect.

Statements

Members are entitled to request that the company circulate a statement relating to any business at a meeting with the notice of the meeting, or if the notice of the meeting has already been issued the statement should be circulated separately. The company can request that the costs of distribution of the statement are reimbursed by the requisitionist(s). Companies need not circulate statements that are defamatory, vexatious or frivolous.

Stop and Think 10.3

As noted above, 100 members, acting together can put forward resolutions at a listed company's general meeting. However this remains a relatively rare occurrence. Why might this be the case?

Test Yourself 10.1

1.   **How many people must attend a meeting for it to be valid?**

2.   **Do all participants in a meeting need to be in the same room?**

3.   **Is a meeting always required to consider a resolution of the members?**

4.   **Can members propose their own resolutions?**

3 Members' meetings

3.1 Types and purpose of meetings

General

Meetings of members are called general meetings and, provided appropriate notice has been given and a quorum is present, may consider any business. The more common types of business put to general meetings are resolutions relating to:

◆ share capital either to authorise the directors to issue additional shares, waive rights of pre-emption, approve purchases of shares, redemptions and **bonus issues**;

◆ create a new class of shares or vary existing share rights;

◆ approve matters relating to the directors such as substantial property transactions, some other matter in which the directors are conflicted;

◆ appointments or removal of directors;

◆ amendments to the articles of association; and

◆ changing the registration of the company, such as a conversion from private to public, and finally resolutions relating to its closure or liquidation.

bonus issue
Issue of additional shares to existing shareholders, in proportion to their current holding, already paid up in full out of the distributable reserves of the company.

Annual

All public companies are required to hold an annual general (AGM) meeting each year. Although an AGM can consider any business, their primary purpose is to: receive the reports of the directors, financial statements, remuneration report (if any), rotation and re-appointment of directors, re-appointment of auditors, declaration of final dividend and renewal of any annual authorities relating to the directors' authority to issue shares and waiver of pre-emption rights.

Although private companies can also hold AGMs it is often better to refer to them as an annual meeting of the members. The Act has specific requirements for an AGM and the articles may have specific items of business to be dealt with such as directors' rotation, re-appointment of auditors etc. which, if omitted, may well have unintended results especially if the AGM is not held regularly.

Class

These are like general meetings but only members of the specific class are entitled to attend, even if the class has no voting rights. Class meetings are normally only required if there is a proposal to amend the articles and, in particular, rights attaching to shares, and the changes amend the class rights. It is not possible to amend class rights, even indirectly, without the consent of the affected class.

All the usual rules for the convening, holding and notification of results of a general meeting apply to a class meeting with appropriate amendment.

Court

Very occasionally a company might be required to convene court meetings. These are meetings associated with an application to court (e.g. to approve a reduction of capital or scheme of arrangement).

3.2　Types of resolution

At members' meetings there are two types of resolution: ordinary and special. The main difference being the majority required to pass each type of resolution.

Ordinary

An ordinary resolution simply requires a majority of those voting to vote in favour of the resolution for it to be approved.

Special

A special resolution requires 75% of those voting to vote in favour of it.

A special resolution is only required where this is a specific requirement of the Act or, rarely, the articles may require a special resolution for certain resolutions. Examples where a special resolution is required include changes of company name and amending the articles.

The notice convening the meeting must identify special resolutions.

3.3　Notice of meetings

Although the Act sets out minimum notice periods, it is perfectly acceptable to give longer notice. Care must also be taken to check the articles of the company as these might contain a longer notice period which will overrule that contained in the Act. In particular, companies with pre-2006 articles may well have longer notice periods especially for meetings where special resolutions are to be considered.

Convening

Except where a valid request from members to convene a meeting has not been acted on by the directors, all meetings of the members are convened under the authority of the directors of the company by issuing a notice of meeting to all members entitled to attend and vote at the meeting.

As general meetings are convened under the authority of the directors the notice is normally signed by a director or the company secretary and stated as being 'by order of the board'.

Content

The notice must contain as a minimum the following details:

◆　name of the company;

◆　time, date and place of the meeting;

◆　general nature of the business to be conducted (s.311). However, when a special resolution is to be proposed, its full text must be set out and it must be identified as a special resolution (s. 283(6));

◆ the notice must contain a statement making it clear that all members are entitled to appoint one or more proxies to attend and vote on their behalf and that the proxy need not themselves be a member of the company (s. 325) The articles cannot require that notice of appointment of a proxy be deposited more than 48 hours prior to the commencement of the meeting (excluding non-business days) (s. 327); and

◆ notice of an annual general meeting of a public company must state that the meeting is to be an annual general meeting (s. 337).

Notice periods

Section 307 of the Act sets out minimum notice periods for members' meetings as follows:

◆ general meeting of a private company: 14 days;

◆ annual general meeting of a public company: 21 days;

◆ general meeting of a public company that is not a traded company: 14 days.

For traded companies the notice periods are set out in s. 307A, as follows:

◆ general meetings where specified conditions met: 14 days;

◆ all other general meetings: 21 days.

For a general meeting of a traded company to be held on 14 days' notice, the circumstances specified in s. 307A must be met. These are as follows:

◆ the meeting is not an annual general meeting;

◆ members are offered an electronic voting facility; and

◆ a special resolution has been passed to reduce the notice period to 14 days either at the immediately preceding AGM or at a general meeting held since the last AGM.

If all three conditions are met, the notice period will be 14 days. In all other cases, 21 days' notice will be required.

In all cases, notice periods refer to 'clear days' which exclude the day the notice is given (or deemed to be given) and the day of the meeting itself (s. 360) It is important to check the articles as the definition of clear days and when notice is deemed given can vary considerably from company to company.

Under the model articles and s. 1147, delivery of documents by either post or by electronic means is deemed to have been given 48 hours after posting or the electronic message has been sent.

Short notice

Although the Act sets out minimum notice periods the members themselves are permitted to agree to meetings being held on shorter notice. This concession only has practical use for companies with a small number of shareholders as for private companies the requirement is that a majority of the shares together holding not less than 90% of the voting rights must agree to the short notice. This 90% hurdle can be increased by the articles to not more than 95%. For a public company the short notice must be agreed by 95% of members except in the case of an AGM where agreement is required of all members.

Although not a legal requirement, it is recommended that agreement to short notice be obtained in writing in case there is any later question as to the legality of a meeting held on short notice.

Where short notice is agreed to, notice must still be given to all members entitled to attend and vote at the meeting.

Special notice
For a few resolutions special notice must be given. Special notice requires that notice is given to the company at least 28 days before the date of the meeting and that notice of the special notice be given to members at the same time as the notice of the meeting. Except for requisitioned resolutions the special notice is given by one of the directors.

Stop and Think 10.4

Giving proper notice of a members' meeting is vital as otherwise any business conducted might be declared invalid. Consider the difference to the last day of posting if the articles of association stipulate the notice is deemed given 24 or 48 hours after posting or immediately or 24 hours after sending by electronic means or if the definition of clear days' notice is changed from excluding to including the date notice is given.

3.4 Proxies

A proxy is a person appointed by a member to attend and vote at a members' meeting on their behalf.

Right to appoint
All members have the right to appoint one or more proxies to attend and vote on their behalf; any provision in a company's articles to the contrary is not valid.

Appointment process
The appointment of a proxy is made by lodging a form of proxy with the company, often at its registered office or the office of its share registrar. The Act sets out a template form of proxy although most companies will usually issue a form of proxy for completion by members with the notice of meeting. Where forms of proxy are issued, these must be sent to all members.

As set out in the Act, forms of proxy should be submitted not less than 48 hours prior to the meeting. This period cannot be increased although companies may accept shorter notice if they wish.

The majority of forms of proxy automatically appoint the chairman of the board of directors as the proxy unless some other person is expressly appointed. The form of proxy will allow the appointee to specify how their proxy should vote or if no instructions are provided it is for the proxy to decide how to vote, if at all.

Appointing a form of proxy does not preclude the member from attending the meeting.

Revocation
A form of proxy is automatically revoked if another form of proxy is received or may be revoked at any time by the member by providing written notice to that effect.

Stop and Think 10.5

It is very common for companies to provide a form of proxy for use by members unable to attend general meeting. Groups of disaffected members will often amend this form and pre-populate the voting instructions, circulate these for signature by like-minded members and lodge them at the last minute.

However, care must be taken as if there are any problems with the forms of proxy there might not be any tie to correct them prior to the deadline for the receipt of proxies. Additionally although the articles of association will often provide for proxies to be permitted in any usual form 'approved by the directors' this wording can be used to exclude any forms with pre-printed voting instructions on the basis that those forms of proxy were not in the form approved by the directors.

3.5 Quorum

The Act requires that for general meetings the quorum is two members present in person or by proxy. The exception being that for sole member companies the quorum is reduced to one. Where a quorum is met by one or both members being present by proxy there must be two persons at the meeting and one person cannot represent all members.

The articles must be checked, however, as these may provide that the quorum is greater than the level set out in the Act.

Where there is a shareholders' or investors' agreement in place these often increase the quorum and/ or stipulate that it must include a specific shareholder, usually the majority holder.

3.6 Attendance by non-members

Members, proxies and corporate representatives, directors and auditors, are entitled to receive notice of and attend members' meetings. Auditors are entitled to speak at general meetings but only on matters that concern them as auditor (s. 502). Other persons may attend with the consent of the chair, but cannot vote and would not normally be allowed to speak.

3.7 Role and responsibilities of the chair

The role of the chair at a shareholders' meeting is to ensure that the meeting is properly and fairly conducted, allowing all opinions to be expressed. The company's articles will also usually give the chair specific powers relating to the conduct of meetings.

The model articles state that the chair of the board of directors will also be chair for general meetings. If the chair is not present, then another director (e.g. a deputy chair or vice-chair) takes the chair. In the absence of any director, one of the members present takes the chair.

Section 319 states that subject to any provisions in the company's articles, any member may be elected by the meeting to be chair of that meeting. Section 328 permits a proxy holder to be elected chair of the meeting subject to any provisions in the articles.

3.8 Voting

Voting at members' meetings is undertaken in one of two ways – either on a show of hands or via a poll. In both cases, for a vote to count, it must be cast either for or against the resolution. Although forms of proxy and frequently even on a show of hands there is an option for members to indicate an abstention. An abstention is not a vote in law and does not affect the result of the vote but can be used to signal a member's discontent without voting against.

Show of hands

On a show of hands each member voting has one vote each even if they represent more than one member. Voting on a show of hands is very much quicker than voting via a poll, particularly where the vote is decisively for or against the resolution.

A major disadvantage of voting on a show of hands is that no account is taken of any forms of proxy received. As the chairman is likely to know the proxy count they should demand a poll vote if the vote is close or if the inclusion of the proxy votes might arrive at a different outcome. However, there is no compulsion on the chairman to do so.

Although the articles may well contain different provisions s. 324 provides that five or more members or any member(s) holding not less than 10% of the voting rights can demand a poll. Any demand for a poll should be made either before or upon the declaration of the vote on a show of hands.

Poll
On a poll vote, each member voting has one vote for each share held or, if different, according to the votes set out in the articles. The votes of any members voting by proxy are also included. The articles will contain provisions

detailing how and when a poll vote should be conducted. Usually the process leaves considerable discretion to the chair, but it is usually most convenient to hold it at the end of the meeting. This will also facilitate polls being taken on multiple resolutions at the same time rather than delaying the meeting each time a poll is required.

If attendance at the meeting is poor or new information relevant to the resolution has been given to the meeting it can be held at a later date to give all members the opportunity to consider the new information and vote on the resolution.

Stop and Think 10.6

The organisation of general meetings and conduct of voting is usually left entirely in the hands of the company secretary. Voting on a show of hands is much quicker than voting on a poll but provides smaller shareholders with a greater voice. A meeting of, say 50 members, with a vocal activist group of 25 members each holding one share can easily dominate a meeting and make it appear that a particular resolution has been overwhelmingly approved or defeated on a show of hands, whereas if a poll were conducted, the opposite might well be the case.

Unless a poll vote is to be taken on all resolutions it is for the company secretary, in conjunction with the chair, to decide whether a poll should be taken or to rely on the show of hands. This decision will be taken in the knowledge of the proxies already submitted and possibly also in the knowledge of how many votes those members actually present represent.

In order to ensure 'fair play' it is best practice to announce the details of proxy votes received if a poll is not called for.

3.9 Written resolutions of members

As noted earlier, the default position for private companies is not to hold general meetings but to circulate resolutions in writing for members to vote upon and return (ss. 292–295).

As with a general meeting, most resolutions will be proposed and circulated by the company directors but it is possible for members to request that specific resolutions be circulated and if the directors fail to do so, may circulate the resolution themselves.

The process to circulate a written resolution is as follows:

◆ The directors circulate the full text of the resolution(s), either in hard copy or electronically, to all members entitled to attend and vote at a general meeting.

◆ The members consider the resolution(s) and signify their consent to some or all resolutions and return either in hard copy or electronically, a document identifying the relevant resolutions and signifying their consent.

◆ A written resolution is approved when the necessary majority, determined according to their shareholding, is reached.

◆ If the necessary majority has not been reached within 28 days of the resolution being circulated, it is deemed to have been defeated.

3.10 Unanimity rule

Where all the members consent to a resolution it will be approved under the so-called unanimity rule even if none of the necessary formalities have been observed; there being no dissent, the resolution is bound to have been approved and there are no dissenting members to object.

Stop and Think 10.7

The unanimity rule is based upon common law and is not contained in the Companies Act and is a rare example of the practicalities of the matter taking precedence over the letter of the law.

Consider in what circumstances members might agree something between themselves and inform the company/directors of their decisions without a meeting being convened or written resolution circulated.

3.11 Communicating with members

As noted in Chapter 9, a company may circulate resolutions either in hard copy or electronically provided specific or general consent or deemed consent has been obtained from members.

Paper communications
Hard copy communication remains the default method and notices and written resolutions must be sent to the address provided by the member and recorded in the register of members or, failing that, to their last-known address.

Electronic communications
Where a member has consented, notices and written resolutions may be circulated by the company sending the documents to the electronic address supplied by the member.

Use of website
Alternatively, and in the case of deemed consent, the documents may be made available on a website and the members notified either electronically or by hard copy notification of the web address where the documents can be viewed and downloaded.

Test Yourself 10.2

1. What are the different types of meeting?

2. What must be included in the notice of an annual general meeting?

3. How soon must the requisite majority be obtained to approve a members' written resolution?

4. How must the documents to convene a members' meeting be circulated?

5. What is the notice period for a members' meeting?

Stop and Think 10.8

Use of electronic or website communications were introduced to provide a more effective channel of communication for certain members as well as offering cost savings over traditional hard copy postage.

Consider the practical steps a company will need to take and potential time-scale to enable it to take advantage of electronic or website communication without incurring significant cost to do so.

4 Directors' meetings

As has been discussed in earlier chapters, CA 2006 is much less prescriptive in the running of directors' meetings. It is left to the directors to manage their meetings to suit their needs.

4.1 Types of meeting

In companies with a mix of executive and non-executive directors the management of the company is often divided into two elements. Formal structured board meetings setting corporate strategy and evaluating the performance of the company against that strategy and more informal flexible executive management meetings where the day-to-day business decisions to implement and deliver the corporate strategy are made and performance measured against a whole array of key performance indicators (KPIs).

In smaller businesses and those without non-executive directors, formal board meetings are rarely held; most discussions and decisions are made informally or at management meetings held on an 'as required' basis.

Management meetings
These will usually be held frequently, often at regular pre-determined intervals such as weekly, fortnightly or monthly. There will be a general agenda with the

exact business determined by actual performance of the various departments or divisions.

Any minutes might be limited to action points with little, if any, record of the discussions leading to those decisions or actions.

Board meetings

These will usually be held at longer intervals than the management meetings. The frequency will depend entirely on the board or chair's preference and the stage of the company's evolution – an early-stage company might have more frequent meetings, whereas a much more developed and stable business might only need a light-touch approach from the board.

Formal board minutes will be kept, recording not only the decisions but the rationale for those decisions. Historically, board minutes were written very much as an internal record of business decisions. However, particularly in industries with external regulators, minutes are a primary source of information about the performance of the board and management and minutes are increasingly written with this external audience in mind.

Stop and Think 10.9

As a company secretary you are asked to prepare a briefing paper highlighting the difference between a directors' meeting and an executive management meetings. What examples of agenda items might you expect to be included on the board agenda and not an executive management meeting?

4.2 Convening

Any director or the company secretary at the request of a director can convene a directors' meeting. Where the meetings are held at regular intervals with meeting dates, agreed weeks or months in advance, the company secretary will not require specific authority to convene each meeting.

4.3 Notice

There is no set format or content for the notice of a directors' meeting nor are there prescribed notice periods with the legislation simply requiring that reasonable notice be given.

Best practice guidance is that notice of a directors' meeting should state the name of the company, the date, time and place of the meeting and an agenda. Some boards with regular meetings will have a set agenda with ad hoc items being brought up under 'any other business'; companies who hold irregular meetings will have agendas drawn up for each one.

The length of notice will depend entirely on the urgency of the business, the location of the directors and the content of the board papers accompanying the notice. In all cases, directors should have sufficient time to read the board papers in advance of the meeting.

For urgent meetings or meetings of directors located in the same building, reasonable notice might be as little as a few hours. In contrast, in a company with directors located across different countries and time zones or where the board papers amount to several hundred papers, a week or more might constitute reasonable notice.

4.4 Quorum

The articles will set out the quorum for directors' meetings and will often provide that this can be amended by the directors themselves. The model articles provide that the quorum should be two directors.

The quorum must be present at the commencement of the meeting and whenever any decisions are to be voted upon. An inquorate meeting cannot validly make any decisions.

Directors do not need to be present in person. The articles will usually provide that, provided they can hear the discussions and participate in the meeting, they can participate via audio visual or teleconferencing.

4.5 Conflicts of interest

Directors are required to declare any interests which either conflict or might conflict with the interests of the company. It is most common for directors to declare their general interests on appointment and to confirm these on a regular basis. This could be annually, half-yearly or quarterly, depending on the size and nature of the company. It is also good practice for interests relating to any items of business on the agenda to be declared at the start of the meeting.

Where a director has a significant conflict or a direct interest in a proposed transaction this might require approval of the members either by written resolution or at a general meeting. Such transaction will often be seen in property development companies where a director purchases a property built by the company.

Stop and Think 10.10

Ensuring directors' conflicts of interest are appropriately recorded and recognised is a key role for the company secretary.

In addition to request for declarations of any new conflicts at each directors' meeting, detailed guidance should be provided at the induction of new directors. This should be regularly updated and refreshed.

4.6 Attendance by non-directors

Only directors have the right to attend directors' meetings. Any other person attends with the consent of the meeting.

4.7 Chairing board meetings

It is for the board members collectively to elect one of their number to act as chair. For listed companies, the UK Corporate Governance Code sets out guidance on the election of a chair to ensure their independence from the executive management team and length of service.

The chair should ensure that all points of view are discussed on any issue whilst avoiding repetition. Discussion should be pertinent to the matter under consideration and should not be allowed to digress into other areas.

Although directors carry collective responsibility for their decisions, formal votes at directors' meetings are rare, with most decisions being agreed following sufficient discussion to resolve any uncertainties or concerns. Where unanimity is not possible, the matter will usually be deferred to another meeting.

In the event of a director not agreeing with any decision this should be minuted.

The articles may give the chair a second or casting vote if there are an equal number of votes. While the use of such a casting vote is entirely at the chair's discretion, it is suggested that this should only be used to defeat the resolution, on the basis that there is no majority in favour of it. In practice however, it is unusual for decisions of directors to proceed unless there is unanimity or, failing that, a healthy majority in favour.

Chairing a board is much more than just ensuring the smooth running of directors' meetings. The chair should lead by example: demonstrating ethical leadership, providing advice and support to the executive team (especially the chief executive) while not straying into executive decision making.

A good chair will promote good relationships with all directors and senior managers, encouraging them to use all their skills, qualifications and experience to provide an appropriate forum to set and monitor strategy, create value and ensure accountability. The chair is responsible for ensuring the board regularly reviews its own performance collectively and individually and that there are appropriate resources to develop directors. The chair and other independent directors should ensure effective communication with shareholders in general – and with the major shareholders specifically – to ensure their views are known to the board.

Stop and Think 10.11

An effective chair is crucial to the correct functioning of the board of directors.

A good chair facilitates appropriate consideration of agenda items ensuring sufficient time is allocated and allowing all views to be heard with equal weight.

Consider the impact that a domineering outspoken chair might have and the detrimental effect this is likely to have on proper board discussion and evaluation of agenda items.

4.8 How to make meetings effective

The effectiveness of directors' meetings can be improved by following some basic rules:

- ensuring that sufficient notice is given, including the issue of board papers to allow directors sufficient time to read and understand the items to be discussed;
- high-quality board documentation – ensuring the board papers only contain relevant information and ideally include a short executive summary and a clear statement of the action required of the directors;
- ensuring the board and/or participants have a clear understanding of their role;
- allowing sufficient time for debate and challenge;
- good time management ensuring both sufficient time is spent considering items but that not too much time is devoted to any item;
- reflecting on previous decisions, especially the decision-making process where the outcomes were poor, can help improve the board's future effectiveness.

4.9 Minutes

Although CA 2006 requires that minutes of the proceedings at meetings of the directors are kept, there is no further clarification on the detail or format of those minutes (s. 248). As a minimum, the minutes should record decisions reached together with a summary of the key points leading to the decision to allow the reader an understanding of the discussion.

Due to the increase in regulatory oversight and reviews of the decision-making process, minutes will now often include details of any challenges raised during the discussions and review of any response to those challenges and monitor any actions requested by the directors.

The importance of accurate minute taking cannot be overemphasised.

The chair, in conjunction with the company secretary, will determine how much of the discussion should be reflected in the minutes and whether this should be in the form of suitable narrative, formal resolutions, action points or follow-up actions.

Stop and Think 10.12

All company secretaries, companies and boards have their own style of minutes. Consider the benefits or disadvantages of the following:

◆ **verbatim record versus action points only;**

◆ **formal resolutions versus full record of discussion;**

◆ **reproducing extracts from board papers versus cross-referencing to those reports.**

4.10 The role of committees

Boards comprising both executive and non-executive directors will often constitute committees of the board to provide more detailed independent oversight of certain areas. Listed companies are recommended by the UK Corporate Governance Code to establish several standing board committees including audit, risk, remuneration and nominations committees or to explain why these are not appropriate.

A majority of the members of these committees should be independent of the executive team and, especially in the case of the chair of each committee, have an appropriate level of qualification and experience. In two significant areas, the remuneration and audit committees, the membership should be entirely independent non-executives to provide, as far as possible, a neutral view to setting the executive remuneration policy and agreeing the scope and terms of the external audit, including the appointment of the external auditor.

Board committees can devote more time to the detail of their focus than is possible for the full board.

While the board makes use of committees to assist in its oversight of their area of interest, it retains responsibility for and makes the final decisions in all those areas.

Test Yourself 10.3

1. **What are the sorts of meetings that directors might regularly hold?**

2. **What notice must be given for a directors' meeting?**

3. **Must directors disclose conflicts of interest?**

4. **Can a meeting where the number of directors present falls below the quorum continue?**

Chapter summary

◆ The grant or exercise of certain authorities requires a formal resolution of the members or directors.

◆ Meetings generally require two or more people to be present but they need not be in the same place.

- There are strict rules governing the convening and holding of members' meetings but there is much more flexibility regarding directors' meetings.
- Almost all members' resolutions may be approved by written resolution rather than convening a physical meeting.
- Communications with members are in hard copy by default, but providing the necessary consent is obtained may be by electronic communication or via a website.
- Members are entitled to appoint a proxy to attend and vote at meetings on their behalf.
- Directors must disclose conflicts of interest.

Part four

Introduction to finance and accounting

This part introduces the components of financial documentation and the principles of financial decision-making.

The aim of this module is to provide a basic level of understanding of accounting and finance. As well as an overview of basic accounting terms and concepts, you will learn the importance of financial reporting and how financial statements and reports can be used for analysis that informs decision making for both internal and external stakeholders, such as management and investors.

At the end of this part, you will be able to:

- Identify costs, revenue and profit, and understand profit margins
- Understand the principles and objectives of financial reporting
- Demonstrate a basic knowledge of accounting
- Understand and apply the principles of double-entry book-keeping

- Consider how financial information can be analysed for various audiences
- Understand the principles of management accounting
- Understand the principles of financial decision making and the impact of financial decisions on businesses

Chapter eleven
Revenue, costs and profit

CONTENTS

1. Introduction

This chapter outlines the basic concepts of business: revenue, costs and profit. The definitions of costs, expenses and expenditure are provided, along with an understanding of where business revenue comes from and why profit is important, as well as an introduction to profit margins.

2. Revenue

First, let's look at what revenue is and how it is measured.

2.1 What is revenue?

Revenue is defined as the money a business receives. In finance, revenue is usually measured over a specific period of time (e.g. a year), and in the currency the business operates in – for a business based in the UK, this is usually British pounds sterling (£).

For a business that sells toys at a price of £10 each and sells 3 toys, the revenue it will receive from these sales is £10 × 3 = £30, or:

Revenue = Sale price × Number of products sold

If products (or **goods**) are sold at different prices then total revenue is the sum of the prices at which the goods are sold.

goods
Another name for products, or items to be sold by the business in the course of its trade.

Worked example 11.1

Kanye decides to start a business selling expensive branded T-shirts. He prices them at £80 each, and in the first week he sells 125 T-shirts to the general public. Kanye also invited 25 VIPs to purchase his T-shirts at a discount, so during the week each VIP buys a T-shirt for £60. How much revenue has Kanye made in total during his first week of business?

Answer:

Amount of revenue made when selling to general public:

Price × number of items sold at that price = £80 × 125 T-shirts = £10,000

Amount of revenue made from VIPs:

Price × number of items sold at that price = £60 × 25 T-shirts = £1,500

Total revenue = £10,000 + £1,500 = £11,500

Therefore, in his first week of business, Kanye made £11,500 in revenue.

entity
A person, organisation or business with a separately identifiable and legal existence.

Note that a business is a separate **entity** from the people who own it, therefore the business's activities should be considered separately from the owners' activities. This is known as the **separate entity concept** or sometimes the **business entity concept**. In Worked Example 11.1, any other money Kanye is earning (or spending) that doesn't relate to his T-shirt business will not be looked at when examining the activities of that business.

Alternative names for revenue include:

◆   **turnover**

sales
The money a business receives from trading. Often used interchangeably in a company's accounts with income, revenue or turnover.

◆   **sales**, or occasionally **net sales**

◆   **income**, or occasionally gross income.

A business can generate revenue in a number of ways.

net sales
Technically, this is the sales figure minus any returns or refunds. However, it is occasionally used in place of sales or turnover.

2.2 Where does revenue come from?

Sources of revenue include:

◆   sales of goods or services

◆   interest income

income (revenue/ turnover)
The money a business receives.

◆   royalties

◆   other income.

Sales of goods or services

Most business revenue comes from the sale of goods and/or services. Businesses sell physical goods (such as Kanye's T-shirts in the above example) to customers, and the money they receive from selling these items makes up the business's revenue.

Alternatively, businesses can sell **services**, rather than physical goods – think of your internet service provider, whom you pay for internet access, rather than for a tangible item. The internet service company's revenue will come from people paying them for internet access.

Some businesses sell goods and services, and the business's revenue will come from both. A garage which sells car parts (goods) where you can also pay mechanics for car maintenance (services) will make income from both the sale of goods and services.

Interest income
Also known as **interest receivable**, this is interest earned from, for example, money in a bank account.

Royalties
These include **earnings** from patents, copyrights or other copyrighted material, such as books and music.

Other income
This can include income from:

◆ the sale of an **asset** (such as property or vehicles)

◆ the sale of a business

◆ one-off items that generate income.

3. Costs and expenditure

As well as income that the business generates and receives, there are also items or services that the business has to pay for, such as staff wages. These are known as the business's **costs**, **expenses** or **expenditure**. These terms are often used interchangeably, but each actually means something slightly different.

3.1 The difference between expenditure, expenses and costs

Expenditure is money spent (on an item, or a service, etc.) by the business.

An expense is an amount paid for an item or service that is being, or has been, used in the business. It often refers to a payment – or expenditure – that a business makes regularly over a specific time period, like office rent (rental expense), utilities (i.e. payments for electricity, gas, water), wages or advertising. 'Expense' is a term often used in a business's accounting records and financial statements – more on that later.

A cost is an amount that has to be spent to buy or obtain something. A more thorough definition would be 'a resource sacrificed or foregone to achieve a specific outcome' as cost is not always financial. While 'expense' and 'cost' are terms often substituted for each other, 'cost' is often used in management accounting or business strategy.

---

service
An item that is not a physical/tangible good that is sold as part of a business's trade. Examples include the provision of internet services, or a self-employed graphic designer selling their labour.

interest receivable
The interest income earned by a business. Often this is bank interest paid on the money the business holds in a bank account.

earnings
The money earned by the business, either as profit or income.

asset
An item a business owns that either generates cash or has the potential to.

cost
An amount that has to be spent to buy or obtain something. A cost is not always financial.

expenditure
This is money spent (on an item, or a service, etc.) by a business.

expense
This is an amount paid for an item or service that is being, or has been, used in the business. It often refers to a payment – or expenditure – that a business makes regularly over a specific time period.

Test yourself 11.1

For each of the following, state whether the item is a revenue/income item, or a cost/expense item:

◆   **rental income**

◆   **office rent**

◆   **wages**

◆   **bank interest received**

◆   **bank interest paid**

◆   **interest on loan payments**

◆   **purchase of T-shirts to sell later**

◆   **accounting software expenditure**

◆   **book royalties.**

Costs are often broken down into further categories:

◆   fixed costs and variable costs

◆   direct costs and indirect costs.

3.2   Fixed costs and variable costs

Costs are sometimes classified by a business as either fixed costs or variable costs.

fixed cost
This is a cost or expenditure amount that is unchanged (i.e. fixed) regardless of how much work is done or how much output is produced.

Fixed costs are costs or expenditure amounts that are unchanged (i.e. fixed) regardless of how much work is done or how much output is produced. See Figure 11.1.

Cost/revenue
(£)

Fixed costs

Quantity

Figure 11.1 Graph showing fixed costs

Examples of fixed costs are:

◆ rent

◆ business rates (i.e. local council tax on business properties)

◆ business insurance

◆ utilities (i.e. water bills, electricity and gas bills)

◆ legal and accountancy fees

◆ managers' wages.

Variable costs are costs that vary with how much work is done or how much output is produced. As activity rises, variable costs increase; and vice versa. See Figure 11.2.

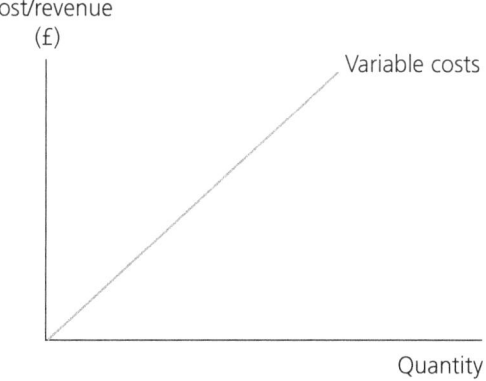

Figure 11.2: Graph showing variable costs

Examples include:

◆ the cost of **raw materials** used to make the business's product – the more products that are made for sale, the more raw materials need to be acquired

◆ transport or **distribution costs** in cases where the more products are sold and delivered, the more workers/lorries/fuel etc. is needed to transport goods to customers

◆ staff or labour costs where this is dependent on time or quantity (e.g. if a product requires a business to pay a worker £20 to make it, then the labour cost of two products is £40, and the labour cost of 15 products is £300).

Some costs cannot be easily classified as fixed or variable (e.g. telephone expenses). However, some costs have both a fixed part and a variable part (e.g. managers' wages which have a performance-related bonus element). These are known as **semi-fixed costs** or, more usually, as **semi-variable costs**.

3.3 Indirect costs and direct costs

Another way costs are broken down are as indirect costs or direct costs.

Indirect costs are costs or expenses that are necessary to operate the business, but which do not relate directly to the production or sale of the

variable cost
This is a cost that varies with how much work is done or how much output is produced.

raw materials
These are the basic materials from which a business's products are made, especially for manufacturing businesses.

distribution costs
In an income statement, these are expenses involved in distributing a business's goods or services.

semi-fixed cost (semi-variable cost)
A cost which has a fixed cost part and a variable cost part.

indirect cost (overhead)
A cost or expense that is necessary to operate the business, but which does not relate directly to the production or sale of the business's products or services.

business's products or services. Another name for indirect costs is **overheads**. Examples are:

◆ utilities

◆ rent

◆ administrative costs

◆ marketing expenses

◆ interest paid on overdraft or loan

◆ insurance

◆ accountancy and legal fees.

direct cost
This is a cost or expense that relates specifically to the production or sale of the business's products or services.

Direct costs are costs or expenses that relate specifically to the production or sale of the business's products or services. These can include:

◆ wages

◆ raw materials

inventory
Items the business intends to sell in the course of its trade.

◆ the purchase of **inventory** (also known as **stock**), which is defined as items the business intends to sell in the course of its trade

stock
In this case, another name for inventory or finished goods.

◆ transport costs – either **carriage inwards** (or **carriage in**), which is the cost, paid for by the business rather than the supplier, of delivering purchases to the business; or **carriage outwards** (also known as **carriage out**), which is the cost of delivering goods to customers that is paid for by the business and not the customer.

statement of profit or loss (income/P&L statement)
A statement showing a business's financial performance over a specified period.

However, in a business's **accounting records**, costs and expenses are usually categorised differently. Nowhere is this more apparent than in a business's **statement of profit or loss** (also known as the **income statement**, or formerly **profit and loss account**).

3.4   How income and expenses appear on a statement of profit or loss

The statement of profit or loss (sometimes shortened to P&L statement, or P&L account) shows a business's total revenue (or income) and deducts total expenses for the period, resulting in a profit or loss – it is one of the primary financial statements used to show how a business performed over a given period of time. An example is given in Figure 11.3 below.

Alenko Ltd
Statement of profit or loss for the year ended 31 December 2018

	£
Sales	209,956
Cost of sales	(99,834)
Gross Profit	110,122
Less: Operating expenses	

– Selling and distribution costs	(26,933)
– Administrative expenses	(54,845)
Operating profit	28,344
Less: Finance costs	
– Interest payable	(5,148)
Profit before taxation	23,196

Figure 11.3: Example of an income statement

The numbers in brackets indicate subtracted amounts – note how costs and expenses are subtracted from income to obtain the profit or loss for the period. (Note that 'operating profit' is not always a line that appears in a basic P&L statement – often we are given the revenue figure in the top line, followed by a list of expenses before getting to the profit or loss at the bottom.)

The preparation of a profit and loss statement will be explained in Chapter 12, but for now, we will look at how costs and expenses are classified on the P&L statement.

3.5 Cost of sales (or cost of goods sold)

A business's **cost of sales** (also known as **cost of goods sold**, or COGS for short) are expenses relating directly to the make or manufacture of the products sold by the business in the course of its trade. It is a term often used by merchanting businesses (i.e. those that sell goods) rather than service industry businesses (which provide services).

cost of sales
Expenses relating directly to the make or manufacture of the products sold by the business in the course of its trade.

Cost of sales usually includes the following:

◈ **raw materials**, which are the basic materials that make a product the business intends to sell as part of its trade;

◈ **inventory** (also known as **stock** or **finished goods**), which are goods the business holds with the intention of selling in its trade, but have not yet been sold; and

◈ **work in progress**, WIP for short; these are goods that are in the process of being made or manufactured but have not yet been finished.

work in progress (WIP)
This is a business's product which is in the process of being made or manufactured for trade, but is not yet finished or ready for sale.

Staff wages and other labour costs that relate to the make or manufacture of these goods can also be included in the cost of sales figure.

Cost of sales can sometimes include the **depreciation** of plant and machinery used to manufacture goods the business sells. Since plant and machinery eventually wears out and needs to be replaced, a business will account for this by estimating how much the value of the plant and machinery (or any other tangible **asset** used in the business, such as vehicles) has reduced by over a given period of time. This reduction is known as a **depreciation expense**, and is accounted for as an expense even though no actual money has been spent or received. Depreciation, therefore, is an allocation of the cost of an asset over its useful life.

depreciation
This is an allocation of the cost of an asset over its useful life, and is accounted for as an expense in a business's accounts even though no actual money has been spent or received.

3.6 Selling and distribution costs

Selling and distribution costs include all expenses involved in marketing, selling and distributing a business's goods or services. This can include the wages of staff working in those departments, vehicle and transportation costs (which could include depreciation), advertising and promotion costs, etc. These are sometimes known as **selling expenses** or **selling and marketing expenses**.

3.7 Administrative expenses

Administrative expenses, or **administration costs**, are expenses relating to the administration or administrative systems the business runs on, such as office rent, business rates, telephone costs, postage and stationery expenses, computer and software expenses and the salaries of admin staff.

amortisation
The depreciation of an intangible asset.

Depreciation is an expense that can be included in this category too (e.g. if it relates to the computer hardware used to run the business), as well as **amortisation**, which is the depreciation of intangible assets such as **business goodwill**. (Goodwill is the premium that a business is prepared to pay when buying another business for more than the business is worth. As it does not physically exist, it is often estimated and depreciated yearly through an amortisation expense.)

3.8 Finance costs

finance costs (finance expenses/charges)
Expenses relating to the financing of a business, such as bank charges or interest paid on loans and overdrafts.

Finance costs, also known as **finance expenses** or **finance charges** are expenses relating to the financing of a business and include:

◆   interest paid on loans or overdrafts (interest expense)
◆   bank charges
◆   other borrowing/financing charges or fees.

Stop and think 11.1

Think about the costs and expenses the business you work for might have. Make a list of some of them – which expense category (cost of sales, selling and distribution costs, administration expenses, finance costs) might they fall under? Could some of them potentially be classified under more than one category?

start-up costs
The expenditures made in starting a business, or costs that need to be considered in starting a business. Also known as pre-trade expenses.

3.9 Start-up costs

Start-up costs, also known as pre-trade expenses, are the expenditures made in starting a business or costs that need to be considered in starting a business. They can be useful to know, especially when performing economic analysis.

Types of start-up cost can include:

◆ rent of premises

◆ business insurance

◆ staff recruitment fees

◆ employee uniforms, if needed

◆ initial stock or materials

◆ fixtures and fittings (i.e. things like décor, lights, office furniture, heaters)

◆ legal and accountancy advice

◆ financing costs

◆ marketing costs for launch of the business.

Businesses may try to keep start-up costs to a minimum, as it might take a while to receive income from the business's trade, but knowing one's start-up costs can be useful when writing a business plan – or even for calculating what some of the likely overheads of the business might be, as well as likely fixed and variable costs.

3.10 Operating (running) costs

Operating costs (or **running costs**) are also known as **operating expenses**, and are costs and expenses that relate to the operating of the business, but not necessarily directly to the manufacture or making of the business's products or services to be sold. These include selling and distribution costs, administrative expenses, and sometimes depreciation or amortisation – but not usually finance costs such as interest paid on bank loans or overdrafts.

Operating expenses is the term often used by service industry businesses in place of cost of sales (or COGS), which tends to refer to a physical product that is made and sold rather than a service that is provided or delivered. For a service industry business, operating expenses can sometimes relate directly to operations to deliver services provided by the business.

3.11 Total cost

Total cost is the total expense a business incurs to reach a particular level of output. If the total cost is divided by the quantity produced, the business can obtain its **average cost** or **unit cost**, and estimate how efficient it is or how much it will cost to produce at a certain level of output.

The total cost is made up of fixed costs, which remain constant at any level of output, and variable costs, which change according to the business's level of output. See the graphs in Figure 11.4.

operating (operating expenses/running costs)
The costs and expenses that relate to the operating of the business, but not necessarily directly to the manufacture or making of the business's products or services to be sold.

total cost
The total expense a business incurs to reach a particular level of output.

unit cost (average cost)
The total cost per unit produced.

Figure 11.4: Examples of graphs showing total costs

Cost/revenue (£)

Total costs

Variable costs

Fixed costs

Quantity

Cost & revenue

Total costs

Total variable costs

Total fixed costs

Output

At a zero level of output (i.e. if no goods were produced by the business to sell) total cost would be equal to fixed costs.

Total cost = Fixed costs + (Variable costs per unit × Quantity of goods produced)

Worked example 11.2

In January, John Shepard's hobby business made 40 toy spaceships to sell. Each toy is handmade by Shepard in his workshop. He buys blocks of wood at £10 each to make each spaceship. Shepard's only other costs (apart from the tools he has already bought) consist of his electricity and water bills, which come to £25 a month combined, and cost him the same regardless of how many toy spaceships he makes. What is the total cost for that month for Shepard's hobby business?

Answer:

Fixed costs = £25, while Variable costs per unit = £10

Total cost = Fixed costs + (Variable costs per unit × Quantity of goods produced)

= £25 + (£10 × 40) = £25 + £400 = £425

Total variable costs and total fixed costs
The **total variable costs** are the variable costs per unit multiplied by the number of goods produced. Sometimes **average variable cost** (see below) is used in place of variable costs per unit, if the variable cost per unit is not available.

Total variable costs = Variable costs per unit × Quantity of goods produced

Or

Total variable costs = Average variable cost × Quantity of goods produced

Therefore, **total fixed costs** can be calculated by subtracting total variable cost from total cost.

Total fixed cost = Total cost − Total variable cost

Average fixed cost and average variable cost

The **average fixed cost** can be calculated by dividing the total fixed costs by the quantity of goods produced. Average variable cost can be worked out by dividing the total variable costs by the quantity produced. In other words:

Average fixed cost = Total fixed costs ÷ Quantity of goods produced

Average variable cost = Total variable costs ÷ Quantity of goods produced

Marginal cost

Finally, the **marginal costs** figure represents how total costs change as output changes. So, if a business wanted to calculate the cost of, say, producing one extra unit, the marginal cost calculation would be the one to use.

marginal cost
A figure representing how total costs change as output changes.

Marginal cost = Change in total cost ÷ Change in quantity produced

Test yourself 11.2

For John Shepard's hobby business in Worked Example 11.2, calculate the following:

1. **His average fixed cost**

2. **His marginal cost.**

4. Profit

The purpose of a business is to make a **profit** for the owners.

4.1 What is profit and/or loss?

Profit is the amount by which the revenue the business generates is greater than the business's expenses (or costs paid) for the trading period. In other words:

Profit = income − expenses

If the profit figure is negative (i.e. the business's expenses exceeded the income it received), then the business is said to have made a **loss**.

There are several profit and loss metrics a business may look at:

◆ gross profit

◆ net profit

◆ operating profit and/or **EBIT** (see section 4.4 of this chapter)

◆ **EBITDA** (see section 4.5 of this chapter).

Generally speaking, in finance, **gross** refers to the total amount before anything is deducted, while **net** refers to the amount after deductions are made.

profit
The amount left when a business's expenses (or costs paid) is subtracted from the revenue it earned for a trading period. A business exists to make a profit for its owners.

EBIT
Earnings before interest and tax. Most of the time it is the same as the operating profit.

EBITDA
(earnings before interest, tax, depreciation and amortisation) A way of measuring a company's profitability without the effects of financing, tax or accounting treatments taken into account.

4.2 Gross profit

Gross profit is the amount made from total sales (or revenue, or turnover) minus the cost of sales. In other words,

Gross profit = sales – **cost of goods sold (COGS)**

You will have seen this in Figure 11.3.

cost of goods sold (COGS)
Also known as cost of sales.

Note that the 'sales' figure should not include **sales returns**, which are sales made to customers that were later refunded (e.g. purchases returned to a shop because the customer no longer wanted the goods and got their money back).

The gross profit figure is useful for seeing how much profit a business is making on its products or services before any incidental business costs or expenses are taken into account. It can be used to see how much money is left over for the rest of the business's operations, and also to calculate the gross profit margin (see page 196).

4.3 Net profit

net profit
The amount left when all costs have been taken into account. Used to see how well the business is performing overall.

Net profit is the amount left when all expenses – COGS included – are deducted from total income (or revenue, or turnover). Often the total income figure coincides with the sales figure, but for businesses that received income from sources other than their main trade, the business's total income will be higher than the income from its trade sales. (As with all the profit calculations in this section, sales returns should not be included in the sales figure.)

Net profit = total income – total expenses

= gross profit – all other expenses

The net profit figure is useful for seeing how well the business is performing overall, once all costs have been taken into account, and will be used in calculating the net profit margin later.

4.4 Operating profit and Earnings before interest and tax (EBIT)

Operating profit is the amount of profit that's left after COGS and what are known as **operating expenses** are deducted from total income (or revenue, or turnover). Unlike net profit, not all expenses are included when calculating operating profit (e.g. finance costs such as interest expenses are not included).

Operating profit = sales – (COGS + operating expenses)

= gross profit – operating expenses

Operating profit is also known as **profit from operations** – the profit a business's operations has generated before financing (i.e. interest paid and received) and tax is taken into account. Interest rates and taxation rules are outside of a business's control, which is why these are not included in the calculation.

Operating profit is usually the same as a business's **earnings before interest and tax**, or **EBIT** for short. Whenever it differs, however, the difference is usually small and comes from the fact that the operating profit calculation does not include certain profits or losses that are not part of the operations of a business – such as profits on the sale of businesses – whereas EBIT does include this **non-operating income**.

non-operating income
Income received by a business that is not from its trade.

EBIT = revenue excluding interest income – (COGS + operating expenses)

4.5 EBITDA

Another profit measure is **EBITDA** (as opposed to EBIT), which stands for **earnings before interest, tax, depreciation and amortisation**.

EBITDA = EBIT (if EBIT does not include depreciation or amortisation expense)

or: EBITDA = EBIT + depreciation + amortisation (if it does)

EBITDA is a way of measuring a company's profitability without the effects of financing, tax or accounting treatments being taken into account. Depreciation and amortisation are recorded as expenses in a business's accounts – but they are determined by whatever accounting treatment the business is using to depreciate its assets, rather than any money physically paid or received.

By removing depreciation and amortisation (as well as taxation, and the effect of management's choice of financing) in the EBITDA calculation, it is easier to get a less distorted view of how a business is actually performing.

Test yourself 11.3

Calculate net profit, operating profit, EBIT and EBITDA for the following business.

◆ **net sales made during the year £1,600,000**

◆ **cost of goods sold £700,000**

◆ **selling and distribution expenses £100,000**

◆ **wages and salaries £300,000**

◆ **administrative expenses £350,000 (which includes £25,000 for amortisation of business goodwill, and £75,000 for depreciation of plant and machinery)**

◆ **income from sale of business premises £250,000**

◆ **interest paid on overdraft £50,000.**

4.6 Profit margins

Profit margins are a way of measuring a business's profitability. They are expressed as a percentage – and can be more useful than giving profit as a figure without any context or without any way of discerning whether the profit

profit margin
A ratio, expressed as a percentage, used to measure and analyse a business's profitability.

figure is in line with expectations when compared with the rest of the business's financial information.

There are three different profit margins a business might look at, and these can be derived from some of the profit calculations above.

Gross profit margin expresses gross profit as a percentage of sales or revenue.

Gross profit margin % = (gross profit ÷ revenue) × 100

Operating profit margin (or **operating margin**) expresses operating profit as a percentage of sales or revenue.

Operating profit margin % = (operating profit ÷ revenue) × 100

Net profit margin expresses net profit as a percentage of sales or revenue.

Net profit margin % = (net profit ÷ revenue) × 100

Worked example 11.3

Remember Kanye, with his business selling expensive T-shirts. In his first two months of business, he makes £100,000 in revenue. The T-shirts he imports for sale cost him a total of £25,000 to design, manufacture and deliver, while his marketing and administrative expenses for the month come to £40,000.

In addition, Kanye paid £5,000 in interest on a loan he took out from the bank to finance his fledgling business.

Calculate the following:

◆   Kanye's gross profit and gross profit margin

◆   Kanye's operating profit and operating margin

◆   Kanye's net profit and net profit margin.

Answers:

Gross profit = sales − cost of sales = 100,000 − 25,000 = £75,000

Gross profit margin = gross profit/revenue × 100 = 75,000/100,000 = 75%

Operating profit = gross profit − operating expenses = 75,000 − 40,000 = £35,000

Operating margin = operating profit/revenue × 100 = 35,000/100,000 = 35%

Net profit = total income − total expenses = 100,000 − (25,000 + 40,000 + 5,000)

= 100,000 − 70,000 = £30,000

Net profit margin = net profit/revenue × 100 = 30,000/100,000 = 30%

4.7 Profit and business entity

While the purpose of a business is to make a profit for the owners, the owners of the business depend on the type of entity the business is. As we shall see in the next chapter, this can affect the business's profit-generating aims and activities, as well as how it reports financial information.

There are three main types of UK business entity:

◆ sole trader

◆ partnership

◆ company.

Not-for-profit organisations are another type of entity. Although they do not aim to make a profit, the concepts of revenue, expenses and profit still apply. Accounting records must be kept of all their financial transactions.

Sole traders, partnerships and companies are covered in Part One, but here is an informal recap of each.

Sole trader

A **sole trader** business is one owned and run by an individual person. Examples include plumbers and freelance journalists. Sometimes sole traders employ other people – a builder might employ an accountant, or the owner of a small corner shop might employ shop assistants.

Partnership

A **partnership** is owned and run by two or more individuals. It is similar to a sole trader and can employ people, but often a legal contract known as the partnership agreement is drawn up, which specifies (among other things) how profits are to be shared between the partners.

Company

From a legal standpoint, the owners of sole traders and partnerships are not considered separate from the business itself. If a sole trader or partnership owes money, the owners may have to sell or use some of their own personal assets – even the house they live in – to pay the money their business owes.

A **company**, on the other hand, is a legal entity in its own right, incorporated under legislation (in the UK, the Companies Act 2006) it is governed by. The owners of a company own **shares** in that company, and are called **shareholders**. If the company owes money, any losses shareholders make is limited to the amount of money they put into the company, which is represented by the shares they own (limited liability).

There are two types of limited liability companies:

◆ **Private limited companies** usually have only a few shareholders and the shares cannot be offered to the general public or bought and sold on a stock exchange. Private limited companies have the word 'Limited' after the company name, or 'Ltd' for short;

share
A portion of a company's capital which legally represents a unit of ownership in that company. Shares entitle the person(s) owning them to voting rights at the company's annual general meeting, as well as a proportion of the company's profits. A listed company's shares can be purchased and sold on a public stock exchange, but a private limited company's shares cannot.

◆ **Public limited companies** are those whose shares can be traded and owned by the public, whether via a recognised stock exchange (in which case, the company is said to be **listed** on that stock exchange) or another way. Public limited companies have the abbreviation 'plc' after the company's name.

Stop and think 11.2

What other sole trader businesses, partnerships and companies (private limited and/or listed) can you think of? How is profit important to each of these businesses?

Chapter summary

◆ Revenue is the money a business receives, measured over a specific period of time. Revenue can be received from several sources.

◆ Costs can be fixed or variable; direct or indirect. There are slight differences between the definition of costs, expenses and expenditure but they are often used interchangeably.

◆ Cost of sales are expenses relating directly to the make or manufacture of the products sold by the business.

◆ Depreciation is an estimation of how much an asset's value has reduced by over a period of time. Amortisation is depreciation of intangible assets.

◆ Selling and distribution costs are the expenses involved in marketing, selling and distributing a business's goods or services. Administration expenses relate to the business's administration. Finance expenses relate to business financing.

◆ Total cost is the sum of all fixed and variable costs a business incurs to reach a particular output level. Total variable cost is the sum of all the variable costs a business incurs, while total fixed cost is the sum of all the fixed costs a business incurs. Average or unit cost is the total cost divided by the quantity of goods produced. Marginal costs represent how total costs change as output changes.

◆ Profit is the difference between a business's income and its expenses (called a loss if profit is negative). Commonly used profit measures are gross profit, net profit, operating profit, EBIT and EBITDA.

◆ Profit margins indicate profitability by expressing profit as a percentage of revenue. The three main types are gross profit margin, net profit margin and operating margin.

◆ A sole trader is a business run by one individual, while a partnership is run by more than one individual and a company is owned by its shareholders.

Chapter twelve
Financial accounting and management

CONTENTS

1. Introduction

This chapter outlines the purpose and objective of financial reporting, and financial reporting standards – before delving into the components that make up financial statements, giving a basic understanding of accounting as well as the types of financial analysis (along with their advantages and disadvantages) that can be performed on the financial statements.

2. The purpose of financial reporting

In order for a business to keep itself accountable and inform the various people interested in its financial performance (these people are known as **stakeholders**, and can include other businesses as well as individuals) some form of financial reporting has to be done so that these stakeholders can make decisions about the business.

stakeholders
People or organisations with an interest in a business, especially in its financial performance and/ or activities. This interest (or stake) in the business can be financial or non-financial.

2.1 Overview of financial reporting

Financial reporting is the provision of financial information about a business entity (for example, a company) to those outside the entity (i.e. external users) in a way that's useful to them to:

- make economic decisions about the entity
- assess how well the entity is being managed.

It can also be useful for those inside the business entity (i.e. internal users), but is primarily for the benefit of external users of the entity's financial information.

These internal and external users – the **stakeholders** – can include the business's employees or management, customers, lenders, suppliers, investors or potential investors, governments and their tax authorities (in the UK the tax authority is Her Majesty's Revenue & Customs or HMRC) or the general public.

financial statements (or accounts)
These are a summary of an entity's performance over a given time period (often a year), and its financial position at the end of that period.

The main way of providing this financial information, particularly to external users, is via yearly **financial statements** prepared by an accountant. The financial statements are a summary of both the entity's performance over a given time period (in this case a year) and its financial position at the end of that period. Financial statements are sometimes referred to as 'accounts', and the terms are often used interchangeably.

While financial statements are yearly, financial information can also be made available half-yearly or sometimes even quarterly. However, the annual financial statements have to be presented in a format approved by the government of the jurisdiction the business operates in.

accounting standards
Rules and guidelines setting out proper accounting practice for the benefit of those who prepare, analyse and use an entity's financial statements.

Financial reporting, therefore, is governed by local and international **accounting standards**. These set out proper accounting practice for the benefit of those who prepare, analyse and use an entity's financial statements. They create a common understanding on how particular items should be treated and displayed. Large multinational companies or companies that are **listed** on a stock exchange, are examples of entities that will need to use international accounting standards.

In the UK, all companies are required by law to prepare financial statements and issue these to their shareholders, as well as file them at Companies House. Publication of financial information is one of the requirements of **limited liability status**, so financial statements filed at Companies House are held on public record. However, smaller companies can take advantage of reporting exemptions that reduce the amount of information made publicly available in their financial statements.

2.2 Objectives of financial reporting

Early drafts of the Conceptual Framework for Financial Reporting (also known as the **International Financial Reporting Standards (IFRS)** Framework) stated the objective of financial reporting is 'to provide financial information about the reporting entity that is useful to existing and potential investors, lenders and other creditors in making decisions about providing resources to the entity'.

This 'financial information by the reporting entity' (i.e. the business or entity doing the financial reporting) is, as noted above, usually provided in the form of financial statements.

2.3 Types of financial reporting standards

In the UK, there are two systems of financial reporting standards that entities must adhere to:

◆ **UK GAAP** (Generally Accepted Accounting Practice) or
◆ **IFRS** (International Financial Reporting Standards).

Each of these has different reporting requirements.

IFRS

IFRS is the set of internationally agreed financial reporting and accounting standards that all types of entity can use.

The benefit of choosing to report financial information under IFRS is that, because they are global standards, users from anywhere in the world can understand the information provided and how financial items have been treated. Multinational organisations, for example, may find reporting under IFRS less of a burden than complying with all the local/national reporting requirements where they have entities located – especially if they have to adjust these figures again to comply with the reporting laws of their home country when preparing **consolidated financial statements**, also known as group financial statements or group accounts.

Under EU law, all companies whose **securities** (i.e. stocks and shares) are listed and traded on an EU-recognised public **stock exchange** (e.g. the London Stock Exchange) are required to prepare their group financial statements under IFRS.

Some differences exist between IFRS and UK GAAP. One difference between the two is that financial statements prepared under UK GAAP must give a 'true and fair view' of the entity's financial position and financial performance, whereas under IFRS the financial statements must 'present fairly' this same information.

Under IFRS IAS 1 (International Accounting Standard 1): 'Fair presentation requires the faithful representation of the effects of transactions, other events, and conditions in accordance with the definitions and recognition criteria for assets, liabilities, income and expenses … The application of IFRSs, with additional disclosure when necessary, is presumed to result in financial statements that achieve a fair presentation.' Other slight differences between IFRS and UK GAAP reflect how certain items are accounted for and presented in the financial statements.

While IFRS is available for anyone to apply, UK entities that do not need to apply IFRS – particularly small companies – may find the reporting requirements under UK GAAP less onerous.

UK GAAP

UK GAAP is the set of accounting standards that establish how financial statements for companies must be prepared in the UK. By law, financial statements (or accounts) must be prepared in accordance with the Companies Act 2006, which sets out the minimum reporting requirements for companies and requires them to file their financial statements at Companies House, which then makes them available to the public.

The new UK GAAP became effective for UK entities from 1 January 2015, and is based on five financial reporting standards (FRSs). FRS 100 (Application

generally accepted accounting practice (GAAP)
A set of accounting standards that establish how financial statements for companies must be prepared in the jurisdiction that the company is governed by.

IFRS
This stands for International Financial Reporting Standards and is the set of internationally agreed financial reporting and accounting standards that all types of entity can use.

consolidated financial statements (group accounts)
Financial statements of a group of companies presented as if they are a single entity.

securities
This is the collective name for items that can be publicly traded on a stock exchange which holds a financial value, such as equities (e.g. shares) or debts (e.g. bonds). Also known as stocks and shares.

stock
In this case, this is another name for company shares and/or bonds.

stock exchange
A financial market in which shares, bonds and other securities can be bought and sold.

of Financial Reporting Requirements) sets out the new financial reporting regime, explaining which types of entity were required to prepare their financial statements in accordance with the relevant accounting standards.

The five financial reporting standards comprising UK GAAP are:

◆ FRS 101, Reduced Disclosure Framework, for exemptions available to certain types of UK entity reporting under IFRS.

◆ FRS 102, the Financial Reporting Standard which applies to most UK entities who do not need to report under IFRS.

◆ FRS 103, Insurance Contracts, which set out the requirements and guidance for insurance contracts.

◆ FRS 104, Interim Financial Reporting, which provides guidance on interim financial reports (i.e. financial reports for a time period shorter than a year).

◆ FRS 105, the Financial Reporting Standard applicable to the micro-entities regime, under which the very smallest businesses can report reduced information.

FRS 105 permits **micro-entities** to report less financial information than larger businesses have to. Micro-entities are defined as certain types of entity which meet two of the following criteria over a 12-month reporting period:

◆ turnover: up to £632,000 (adjusted for periods longer or shorter than 12 months)

◆ balance sheet (net assets): up to £316,000 or

◆ average number of employees: up to 10.

Some **small and medium-sized entities (SMEs)** are also able to apply exemptions under UK GAAP, although they do not have as many reporting exemptions as micro-entities. SMEs used to be able to file abbreviated accounts at Companies House and you may still see these; however, for accounting periods beginning on or after 1 January 2016, the reporting requirements have changed.

SMEs are made up of those entities that fit the criteria for either **small** or **medium-sized companies**, as explained below – the figures in brackets are the limits that apply to accounting periods that start on or after 1 January 2016.

Small companies are defined as those that meet two of the following criteria over a 12-month reporting period:

◆ turnover: not more than £10.2 million (previously £6.5 million);

◆ balance sheet (net assets): not more than £5.1 million (previously £3.26 million); or

◆ average number of employees: not more than 50.

Medium-sized companies are those that meet two of the following criteria over a 12-month reporting period:

◆ turnover: not more than £36 million (previously £25.9 million);

◆ balance sheet (net assets): not more than £18 million (previously £12.9 million); or

◆ average number of employees: not more than 250.

Large companies are those entities in excess of the criteria for medium-sized companies.

Small companies can report either under FRS 105 if they qualify as micro-entities or under section 1A of FRS 102 – which replaced the Financial Reporting Standard for Small Entities (FRSSE) from 1 January 2016. Section 1A FRS 102 does not require small entities to disclose as much information as medium-sized or large entities – for example, there is no requirement for small entities to produce a cashflow statement (more on what this is later).

Generally accepted accounting practice (or generally accepted accounting principles) can vary between countries. For example, in the USA, traditionally US GAAP requirements have been based on detailed sets of rules to cover as many eventualities as possible, whereas UK GAAP sets out more general principles which require those who prepare financial statements to justify how and why their treatment of financial information adheres to these principles.

Test yourself 12.1

While any UK company is allowed to report under IFRS, can any of the following companies report under UK GAAP? If so, do they report under FRS 102, FRS 105, or section 1A of FRS 102?

◆ **A UK-listed company, X plc, with 25 employees and a turnover of £9 million.**

◆ **A non-listed UK limited company, X Ltd, with 25 employees and a turnover of £9 million.**

◆ **A non-listed UK limited company, Y Ltd, with 251 employees and a turnover of £40 million.**

◆ **A non-listed UK limited company, Z Ltd, with two employees and a turnover of £490,000.**

2.4 Characteristics of financial statements

When considering financial reporting and disclosure requirements, it is important to think about whether the financial information being included and presented will be useful. The Conceptual Framework for Financial Reporting sets out the qualitative characteristics of financial statements reported under IFRS as follows.

The fundamental qualitative characteristics of financial statements are:

◆ relevance

◆ faithful representation.

The enhancing qualitative characteristics (i.e. the qualitative characteristics that enhance the usefulness of information that is relevant and faithfully represented) are:

- understandability
- comparability
- verifiability
- timeliness.

Relevance

Financial information is relevant if it has the ability to influence the economic decisions a user of the financial statements might make. Information that has predictive value or confirmatory value – or both – is capable of influencing a user's economic decisions.

materiality
A concept that describes whether an item's omission or misstatement could influence the decision taken by users of financial statements, or cause those financial statements to not faithfully represent the economic substance of the information contained.

Relevance is affected by **materiality**. Materiality is a fundamental concept in financial reporting, but it does not have an exact definition. Information is said to be **material** if its omission or misstatement could influence the decision taken by users of financial statements, or cause the financial statements to either not present a true and fair view (under UK GAAP) or not represent faithfully the economic substance of the information in the accounts (under IFRS).

Generally materiality is relative to the size and circumstances of the business and/or the nature of the item under consideration. For example, one business in one industry may consider a particular item that is worth 1% of its gross profit to be material information to disclose further details about, whereas another business in another industry – with, say, a smaller gross profit – may consider that same item worth 1% of its gross profit as immaterial, either by size or nature.

Faithful representation

Financial reports must represent economic events and transactions – in words and numbers – in a way that aims to be, as far as is possible:

- complete
- neutral (i.e. without bias) and
- free from error.

A faithful representation is not enough on its own – financial information must be both relevant and faithfully represented in order to be useful.

Understandability

This means that information in the financial statements must be understandable, and presented and categorised in such a way that users with a reasonable knowledge of business and accounting can understand it.

Comparability

Comparability means that information in the financial statements is useful if one can compare it with the information for previous periods, or information about another entity.

For example, a company director may want to compare the current year's turnover with last year's turnover figure, to check if the company is making more sales than last year – or even compare it with the current year turnovers of other companies in the same industry, to see how the company is performing compared to other similar companies.

In order to make sure that information can be compared easily, it helps if there is:

◆ consistency – adopting the same financial reporting and accounting policies from one period to the next, or adopting the same policies as other businesses; and

◆ disclosure of these financial reporting and accounting policies in the financial statements – and of any changes made to these policies, which is necessary for the proper interpretation of financial information.

This is a major reason for the existence of accounting rules and financial reporting standards, both national and global.

Verifiability

Verifiability means that different knowledgeable and independent observers could reach consensus, although not necessarily complete agreement, that a particular depiction is a faithful representation. Verifiability helps to assure users that information represents faithfully the economic phenomena it purports to represent.

Timeliness

Providing information in a timely manner means the information should be made available in time for a user to make decisions. Generally, older information is less useful – but users might need it to examine and assess trends for some financial items.

Stop and think 12.1

What constraints might there be on how financial information is reported?

3. Components of financial statements

Financial statements are usually prepared on the assumption that the reporting entity is a **going concern** (i.e. the business has no intention to **liquidate** or be brought to an end) and is likely to operate for the 'foreseeable future'. This usually means over at least the next 12 months.

going concern
A business that is a going concern has no intention to liquidate, or be brought to an end, and is likely to operate for the 'foreseeable future' (usually meaning at least the next 12 months).

Financial statements are the summary – produced in an approved financial reporting format – of a business's financial records over a period of time (usually a year). The process of making up these financial records, which document and summarise a business's transactions, is known as **accounting**.

3.1 Recording financial data

The business's financial data is recorded in **ledgers** and **books of prime entry**.

The ledgers are:

- the nominal ledger (or general ledger)
- the sales ledger
- the purchase ledger.

The books of prime entry are:

- the sales day book
- the purchases day book
- the cash book
- the petty cash book
- the journal.

Sometimes a 'sales returns day book' exists, but this is often subsumed into the sales day book; in this case a 'purchase returns day book' may also exist, although this is often subsumed into the purchases day book.

Before computers, these were physical books of record that were filled out by hand in a process known as **double entry bookkeeping** (more on that later). The terminology still used today harks back to the pre-digital era (e.g. the accounting system for recording transactions is still sometimes referred to as the 'the books'). Nowadays these books of record are entered into accounting software rather than filled out by hand.

Ledgers and ledger accounting
Ledger accounting is just another term for bookkeeping and the 'books' used in bookkeeping refer to the ledgers and the day books. The most important ledger is the **nominal ledger**, also known as the general ledger.

The sales ledger is not part of a double entry system, and serves as a record of individual **receivables** (i.e. people or companies that owe the business money, also known as **debtors**) as a memorandum. The purchase ledger functions the same way, but is a record of individual **payables** (i.e. people or companies that the business owes money to, also known as **creditors**).

The nominal ledger contains a number of different 'accounts' for each type of item, regardless of whether it is an income or expense item, and is probably the most important ledger in a double-entry bookkeeping system.

ledger
In bookkeeping, this is one of the main books in which a business's financial data is recorded.

books of prime entry
In bookkeeping, these are used to record a business's financial transactions before they are fed through to one of the ledgers.

debtors (receivables)
The people/other businesses that owe money to the business.

creditors (payables)
The people/other businesses the business owes money to.

Books of prime entry

These are where the business's main financial transactions are recorded and fed through to the accounts in the nominal ledger. They function as follows:

◆ the sales day book – this is a book for recording sales made to customers on **credit** (i.e. with the customer owing the business money for the sale to be paid at a later date specified on the invoice);

◆ the purchases day book – this is a book for recording what the business spent money on or bought on credit. A **debt** is the amount the business owes;

◆ the cash book – this is for recording cash transactions, whether that is money the business receives or spends;

◆ the petty cash book – keeps a record of **petty cash**, which is a small amount of physical cash a business keeps on hand in a drawer or a safe, rather than in the bank, to make small cash payments when necessary (the maximum petty cash limit is called an **imprest** or **float**);

◆ the journal – this is for recording any transactions that do not go in the other books of prime entry, including any adjustments or correction of errors made in recording transactions in the other day books.

The ledgers and books or prime entry are filled in using a process known as double entry bookkeeping.

3.2 Double-entry bookkeeping

Bookkeeping is the keeping of records of the financial affairs of a business, usually in books (like the ledgers and books of prime entry). **Double-entry bookkeeping** is based on the concept that every economic transaction has two parts – a positive entry and a negative entry, and will therefore affect two ledger accounts.

An entry in one account requires a corresponding opposite entry in a different account – for example, the purchase of a company car in cash will require the transaction to be recorded in the ledger account for company vehicles (added to the account at the price it was purchased for) and recorded in the cash account or day book (subtracted from the current cash amount at the price it was purchased for). These double entries are called **debits** and **credits** – if one ledger account is debited with £X, another must be credited with £X.

Debit is often shortened to DR and goes on the left side of an account, while credit is shortened to CR and goes on the right side. One way to remember which sides debits and credits appear is the following mnemonic: in the UK we DRive on the left and CRash on the right.

The details of how to do double-entry bookkeeping (and how to use each ledger or day book) are outside the scope of this course, but what you do need to know is that double-entry accounting makes up the foundation of all businesses' recorded financial transactions.

debt
An amount that the business owes.

petty cash
A small amount of physical cash a business keeps on hand in a drawer or a safe, rather than in the bank, to make small cash payments when necessary.

float (imprest)
An amount (often the maximum) that a business holds in petty cash.

double-entry bookkeeping
A method of bookkeeping based on the concept that every economic transaction has two parts – a positive entry and a corresponding negative entry, and will therefore affect two ledger accounts.

debit
In bookkeeping, this is an entry recording an amount of money paid by or owed to a business as one half of a transaction's double entry (DR for short).

credit
Either (a) in bookkeeping, an entry recording an amount of money received or owed by a business as one half of a transaction's double entry (CR for short); or (b) the state of a business receiving goods or services before paying for them while being trusted to pay what they owe in the future.

trial balance
A statement, created from the business's bookkeeping system, of all the debits and credits representing the business's financial transactions over an accounting period.

balance sheet
Another name for the statement of financial position.

statement of financial position
This provides a snapshot of the business's financial position at a point in time, usually at the end of an accounting period, showing the business's assets, liabilities and equity at that date. Also known as the balance sheet.

The information in the nominal ledger is used to make up a **trial balance** (more on this later) at the end of a period – usually at the year-end – which then feeds the information through to the **income statement** (or statement of profit or loss, or profit and loss account) and the **balance sheet** (or **statement of financial position**).

We've already seen a very basic example of an income statement in Chapter 11, but an example of a very basic balance sheet is shown in Figure 12.1.

Figure 12.1: A basic balance sheet

**Wrex's sole trader freelancing business
Balance sheet at 31 December 2018**

	£
Assets	
Cash	10,000
Debtors	2,500
Work in progress	500
	13,000
Liabilities	
Creditors	3,000
Outstanding loan amount	1,000
	4,000
Net Assets	**9,000**
CAPITAL	
Opening balance sheet amount	21,000
New capital injected into business	1,000
Drawings	(35,000)
Profit from P&L statement	22,000
Closing Balance Sheet Amount	**9,000**

Note the following from Figure 12.1:

◆   **Assets** are things that the business either owns or expects to receive monetary amounts from (such as cash, debtors or **work in progress** that will be sold once finished). **Liabilities** are monetary amounts the business owes and therefore needs to pay (such as outstanding loans, bank overdrafts or creditor amounts).

◆ **Net assets** are the amount of assets that are left after all liabilities have been accounted for (i.e. net assets = assets − liabilities).

◆ **Capital** is, broadly speaking, the money that is injected into the business or that is used to keep the business operating. For a sole trader, **drawings** are money taken out of the business – usually for the owner's personal use.

◆ The profit (or loss) figure from the profit and loss statement feeds through to the balance sheet, and is included in the calculation of how the business's capital has changed over the period – although balance sheet figures aren't fed through to the profit and loss statement.

◆ The **closing balance sheet amount** (also known as the **closing capital**) is a **reconciliation** of how the capital in the business has changed over the period – it adds any new capital injections and profit to the opening capital figure, then subtracts total drawings or business loss to get the closing capital figure (or closing balance sheet figure).

◆ The net assets figure is equal to the closing balance sheet figure.

The balance sheet's net assets figure – all assets minus all liabilities – is **always equal** to the closing balance sheet figure and illustrates how the balance sheet is a representation of the **accounting equation** in action.

The accounting equation is:

Capital = Assets − Liabilities

or

Assets = Liabilities + Capital

Every time an economic transaction takes place, the accounting equation may change but the relationship between assets, capital and liabilities in the equation will always remain the same. This is the **dual effect of accounting** and it is reflected in the principle of double-entry bookkeeping.

There are two ways of accounting for transactions in the books – under the **cash basis** and under the **accruals basis**:

◆ Cash basis – this is, quite simply, when cash transactions are recorded as and when they happen, or whenever the cash is paid or received. If an invoice is sent to a business, but the business does not pay it before its year-end, then the transaction is not recorded or reflected in the year-end accounts; likewise, if a sale is made but no cash was received by the year-end, the business does not record the sale in its revenue figure. Some simple micro-businesses might use the cash basis of accounting.

◆ Accruals basis – this is when revenues are recorded when they are earned (e.g. when an invoice is sent), rather than when the money is physically received, and expenses are matched with revenues or recorded when they are incurred regardless of when the expense is paid.

capital
In accounting, this is the money injected into the business and/or that is used to keep the business operating.

closing capital/closing balance sheet amount
The reconciliation showing how the capital in the business has changed over an accounting period. The closing balance sheet amount should equal the net assets at the end of the period (i.e. the capital the business 'closes' the period with).

reconciliation
The process that works arithmetically between two sets of recorded figures to check (or confirm) that they are correct. The trial balance is one example of a reconciliation.

accounting equation
This represents the dual effect of accounting, where total equity (or capital) equals net assets (i.e. total assets minus total liabilities).

dual effect of accounting
The principle on which double-entry bookkeeping and the accounting equation are based (i.e. that every economic transaction has two parts and that this dual effect should be recorded in two places).

cash basis (cash accounting)
A way of accounting for transactions by recording them as and when they happen, or whenever the cash is paid or received.

accruals basis
(accrual accounting) A way of accounting for transactions by recording them in the accounting period they are earned or incurred, regardless of when money is paid or received.

Accrual accounting results in a profit and loss statement that reflects profitability more accurately, and thus a balance sheet that reflects assets and liabilities more accurately, and is therefore used by most businesses.

3.3 Trial balance and year-end adjustments

The **trial balance** is a list of all the balances on the all the accounts in the nominal ledger. The total of all debit balances must be equal to the total of all the credit balances – if they are not, then it means a mistake has been made in the bookkeeping entries. Figure 12.2 illustrates an example of a trial balance.

Figure 12.2: Trial balance

Trial balance for Miranda's business for the year ended 31 December 2018

	Dr £	Cr £
Sales		780,000
Cost of sales	356,000	
Office rental expense	60,000	
Staff wages	21,000	
Administrative expenses	8,000	
Insurance	6,000	
Utilities (electricity, heating, water)	15,000	
Distribution costs	27,000	
Sundry expenses	5,000	
Motor vehicles	42,000	
Fixtures and fittings	140,000	
Debtors	53,000	
Creditors		33,500
Cash in bank	48,000	
Cash in hand	500	
Drawings	72,000	
Opening capital at 1 January 2018		40,000
Totals	853,500	853,500

Year-end adjustments are made where necessary before the figures are plugged into the profit and loss statement and balance sheet. Depreciation is one example of a year-end adjustment: it is not an expense where money has to be physically paid to a creditor, but is an accounting adjustment to reflect that assets lose their value as the years pass and eventually need to be replaced.

Year-end adjustments therefore apply the principle of prudence in the preparation of financial statements, as well as the **accruals concept**, which says that revenue and expenses should be recorded in the accounting period in which they occur.

4. Financial statements and their purposes

Financial statements are a formal record of a business's financial performance over a period of time and financial position as at a certain date. They are constructed from the financial records the business has, pulling together the information either from the ledgers and books of prime entry or from the trial balance and journals. They are often known informally as 'the company's accounts'.

There are four basic reports that make up the financial statements as follows:

◆ the **income statement** – also known as the profit and loss statement, sometimes P&L for short
◆ the **statement of financial position** – also known as the balance sheet
◆ the **statement of cash flows** – also known as the cash flow statement
◆ the **statement of income and retained earnings** – also known as the statement of retained earnings.

4.1 The income statement

The income statement, also known as the statement of profit or loss (or sometimes P&L for short), shows a business's financial performance over a period of time, usually a year. It shows the business's income, expenses and profit over a specified period.

year-end adjustment
An accounting adjustment made at the end of the financial year where necessary before the financial statements are prepared.

accrual
(or accrued expense) An adjustment in the accounts or books to reflect an expense payment that falls due in an accounting period but is paid after the period ends.

accruals concept
An accounting concept stating that revenue and expenses should be recorded in the accounting period in which they occur, regardless of when the money is received or paid for them.

statement of cash flows (cash flow statement)
A statement showing how much cash the business is generating from its operations.

statement of income and retained earnings (statement of retained earnings)
A statement that reconciles the changes that have taken place over an accounting period in the retained earnings account.

Figure 12.3: Income statement

XYZ Limited
Income statement for the year ended 31 December 2018 (with prior year comparatives)

	2018 £	2017 £
Turnover	2,957,140	2,139,870
Cost of sales	(1,298,542)	(997,046)
Gross Profit	1,658,598	1,142,824
Distribution costs	(428,986)	(401,933)
Administrative expenses	(536,798)	(499,745)
Operating profit	692,814	241,146
Profit on disposal of freehold property	0	100,525
Unrealised surplus on valuation of property	0	7,500
Income from investments	15,000	15,000
Interest receivable	9,600	9,500
Interest payable	(25,675)	(24,825)
Profit Before Taxation	691,739	348,846
Taxation	(139,362)	(68,134)
Profit After Taxation	552,377	280,712

Figure 12.3 is an example of how an income statement would appear in company accounts. Here, it is evident how the business performed over the period under review – in this case, the year ended 31 December 2018, as seen from the figures in the first column – against the business's performance in the previous period (i.e. the year ended 31 December 2017) which are the figures in the second column.

It is clear, for instance, that XYZ Limited was more profitable in 2018 than in the previous year. During the 12 months to 31 December 2018, XYZ Limited made a profit of £552,377 after tax, while in 2017 the company made a profit after tax of £280,712 – a year-on-year increase of £271,665 (£552,377 minus £280,712).

Being able to compare the figures across income statements from different periods in this way is important. These numerical comparisons can give the reader of the financial statements an idea of how the business is performing from one period to the next. They can also answer any questions that the stakeholders of the business and other users of the financial statements may have. For example, are sales rising in line with expectations? Are costs spiralling out of control? Is profitability increasing? As you can see in the example in Figure 12.3, the answer to that last question is yes – the profit after tax figure almost doubled from 2017 to 2018.

Income statement figures can be compared across more than one period by looking at previous financial statements. Users of the financial statements can use this information to make decisions based on trends in the business's performance (e.g. heading off potential problems either before they arise or before they get any worse).

However, there are other financial statements that can be compared across accounting periods from which useful information can be obtained.

4.2 The statement of financial position

The **statement of financial position**, often called the **balance sheet**, provides a snapshot of the business's financial position at a point in time – usually at the end of an accounting period. Figure 12.4 is an example of what a statement of financial position for a company might look like.

Figure 12.4: Statement of financial position

ABC Limited
Statement of financial position at 31 December 2018 (with prior year comparatives)

	2018 £	2017 £
Non-Current Assets		
Tangible assets	2,324,747	2,228,913
Intangible assets	500,000	500,000
Investments	450,000	450,000
	3,274,747	3,178,913
Current Assets		
Inventory	234,785	199,463
Trade receivables	59,619	53,442
Cash and cash equivalents	37,584	35,521
	331,988	288,426
Current Liabilities		
Trade payables	45,677	41,326
Other creditors	8,467	7,816

Loan amounts falling due within one year	79,000	77,500
	133,144	126,642
Non-Current Liabilities		
Loan amounts falling due after one year	680,500	758,000
Net Assets	2,793,091	2,582,697
Capital and Reserves		
Called-up share capital	100	100
Share premium account	2,007,588	1,878,444
Profit and loss account	785,403	704,153
Total Equity	**2,793,091**	**2,582,697**

The balance sheet is made up of the following components:

◆   assets

◆   liabilities

◆   equity.

Assets

Assets are things that a business *owns* that either generate cash or have the potential to generate cash. For example: inventory, property, office furniture, and vehicles.

There are four different types of asset that are referred to in accounting.

Tangible assets are assets with a physical form, such as land, buildings, plant and equipment, and physical inventory. **Intangible assets** are non-physical or abstract items such as patents, copyrights, trademarks and goodwill.

Fixed assets (or **non-current assets**) are assets that a business owns for long-term use, rather than to sell to customers. Fixed assets can also be tangible assets or intangible assets. Types of fixed asset include:

◆   property (e.g. land and buildings)

◆   office furniture

◆   fixtures and fittings

◆   plant and equipment

◆   goodwill

◆   vehicles for use in the business

◆   patents, copyrights and trademarks needed for the business to operate.

tangible asset
An asset with a physical, touchable (i.e. tangible) form, such as land, buildings, plant and equipment, and physical inventory.

intangible asset
An asset which is a non-physical or abstract item (i.e. intangible), such as patents, copyrights, trademarks and goodwill.

fixed asset (non-current assets)
An asset (tangible or intangible) that a business owns for long-term use, rather than to sell to customers.

Current assets are assets that a business can expect to convert to cash over the course of a year. This includes cash itself, or any item a business expects to sell to customers. As with fixed assets, current assets can also be tangible or intangible. Examples of current assets include:

◆ inventory, also known as **stock;**

◆ raw materials, which may be included in inventory;

◆ cash and cash equivalents (such as petty cash, undeposited cheques);

◆ trade receivables, or trade debtors;

◆ other receivables, or other debtors;

◆ prepayments (prepaid expenses); and

◆ works in progress (WIP).

A business's **total assets** are defined as the sum of all assets the business holds (i.e. total fixed assets plus total current assets).

Total assets = Total fixed assets + Total current assets

Liabilities

Liabilities are things that a business *owes* – amounts that the business has a financial obligation to pay as a result of past transactions or events (e.g. loans, mortgages, overdrafts and amounts due to the business's creditors). Provisions (e.g. for bad and doubtful debts) are also often included in this part of the balance sheet.

Long-term liabilities (or non-current liabilities) are liabilities that a business will settle (pay in full) in more than one year's time and include mortgages and other long-term loans.

Current liabilities are those which a business expects to settle over the course of a year. Examples of current liabilities include:

◆ trade payables, or trade creditors

◆ other payables, or other creditors

◆ deferred income

◆ accruals

◆ bank overdrafts

◆ taxes payable

◆ loan amounts falling due within one year.

A business's **total liabilities** amount is the sum of all liabilities the business owes, both current and non-current.

Total liabilities = Total non-current liabilities + Total current liabilities

current asset
An asset that a business can expect to convert to cash over the course of a year.

total assets
The sum of all assets the business holds.

total liabilities
The sum of all liabilities the business owes, both current and long-term.

Test yourself 12.2

For each of the following items, state whether they are assets or liabilities. If they are assets, consider whether they are (i) fixed assets or current assets or (ii) tangible assets or intangible assets. If they are liabilities, state whether they are long-term liabilities or current liabilities:

◆ office building

◆ petty cash

◆ bank overdraft

◆ commercial mortgage

◆ company cars

◆ patents

◆ trade creditors.

Equity

Equity is a word with many definitions – but in the case of the financial statements, equity represents the ownership interest in the business. If the business was in liquidation (i.e. coming to an end), the equity would be what remains – and therefore what can be returned to the shareholders or owners – after all liabilities have been paid. It can be defined by the **accounting equation**, which is:

Equity = Total assets – Total liabilities

Another name for the business's equity is **net assets**. These are also defined by the accounting equation as total assets minus total liabilities. Therefore, the higher the business's **net assets value**, the higher the value of the business.

For a private limited company, the business and its owners (shareholders) are separate entities, so the business is considered to owe these funds to its owners in the form of **share capital**. While the business continues to exist, the equity of the business will be the difference between the assets it holds and its debts and liabilities.

The ordinary (or nominal) value of a share can be found in a company's memorandum and articles and represents the face value of the share rather than its **market value**. In many cases, the nominal value of a share is £1. So for the example balance sheet in Figure 12.4, if the ordinary value of each share is £1, then the company has 100 shares – making the value of the called up share capital £100. 'Called up share capital' represents the amount of share capital owed by shareholders, but has not yet been paid. The excess value of the shares over their ordinary value is represented by the **share premium account**.

The figure from the profit and loss account comes from the statement of income and retained earnings.

equity
Another name for capital; alternatively, it can refer to shares or shareholdings.

net assets
The amount of assets that are left in the business after all liabilities have been accounted for (i.e. total assets minus total liabilities).

net asset value
The value of what's left in the business after the value of all liabilities have been subtracted from the value of all assets. For the valuation of a listed company, the net asset value can also refer to net assets per share.

market value
The price that an asset can be sold for through the relevant marketplace (e.g. a stock exchange, an auction, an estate agent or retailer).

share premium
The excess value of a share over its ordinary value (or nominal value).

Test yourself 12.3

It is very rare that a company's equity in its financial statements – its net assets – will not be a positive figure, but it occasionally happens. What does it mean, in terms of the accounting equation, when a company's equity is negative? Do you think a company can survive (and keep out of liquidation) in these circumstances?

4.3 The statement of cash flows

The statement of cash flows, more often known as the cash flow statement, shows how much cash the business is generating from its operations. You may even have heard of the saying 'turnover is vanity, profit is sanity, cashflow is reality' – a positive and strong cash flow from a business's operations is one of the best signs that the business is healthy.

Cash inflow is money coming into the business, while **cash outflow** is money going out of the business.

cash inflow/outflow
Money coming into/out of the business.

Figure 12.5 is a basic example of how a cash flow statement could look in a business's accounts.

Figure 12.5: Cash flow statement

YZA Limited
Statement of cash flows for the year ended 31 December 2018
(with prior year comparatives)

	2018 £	2017 £
Cash from:		
– operating activities	672,388	537,191
– investing activities	7,500	7,250
– financing activities	82,345	90,873
Increase in cash	762,233	635,314

Generally, the cashflow statement records cash from different types of activity in the business. These activities typically include:

◆ cash from operating activities: this includes cash inflows and outflows from the business's trading activities, such as the production, sales and delivery of the business's products, payment from customers, advertising, the purchase of raw materials and costs of creating inventory to sell.

◆ cash from investing activities: this includes cash inflows and outflows relating to the business's investments, such as mergers and acquisitions, **dividends** received, and the purchase and sale of fixed assets.

dividend
The money a company pays to its shareholders out of its profits and/or reserves, usually either annually or every six months.

◆   cash from financing activities: this includes cash inflows and outflows relating to financial investors in the business, such as loans received from banks, loan payments made to banks, borrowing, dividends paid out to shareholders, and equity injections (cash) or loans from shareholders.

Reconciliation of operating profit to cash from operating activities

In accounting, a reconciliation is a process that works arithmetically between two sets of recorded figures to check (or confirm) that they are correct.

In the supplementary notes to the accounts, there will often be a reconciliation between the operating profit and the cash from operating activities. The figure that results – the net cash inflow from operations (or even the net cash outflow from operations) – should match the figure for the cash from operating activities figure. This is how users of the financial statements can check that the figures are correct, as well as get an idea from the reconciliation of how efficiently the business turns profit into cashflow.

The cash from operating activities (or cash flow from operations) figure can be obtained via figures from the income statement and balance sheet.

You start with the operating profit in the income statement and add back non-cash expenses such as depreciation of fixed assets and amortisation of intangible assets, and take into account other adjustments such as the change in debtor and creditor amounts over a period. Figure 12.6 is an example of such a reconciliation as it might appear in the notes to the accounts.

Figure 12.6: Reconciliation statement

XYZ Limited
Reconciliation of operating profit to net cash from operating activities (with prior year comparatives)

	2018 £	2017 £
Operating profit	692,814	241,146
Depreciation	100,875	99,764
Amortisation of intangible asset	1,000	1,000
Profit/(loss) on sale of tangible fixed asset	(4,750)	0
Increase/(decrease) in debtors	46,982	(8,758)
Increase/(decrease) in creditors	24,573	19,842
Net Cash Inflow from Operations	861,494	352,994

4.4 The statement of income and retained earnings

Also known as the statement of retained earnings, companies are required to produce this statement under UK GAAP. This statement reconciles the changes that have taken place over an accounting period in the retained earnings account, also known as the 'profit and loss account' on the balance sheet. For a limited company, this reconciliation is generally calculated as follows:

Retained earnings for the year = Opening retained earnings + Profit for the period − Equity dividends paid

As mentioned, the retained earnings for the year figure goes in the profit and loss account on the company's balance sheet, while equity dividends paid (also known as **distributions**) are the dividends paid out to shareholders in the period. An example is given in Figure 12.7.

distributions
Another name for dividends.

Figure 12.7: Statement of retained earnings

ABC Limited
Statement of retained earnings at 31 December 2018 (with prior year comparatives)

	2018 £	2017 £
Retained earnings at 1 January	704,153	648,939
Profit after tax for the period	107,432	99,456
Dividends paid to shareholders	(26,182)	(44,242)
Retained earnings at 31 December	785,403	704,153

Notice that these match the figures given in the 'profit and loss account' in the equity section of the statement of financial position in Figure 12.4.

The retained earnings figures from the start of the period and the end of the period should match the 'profit and loss account' figures for the same dates in the equity section of the balance sheet, and the profit after tax for the period should match the relevant figure in the income statement for the period.

5. Analysing and evaluating financial statements

Financial statements can be analysed by comparing information between different accounting periods. The information that can be obtained from this analysis is useful to both investors and management in the business. Trends can be observed about how the business has performed from one accounting period to the next – or even across several periods – and problems, such as a sharp increase in administrative costs, can be highlighted and tackled before they threaten the business's health.

To observe how a business is performing against its competitors, information and trends from the business's financial statements can be compared against like-for-like information for other businesses in the same industry. They can also be used to forecast how the business is likely to perform over the next year or so.

5.1   Different types of financial statement analysis

The three basic types of analysis that can be performed on financial statements are horizontal, vertical and ratio analysis.

Horizontal analysis

horizontal analysis
A type of financial statement analysis performed by comparing an item against previous periods using the figures on the same horizontal line in that financial statement.

Horizontal analysis – or trend analysis – is when a particular item in a financial statement is compared against previous periods – using the figures on the same horizontal line in the financial statement. For example, if you want to analyse how much the profit before tax has increased in a business from one year to the next, you can compare the relevant figures from the income statement.

For example, if we perform a horizontal analysis of the profit before taxation figures using the income statement in Figure 12.3 on page 212, we can see that profit before taxation almost doubled from 2017 to 2018.

The profit before taxation in 2017 was £348,846 and in 2018 it was £691,739. Therefore, the profit before tax increased by £342,893 over the year – a 98.3% increase.

Vertical analysis

vertical analysis
A type of financial statement analysis performed by comparing an item using figures within the same vertical column of figures on that financial statement.

Where horizontal analysis uses figures on the same horizontal line in a financial statement (from one period to another), **vertical analysis** uses figures within the same vertical column of figures on a financial statement.

Vertical analysis compares items on a financial statement as a percentage of another item within that period.

For example, vertical analysis of an income statement often expresses each line item as a percentage of turnover (e.g. in the income statement Figure 12.3, gross profit in 2018 was 56.1% of turnover: 1,658,598 ÷ 2,957,140 × 100 = 56.1%), and on the balance sheet, vertical analysis often expresses something as a percentage of total assets. For the cash flow statement, items can be expressed as a percentage of total cash and cash equivalents.

The advantage of vertical analysis is that you can compare these percentages against previous periods, and even against other companies. For example, we can see how the above gross profit as a percentage of turnover compares to other companies' income statements in 2018, or even against the same company's income statement in 2017.

Test yourself 12.4

Use the following balance sheet extract to perform both a horizontal analysis and a vertical analysis for each line item above the 'net assets' figure to two decimal places.

For the horizontal analysis, express each line item as a percentage increase/decrease of the 2017 figure; and for the vertical analysis, express each line item as a percentage of total assets for both 2017 and 2018.

	2018 £	2017 £
Total fixed assets	105,000	100,000
Total current assets	57,800	49,500
Total current liabilities	(24,900)	(27,800)
Long-term liabilities	(60,000)	(64,000)
Net assets	**77,900**	**57,700**
Called up share capital	100	100
Profit and loss	77,800	57,600
Total Equity	**77,900**	**57,700**

Ratio analysis

Ratio analysis uses certain ratios to evaluate a business's operating and/or financial performance over time. This can help to pinpoint a business's strengths and weaknesses, which can then inform business strategy; and the success of this strategy can be measured by comparing these ratios over time. Two such ratios are:

◆ **return on assets (ROA)** is defined as net profit divided by total assets. This gives an idea of how efficient the business is at using its assets to generate profit

◆ **return on equity (ROE)** is defined as net profit divided by shareholders' equity. This gives an idea of how able the business is at generating profits from the shareholders' investment in the business.

In other words:

Return on assets (or ROA) = net profit ÷ total assets

Return on equity (or ROE) = net profit ÷ shareholders' equity

These two ratios use information from both the income statement (net profit, or the profit before/after tax figure) and balance sheet (either the total assets figure or the equity figure), but there are other ratios used to evaluate financial and operating performance that are specific to either the income statement or the balance sheet, as follows.

5.2 Analysing the income statement

Horizontal and vertical analysis can be done on any of the primary financial statements (including the cashflow statement), while ROA and ROE require figures from both the income statement (i.e. the net profit figure) and the balance sheet (i.e. either the total assets figure or the shareholders' equity figure).

However, taking each of the primary financial statements by themselves can supply a wealth of information for analysing trends or calculating useful ratios for analysis.

For example, the income statement – or profit and loss statement – can be used to calculate the following ratios:

◆ profit margins

◆ interest cover

◆ break-even point.

We will look at each of these in turn.

Profit margins

We already touched upon these in Chapter 11 on revenue, costs and profit, but here is a recap. **Profit margins** are used to measure and analyse a business's profitability. They are expressed as a percentage, which can be more useful to a user of the financial statements than simply noting the profit figure with no context or comparison.

There are three different profit margins a business might look at, and all of these can be derived from the income statement.

Gross profit margin expresses gross profit as a percentage of sales or revenue:

Gross profit margin % = (gross profit ÷ revenue) × 100

Changes from one year to another for the gross profit margin may have several causes, including (but not limited to) a change in sale prices, a change in the sales mix, a change in the costs of purchase or production, or inventory obsolescence (i.e. inventory which has become unsellable due to lack of demand).

Gross profit margins might be useful for comparing the gross profitability of businesses operating in the same industry, as they are likely to record financial transactions and present their accounts in similar ways; but might not be as useful for comparisons between businesses in different sectors, as expenditure may not be split between cost of sales and other expense types in the same way.

Operating profit margin (also known as **operating margin**) expresses operating profit as a percentage of sales or revenue:

Operating profit margin % = (operating profit ÷ revenue) × 100

Net profit margin (sometimes known as **net margin**) expresses net profit as a percentage of sales or revenue:

Net profit margin % = (net profit ÷ revenue) × 100

Variations between years for the operating margin or net profit margin may be caused by a change in the value of sales – either due to changes in price or sales volume – or changes in non-recurring operating expenses.

Net profit margin can be an indicator of the 'quality' of the business's profits – the higher the profit margin, the higher the profit on each unit sold. Some analysts may feel that higher-margin businesses are less risky than lower-margin businesses, as a decrease in the net profit margin may still mean a business will still be profitable. However, this obviously depends on the type of business or what other ratio calculations indicate.

Interest cover

The **interest cover** (or interest coverage ratio) is one measure of whether a business is generating sufficient profit to pay the interest payments on its outstanding debt – in other words, how many times the business's profits could cover its own interest expenses. It is calculated as follows:

Interest cover = profit before interest payable ÷ interest payable

The profit before interest payable figure includes any income the business received from its **investments** (i.e. assets owned by the business that generate income, such as other businesses or shares or rental properties).

The interest cover measures the margin of safety a business has for paying interest on its debts during the period – which a company will need to survive any financial hardship if it happens.

A business that can meet its interest obligations several times over indicates the business's **solvency**, which shareholders and potential investors will be interested in. A low interest cover figure, especially for a company, might suggest that the business will have difficulty **servicing** its debts (i.e. paying the costs of its debts) if there was a fall in profits, which would risk dividend payouts to shareholders. Interest must be paid first even if profits decline and the company might have to stop paying out dividends to save cash.

Break-even point

The **break-even point** is the point at which a business's revenue is equal to its total expenses. The business has made neither a loss nor a profit – it has 'broken even' – and calculating the point at which a business breaks even is useful for a business in determining production forecasts and planning for profitability.

In order to calculate a business's break-even point, one must remember it is the point at which revenue equals total expenses – or total costs.

Revenue = total costs, or:

(Price × number of units) = fixed costs + (variable cost × number of units)

(Price × number of units) – (variable cost × number of units) = fixed costs

(Price – variable cost) × number of units = fixed costs

interest cover
(interest coverage ratio)
A way of measuring how many times the business's profits could cover its own interest expenses.

investment
An asset owned by a business (or a person) that generates income, such as shares, other businesses or rental properties.

solvency
The ability of a business to pay its financial obligations and stay in business. A business is said to be insolvent if it is unable to pay its debts.

service
To pay the costs of debt (i.e. servicing debt).

Number of units = fixed costs ÷ (price − variable cost)

Therefore, to calculate how many units must be sold before the business breaks even:

Break-even point in units = fixed costs ÷ (price − variable cost per unit)

In other words, the break-even point is equal to the total fixed costs divided by the difference between the unit price and variable cost per unit. Price minus variable cost per unit is called the **contribution margin**, and represents the amount left available to pay the business's fixed costs.

contribution margin
Allows the business to determine how profitable individual products or services. This can help determine what price to sell them for in the future.

5.3 Analysing the statement of financial position

The statement of financial position – or balance sheet – can be used to calculate the following business liquidity ratios:

◆ working capital

◆ current ratio

◆ quick ratio (also known as the acid test or liquidity ratio)

◆ gearing.

There are also some ratios from the year-end balance sheet that can be calculated to give an idea of how efficiently the business was being run from day to day. These ratios make up the **working capital cycle**:

working capital cycle
The time taken by a business to convert its net current assets and current liabilities into cash.

◆ debtors' turnover

◆ creditors' turnover

◆ inventory turnover.

We will look at each of these in turn.

Working capital
A business's **working capital** is the amount that a business requires to meet its short-term financial obligations and commitments. If a business can meet its short-term debts when they are due for payment, it is said to be **solvent** – and in order to be solvent, a business needs enough working capital to:

working capital
The amount that a business requires to meet its short-term financial obligations and commitments.

◆ pay its staff

◆ pay its debts as they fall due

◆ benefit from any discounts offered for prompt payment by its suppliers.

You can calculate a business's working capital by using the following equation:

Working capital = current assets − current liabilities

current ratio
A ratio which measures how adequately a business's current assets can cover its current liabilities.

working capital ratio
Another name for the current ratio.

Current ratio
The **current ratio**, also known as the **working capital ratio**, measures how adequately a business's current assets can cover its current liabilities. It is one type of short-term liquidity ratio that can be used as a quick indicator of a business's ability to meet its payments when they fall due.

Current ratio = current assets ÷ current liabilities

The current ratio (or working capital ratio) can be expressed in the format X:1, and can be useful for spotting potential problems – a low ratio may indicate liquidity problems while a high ratio may indicate a poor use of shareholder or company funds.

The main drawback of the current ratio is that it might not be an accurate indicator of whether a company can actually pay its debts as they fall due, as the current assets figure includes inventories, which might not be so easily converted into cash as the inventories figure might contain slow-moving or even obsolete items. This is where the quick ratio comes in.

Quick ratio

Another type of short-term liquidity ratio, the **quick ratio** (also known as the **acid test ratio** or **liquidity ratio**) eliminates the inventories figure from the current assets used in the current ratio, and gives a better measure of short-term liquidity:

Quick ratio = (current assets – inventories) ÷ current liabilities

or

Quick ratio = (receivables + investments + cash) ÷ current liabilities

Like the current ratio, it can also be expressed as X:1 and a low quick ratio may indicate liquidity problems while a high quick ratio may indicate a poor use of shareholder or company funds.

The potential drawbacks of the quick ratio are that not all receivables may be recoverable (which is also a problem for the current ratio) and that the ratio itself (like the current ratio) may be subject to manipulation – for example, if a company has a positive cash balance at the end of the period and a ratio greater than 1:1, payment of any current liabilities such as trade payables just prior to the accounting period's end will make the ratio look much better than it should be.

Both the current and quick ratios, therefore, should be used in conjunction with other ratio analyses to get a better picture of the business's performance and position.

Gearing

A business's **gearing** measures the ratio between its borrowings (debt) and its share capital and **reserves** (equity). A company that is **highly geared** will have a relatively high debt in comparison to its equity.

There are two equations that can be used to calculate a business's gearing as a percentage:

Gearing = (debt ÷ equity) × 100

or sometimes

Gearing = (debt ÷ (debt + equity)) × 100

quick ratio
A way of measuring short-term liquidity.

acid test ratio
Another name for the quick ratio (also liquidity ratio).

liquidity ratio
Another name for the quick ratio.

gearing
A measure of the ratio between a business's borrowings (debt) and its share capital and reserves (equity).

reserve
An amount a business can use for future payments and/or emergencies in excess of what is already needed for day-to-day operations.

Gearing ratios can give shareholders, potential investors and lenders an idea of how risky a company is and how sensitive any profits and dividends might be to activity levels. A highly geared company might carry a greater risk of insolvency, but if its profits are still growing, returns to shareholders will grow more than for a low-geared company. A low-geared company will be able to borrow more easily and cheaply, but might be seen as being more risky by investors as equity finance can be more expensive long-term.

When looking at gearing, one must also consider any upward revaluations of any non-current assets (e.g. property that has been re-valued to take account of rising land prices) as this can increase shareholders' reserves (and thus increase equity) and decrease the gearing ratio or percentage.

Debtors' turnover

debtors' turnover
(trade receivables collection period/debtor days) The amount of time in days the business's average customer and/or debtor takes to pay the business.

Also known as the **trade receivables collection period** (or more informally as **debtor days**), the **debtors' turnover** measures in number of days the amount of time the business's average customer takes to pay the business on credit (i.e. how many days it takes to recover what the business's trade receivables (or debtors) owe).

Debtors' turnover = (trade receivables ÷ revenue) × 365

If one is able to do so, it is a good idea to exclude cash sales from the revenue figure as cash sales do not create receivables in the accounts. The higher this figure, the longer the business's debtors are taking to pay the business for its goods or services rendered.

A change in debtors' turnover can indicate any of the following:

◆ bad debt or payment collection problems;

◆ a change in the nature of the customer base (e.g. a new customer may place large orders but be slow to pay up); and

◆ a change in the business's settlement terms.

One must also consider whether the receivables figure given in the balance sheet at the end of a period (in the case of the above formula, this would be the balance sheet at the end of a year) gives a reasonable indication of the receivables for the whole period – for example, the receivables figure for a seasonable business could fluctuate quite wildly so the balance sheet figure at the end of the period might not be an accurate reflection of the receivables profile during the period as a whole.

Creditors' turnover

creditors' turnover
Also known as trade payables collection period, or informally as creditor days, this measures the amount of time in days the business takes to pay its suppliers and/or creditors.

Also known as the **trade payables collection period** (or more informally as **creditor days**), the **creditors' turnover** measures in number of days the average amount of time the business takes to pay its suppliers (i.e. how long the business takes to pay its trade payables or creditors).

Credit purchases are often used for this calculation, but if this is not available then cost of sales is used.

Creditors' turnover = (trade payables ÷ credit purchases) × 365

or

Creditors' turnover = (trade payables ÷ cost of sales) × 365

The higher the figure, the longer the business is taking to pay its creditors. On the one hand this can improve short-term cash flow, but on the other hand, a high figure could indicate liquidity problems – and the potential appointment of **receivers** by aggrieved creditors if they remain unpaid.

The same consideration for the trade receivables figure given in the balance sheet at the end of a period applies to the trade payables figure – one should consider whether it gives a reasonable indication of the payables profile as a whole throughout the period.

Inventory turnover
Also known as the **stock turnover** (or more informally as **inventory days**), the **inventory turnover** measures in number of days on average that an item stays in inventory before it is sold. Usually, the lower the number, the better, as it means that the business is selling its products quickly and according to demand:

Inventory turnover = (inventory ÷ cost of sales) × 365

There is also the **inventory turnover ratio**, which measures the number of times inventories are 'turned over' each year, or replaced with new stock for the business to sell. Usually, the higher the number, the better, as it means the business is efficiently managing its inventory levels relative to demand:

Inventory turnover ratio = cost of sales ÷ inventories

A high inventory turnover ratio (which would equate to a low inventory days number) may indicate that the business is managing its inventory levels efficiently and according to demand, but the disadvantage is that a risk of 'stockouts' (i.e. the business running out of stock or inventory to sell) may occur – and even occur frequently.

On the other hand, a low inventory turnover ratio (which would equate to a high inventory days number) indicates either an inefficient use of resources in the business, or potential inventory obsolescence problems.

As with debtors' turnover and creditors' turnover, one must also consider whether the inventory figure given in the balance sheet at the end of the period is an accurate reflection of the business, or whether it distorts the picture of the business's performance.

In an ideal world, the three components of inventory should be considered separately:

◆   finished goods compared to cost of sales

◆   WIP compared to cost of production

◆   raw materials compared to volume of purchases.

receiver
Also known as receivers, this is a person or a company that a court has appointed to manage the finances of a bankrupt business (or person).

inventory turnover (inventory days or stock turnover)
This measures in number of days on average that an item stays in inventory before it is sold. Not to be confused with inventory turnover ratio.

inventory turnover ratio
A ratio which measures the number of times inventories are 'turned over' each year (i.e. replaced with new stock for the business to sell). Not to be confused with inventory turnover.

However, in the absence of these breakdowns, the above inventory turnover (and inventory turnover ratio) will suffice.

Working capital cycle

The last three ratios make up the **working capital cycle**, which is inventory days plus debtors' turnover (or debtor days) minus the creditors' turnover or (creditor days):

Working capital cycle = inventory days + debtor days – creditor days

An increase in this ratio could indicate that the components of working capital are being inefficiently managed.

5.4 Advantages and disadvantages of ratio analysis

Some of the advantages and disadvantages of each individual ratio have been outlined in their explanations in section 5.3. Ratios are of very little use on their own – as noted, many of them have to be compared or used in conjunction with other ratios, numerical analysis and the notes to the financial statements to build up a more complete picture of how well a business is doing at a certain point in time.

However, the clear and obvious advantage of performing the various types of ratio analysis detailed above is that ratios can help users of the financial statements to make economic decisions about the business – as well as identifying any trends, strengths, weaknesses and comparisons with other businesses. Ratios can help to summarise and present financial information in a way that can be more easily understood by more people.

The disadvantage is that ratios calculated on public, published figures can only be of limited use, as the data is incomplete. Ratio analysis also relies on historical data (e.g. figures given for a year that has already passed) so it ignores future actions and events taken by the business's management or any business environment changes. Ratios can also be distorted by differences in accounting policies or based on data which can be manipulated by those preparing the financial statements (especially in the case of estimates that have been included or revalued property and land).

Chapter summary

◆   Financial reporting is required for an entity to keep itself accountable and inform interested parties (stakeholders) of its financial performance. This enables stakeholders to make decisions about the business.

◆   Financial statements or accounts are produced annually to a format approved by the government of the jurisdiction the entity operates in and form a summary of both the entity's performance over the year and its financial position at the end of that year. These are the main way of providing financial information to the stakeholders. There are two systems of financial reporting that entities must adhere to in the UK – UK GAAP and IFRS.

◆ IFRS (International Financial Reporting Standards) is a set of internationally-agreed financial reporting and accounting standards that any type of entity can use. Companies listed and traded on an EU-recognised public stock exchange must report using IFRS.

◆ With UK GAAP (Generally Accepted Accounting Practice), entities are split into micro, small, medium and large based on their turnover, net assets and number of employees. The level of reporting required varies based on which of these the entity falls under. UK GAAP changed in 2015, but you may still find financial statements prepared under the old UK GAAP.

◆ The fundamental qualitative characteristics of financial statements are: relevance and faithful representation; while the enhancing qualitative characteristics of financial statements (that improve the usefulness of the information) are: understandability; comparability; verifiability and timeliness.

◆ Relevant financial information is that which has the ability to influence the economic decisions a user of the statement might make. Material financial information is that which, if omitted or misstated, could influence decisions taken by users of the statement. Faithful representation means financial reports must represent economic events and transactions in a way that aims to be: complete; neutral and free from error.

◆ Understandability of financial information means it should be presented in a way that users with a reasonable knowledge of business and accounting can understand it. Verifiability means the information in the financial statements has been, or can be, independently verified. Comparability refers to how well the information in a financial statement can be compared to previous periods for the same entity or to information about another entity. Timeliness means the information should be made available in time for a user to make decisions.

◆ A business records its financial data in ledgers and books of prime entry using the double-entry bookkeeping process.

◆ The accounting equation is Assets = Liabilities + Capital, and the balance sheet reflects this. The relationship between assets, liabilities and capital is always the same, and is the dual effect of accounting.

◆ There are two ways of accounting for transactions in the books – under the cash basis and under the accruals basis. Most businesses use the accruals basis.

◆ The trial balance is a list of all the balances on the all the accounts in the nominal ledger. Year-end adjustments are made where necessary before the figures are used to make up the financial statements.

◆ Financial statements are a formal record of a business's financial performance over a period of time. There are four basic reports that make up the financial statements: the income statement; the statement of financial position, the statement of cash flows; and the statement of income and retained earnings.

◆ Assets are things that a business owns that either generate cash or have the potential to do so. They may be tangible or intangible, fixed or current.

Meanwhile, liabilities are things that a business owes. They may be either long-term or current. The amount by which a company's total assets exceeds its total liabilities is considered its equity.

◆ There are three basic types of analysis that can be performed on financial statements: horizontal – where you compare values on the same row of a financial statement; vertical – often expressing items as a percentage of turnover within the same column; and ratio analysis – which includes the return on assets and return on equity ratios.

◆ The income statement can be used to calculate profitability ratios such as gross profit, operating profit, net profit and profit margins. The statement of financial position can be used to calculate several business liquidity ratios: working capital, current ratio, quick ratio and gearing.

◆ The working capital cycle is made up of the following three ratios (also calculated from the statement of financial position): debtors' turnover; creditors' turnover; and inventory turnover.

◆ In order to be considered solvent, a business needs enough working capital to: pay its staff, pay its debts as they fall due and benefit from any discounts offered for prompt payment by its suppliers.

Chapter thirteen
Management accounting

CONTENTS

1. Introduction

This chapter defines and outlines the purpose of management accounting, how it compares to financial accounting, and looks at management accounting techniques, systems and analysis.

2. Understanding management accounting

While financial reporting is mainly for the use of external stakeholders of the business, internal stakeholders – such as a company's directors or board members – will need financial information and other types of information about the business reported and measured in a way that enables them to consider and pursue the business's goals.

2.1 What is management accounting?

Management accounting is the sourcing and analysis of financial and non-financial information to provide to the business's management (i.e. directors, board members) so that they can make decisions about the business and its future needs and aims.

2.2 The purpose of management accounting

In order for a business to be run effectively and efficiently – as well as make forecasts or decide on current and future strategy – managers need a wealth of information provided to them regularly and quickly. Financial accounting and reporting is one source of available information, but it is not enough on its own.

Management accounting uses information of all kinds for 'internal use' – and often more frequently and in more detail than what is available in financial statements for external stakeholders – to lead and inform management decisions, control costs and plan for future expansion of the business.

2.3   Integrating management systems

Management accounting needs to interpret financial information (and any relevant non-financial information) from all parts of a business organisation, therefore ideally a business's systems and processes are integrated so that it is easier for the organisation to work as a single unit and provide or communicate accurate information to management in a timely manner.

management accounting system
A business system or process which collects internal financial data from business operations such as sales data, shifts in inventory and changes in raw materials costs, then analyses the information in reports for management to use.

Businesses therefore find it most effective when they select a **management accounting system** that integrates with the business's financial accounting system – doing so increases the timeliness of management reports and eliminates redundant work or duplication.

2.4   Management accounting vs financial accounting

Management accounting is different from financial accounting in some key ways.

◆   Financial accounts are primarily used by external stakeholders; management accounts are used by internal stakeholders.

◆   Financial accounting, which is used to prepare financial statements, is based on historic data (i.e. 'looking backwards'); management accounting uses financial information to analyse trends and statistics to inform future strategy (i.e. 'looking forwards').

◆   Financial accounting prepares and presents summarised information in line with accounting and reporting standards; management accounting communicates information at a more complete level of detail required by management and is not constrained by legislation on how to prepare and present it.

As with financial accounts, management accounts need to be presented in a format that is accurate, understandable, allows comparisons and is either timely or up-to-date.

Stop and think 13.1

What do you think are the advantages and disadvantages of management accounting?

3. Management accounting systems

A **management accounting system** collects financial data from business operations such as sales data, shifts in inventory and changes in raw materials costs, then analyses the information in reports.

The main type of management accounting system is a **cost accounting** system, but there are also inventory management systems, job-costing systems, and price-optimising systems; as well as ways to analyse and evaluate performance and plan for future business activities.

3.1 Cost accounting

Cost accounting is a management accounting method that looks at all of a business's expenses to determine the actual fixed and variable costs associated with making the product or providing the service that the business sells. By so doing, management can see which products, services or business segments are most profitable and can prepare budgets and forecasts accordingly. There are several cost accounting methods.

Standard costing

According to the Chartered Institute of Management Accountants (CIMA), standard costing is 'the planned unit cost of the product, component or service produced in a period. The standard cost may be determined on a number of bases. The main use of standard costs is in performance measurement, control, inventory valuation and in the establishment of selling prices'. It was a method developed more than 100 years ago when most businesses were still manufacturing businesses with repetitive production processes.

The two common ways for determining expected costs (otherwise known as standards) under this method are:

- using past records to estimate labour and material usage; and
- using engineering studies, which may involve a detailed observation or examination of how much material, labour and equipment are used in operations.

This way, pre-determined standards for the use of labour, materials, **overheads** and so on per unit are established. These pre-determined standards can be used where determining the actual costs per unit would be too time-consuming, so these standards are then used as estimates that approximate actual costs.

The pre-determined standard costs are used to value inventories and the cost of goods sold. Where the variance between actual costs and standard costs is small, the variance is included in the cost of goods sold. Significant variances are pro-rated between inventories and cost of goods sold.

The pre-determined standard does not just apply to **direct costs** and **indirect costs** (overheads), but also to the expected input that produces a certain or desired level of output to be sold.

Cost = pre-determined standard price or rate used per unit × standard input

cost accounting
A management accounting method that looks at all of a business's expenses to determine the actual fixed and variable costs associated with making the product, or providing the service, that the business sells.

Normal costing

Normal costing differs from standard costing in that, instead of using pre-determined standard costs for the direct costs (i.e. direct labour and materials), it calculates the actual direct costs used, using the actual direct price or rate multiplied by the actual quantity of that item that was used. However, the rate of overhead used is one that is pre-determined or budgeted for.

Direct costs = actual price or rate of direct cost item per unit × actual input

Indirect costs = pre-determined or budgeted indirect cost per unit × actual input or quantity of overhead allocated

Absorption cost
In management accounting, the cost of all the resources used to produce an item of output or activity.

The cost of all the resources used to produce an item of output or activity is also known as the **absorption cost**. All costs, fixed and variable, are taken into account when calculating the absorption cost of an item, but a distinction is made between direct costs and indirect costs. While establishing direct costs is easier as you can look at internal records on direct materials or direct labour, establishing indirect costs is harder – and overheads are often shared or allocated between departments (or product/service line outputs) on the **basis of apportionment** that seems reasonable or fair.

Basis of apportionment
The way of apportioning an amount between business/production departments using a method that seems the most reasonable or fair.

Actual costing

This is a method of calculating absorption cost using the actual costs and actual quantity of input – or, if calculating the indirect cost (overhead) portion _ using the actual rate of overhead multiplied by the actual quantity of overhead allocated.

If actual costs and inputs can be determined easily and reasonably quickly, then these will be what the business uses as its pre-determined standards – and there would be no difference between this method of costing or the previous two. However, this is not often the case – as arbitrary as that might be, that is why other methods of costing and apportionment are often used.

Worked example 13.1

Garrus owns a manufacturing company, Vakarian Ltd, which makes omni-tools. It establishes a **standard cost card** for the product, which sets out the standard cost of manufacturing each omni-tool:

Resource	Units	Price per unit (£)	Total (£)
Direct material	5kg	£12	60
Direct labour	10 hrs	£15	150
Variable production overhead	10 hrs	£4	40
Standard variable production cost			250

The standard that Vakarian Ltd uses for fixed indirect overheads is based on the company's utility bills and is budgeted at £2,000 per month. Every month, Garrus aims to manufacture and sell 10 omni-tools.

However, one month, the omni-tool manufacturing machine was not calibrated properly, resulting in Garrus having to spend extra time on calibrations to ensure the machine operated at its usual efficiency. Vakarian Ltd managed to make 10 omni-tools that month, but used and wasted an extra 20kg of raw material before the problem was discovered, while direct labour increased by an hour per unit.

In addition, an extra £225 of electricity was consumed by the machine, which bumped up the total utility bill for the month, although the variable production overheads remained the same.

As a result, here are the actual variable production costs per unit for the month – note that an extra 20kg of raw material to produce 10 units means an extra 2kg of material was used per unit:

Resource	Units	Price per unit (£)	Total (£)
Direct material (5kg + 2kg extra)	7 kg	£12	84
Direct labour (10hrs + 1hr extra)	11 hrs	£15	165
Variable production overhead	10 hrs	£4	40
			———
Actual variable production cost			289

And here are the actual costs, normal costs and standard costs for that month.

	Actual costing	Normal costing	Standard costing
Direct costs			
Direct material	840	840	600
Direct labour	1,650	1,650	1,500
Variable production overhead	400	400	400
	2,890	2,890	2,500
Indirect costs			
Utilities for the month	2,225	2,000	2,000
	———	———	———
Total costs of production	5,115	4,890	4,500

Note that normal costing differs from actual costing because under normal costing, indirect costs are calculated using the pre-determined or budgeted indirect cost (or rate), rather than the actual indirect cost/rate.

Activity-based costing (ABC)

The alternative to the traditional method of determining absorption costing is **activity-based costing (ABC)**. It is intended to be a better method for allocating overheads to output, especially in the manufacturing industry, and supposedly provides a better basis for cost control, cost classification and profitability analysis.

Activity-based costing (ABC)
In management accounting, a method of cost accounting to determine the total cost of producing an item or output.

When calculating the absorption cost for a business's product (or a service) that it intends to sell, larger volume items tend to be mathematically allocated more of the total overhead than small volume items – but there are many 'support' activities (such as order processing, packaging and despatch) that are not related to input or output and these activities may fluctuate regardless of how much product is made. Under ABC, overheads are supposed to be allocated to products (or services) on their use of these 'support' activities.

An ABC system is set up in the following way:

cost driver
A factor that causes an activity that creates indirect costs or overheads.

1. Identify the main activities that create indirect costs (overheads).

2. Determine the **cost drivers**, which are the factors that lead to these costs arising (for example, if product packaging is an activity that creates costs, the number of products sold is likely to be the main cost driver).

cost centre
A department or business segment to which costs, particularly indirect costs or overheads, can be allocated for management accounting purposes.

3. Group the costs for these activities into 'cost pools' (sometimes referred to as **cost centres**).

4. Allocate overheads to products according to how much of each cost pool that each product uses.

Test yourself 13.1

A robot manufacturing company has two product lines, Geth Prime and Geth Pyro. Geth Prime is manufactured in standard batch sizes of 250 units, while Geth Pyro is made in standard batch sizes of 1,000 units. Cost information is as below.

	Geth Prime	Geth Pyro
Production run (size)	250 units	1,000 units
Direct materials cost per unit	£35	£20
Direct labour time per unit	0.1 hour	0.05 hours
Direct labour cost per hour	£15	£10
Machine hours per unit	0.06 hours	0.012 hours
Number of set-ups per batch	4	2

Annual overhead costs are as follows:

	£	Annual volume of activity
Set-up costs	600,000	1,200 set-ups
Handling costs	750,000	500 batches (production runs)
Other production overheads	945,000	6,300 machine hours

Using a system of activity-based costing where:

◆ set-up costs are charged to products on the basis of a cost per set-up

◆ handling costs are charged on the basis of a cost per batch/production run

◆ other production overheads are absorbed on a machine hour basis.

Calculate the cost of:

1. Geth Prime

2. Geth Pyro.

Although it has been argued that ABC helps with cost control by controlling the factors that create costs – which is what the identification and consideration of cost drivers can assist in – some management accountants have argued that ABC is costly, time-consuming and not as effective at controlling costs and profits as its proponents assert.

Life cycle costing

A life cycle costing system keeps track of and adds up, the actual costs attributable to each product from the start of the product being created to its end (i.e. over its 'life cycle'). Both revenues and costs for each project are accumulated.

An example would be the design and manufacture of a new car, where the project would take five years and the costs for all associated business activities – from design or research and development right through to customer service – are accumulated. The system would therefore determine the profit made from the project over many years and several accounting periods.

Target costing

A target costing system is when a company plans its targets in advance for the price points, product costs and margins it wants to attain for a new product – but if the company cannot make the product meet these targeted levels, then it cancels the design project entirely. It is therefore in management's interests to continually monitor the product all the way through the product life cycle, from the design stage onwards.

The steps in a target costing system typically involve the following:

1. Conduct market research and develop a product that will satisfy potential customers.

2. Choose a target price that customers are likely to be prepared to pay for and calculate maximum cost to get a targeted gross or operating profit margin that the product must earn.

3. Design and create the product to meet the targeted cost. Design iterations may be needed to decide which design costs the least, as well as sourcing and purchasing components, and outsourcing to reduce costs if necessary.

4. Perform ongoing evaluation of all aspects of the costs during the product's life cycle, aiming to reduce costs (possibly by reducing waste in the production process) for the rest of the project's life.

3.2 Performance evaluation and analysis

A business's management can analyse and evaluate performance to give them a benchmark or guide that they can use for future projects or accounting periods. There are several measures they can use for both financial and non-financial information, but two of them are the use of key performance indicators and balanced scorecards.

Key performance indicators (KPIs)

key performance indicator (KPI)
A measurable value that demonstrates how effectively a company is meeting performance or business objectives.

A **key performance indicator (KPI)** is a quantifiable value that management can use to evaluate how successful an employee, cost centre or an organisation is in meeting performance or business objectives. KPIs can be used to measure both financial and non-financial aims and assess one's success in achieving these.

Examples could include:

◆ percentage of trains arriving at stations on time for a train company;

◆ number of telephone calls handled per hour for a call centre company;

◆ delivery times for a fast food takeaway business;

◆ sales targets per employee for individuals working in a company's sales team;

◆ whether a certain gross profit margin percentage has been achieved; and

◆ whether cost and revenue targets have been met in a management accounting system based on target costing.

benchmarking
A way of determining targets and comparatives by gathering and evaluating relevant data. Once set, benchmarks can be used to measure areas of performance (or underperformance).

One way to determine a KPI is through a process known as **benchmarking**. CIMA defines benchmarking as the 'establishment, through data gathering, of target and comparators, that permits relative levels of performance (and particularly areas of underperformance) to be identified. Adoption of identified best practices should improve performance'.

Benchmarks can be set in four main ways:

◆ **internal benchmarking**: this involves comparing one operating unit or function with another within the business (i.e. internally). This can be done by ascertaining trends and changes by comparing historical data, or comparing different branches – although there is a danger that this method ignores competitors;

◆ **functional benchmarking** (also known as **operational benchmarking**, **activity benchmarking** or **best in class benchmarking**): this is when internal functions are compared to those of the best external practitioners, regardless of their industry (e.g. studying Formula One processes helped British Airways to improve aircraft maintenance, turnaround and refuelling);

◆ **generic benchmarking**: this is when a benchmark is set against a conceptually similar process or metric in another (often unrelated) business or industry (e.g. revenue per employee or return on investment);

◆ **competitive benchmarking**: information is gathered about direct competitors (e.g. through league tables) and performance is compared with these competitors. **Strategic benchmarking** is a type of competitive benchmarking aimed at strategic action and organisational change.

A balanced scorecard can be used to make sure that a wide range of performance measures (KPIs and/or benchmarks) are set.

Balanced scorecards

As businesses have multiple objectives they aim to compete in their markets – and as management has multiple performance measures they will need to track these to ensure that these objectives are being met – the **balanced scorecard** is one method to help manage these and can be used for both financial and non-financial measures.

balanced scorecard
A method of analysing a business, both internally and externally to determine KPIs and/or benchmarks.

A balanced scorecard analyses the following four perspectives:

◆ financial: determining how the company looks to its shareholders, examining financial performance metrics, budgets and ratio analysis;

◆ customer: analysing how customers see the company, gauging their levels of satisfaction and their needs;

◆ learning and growth/innovation: considering where the business can continue to create value and improve, what training and knowledge resources the business has; and

◆ internal business: evaluating business processes, bottlenecks, waste, delays, as well as evaluating what the business excels at.

Once these perspectives have been analysed, KPIs can be developed and any resources the business requires to achieve these can be decided upon. Once targets are set, data can be collected to continually (or periodically) assess whether the KPIs have been met and thus monitor performance.

3.3 Other planning and forecasting techniques

We've seen how cost accounting and performance evaluation can be used to control costs, set future objectives and monitor financial metrics and business aims, but we've only touched briefly on how management accounting concepts can be used for planning and forecasting purposes.

Cost allocation

One problem businesses always face is how they should charge costs between the components of their business, as well as for accounting purposes. Imagine a multinational company, where an employee flies from Sydney to London to work in the company's UK branch for a few weeks. If the company pays for the employee's flight from Sydney to London, how should this cost be allocated? Should this be recorded as a cost paid for by the company's Sydney branch or the London branch, or split between them? Why? What if the employee is normally based in the company's Hong Kong branch, rather than in Australia or the UK – should the Hong Kong branch be allocated the cost (and paying for the employee's flight) instead?

cost object
In management accounting, this is anything a business wants to separately measure costs for. This can be a cost centre, but is not always.

Cost allocation, therefore, is the process of identifying and assigning indirect costs to a **cost object**, which is anything a business wants to separately measure costs for. Examples of cost objects include a product, a business activity, a customer, a department or a regional branch.

Businesses often differ in how they classify costs – an item that is classified as a direct cost in one business can be classified as an indirect cost in another (e.g. electricity costs). When direct costs are assigned to a cost object, this is known as **cost tracing**.

As we have already seen in standard cost accounting, normal costing and activity-based costing, cost allocation is used in management accounting – as well as in financial reporting – to spread costs between departments, cost of sales or items of inventory. This, in turn, can be used in profitability calculations (or profitability ratios) for various levels or segments of the business which, in turn, may be used as the basis for paying staff bonuses or funding additional activities.

As implied by the word 'allocation' there is no precise way costs can be assigned to or split between cost objects, so a business will use whichever approximation management thinks will best help measure financial performance and improve decision making.

financial modelling
A way of analysing a business by using financial models to estimate economic outcomes, forecast future profits and cash flows, and make decisions and recommendations.

Financial modelling

Financial modelling is one way management can analyse a business to estimate economic outcomes and forecast future profits and cash flows. This involves creating a mathematical representation – a model – of the business's financial relationships to examine how different economic situations or events will affect it. A basic example of a financial model is a cash budget, whether this is calculated by hand or on a computer spreadsheet.

Financial models will contain one or more mathematical formulae into which variables can be put to see the impact of these different situations or events. Recommendations are then made on the information given. Many of these will involve estimating the funds to commit to a project or department based on various outcomes and scenarios.

Business funds come from various sources. There is usually no separation between financing from different sources that are going towards specific projects. To obtain a measure with which to evaluate these projects, the cost of each source of finance is calculated and then weighted by how important they are in the project's overall financing amount. This is known as the combined or **weighted average cost of capital (WACC)**. The WACC is the minimum return – expressed as a percentage – that a business must earn on an existing asset base to satisfy its creditors, owners and other providers of capital (money) who will otherwise invest elsewhere.

While business funds – or financing – can come from a range of sources, the two main sources are from equity and from debt. Equity financing raises capital by selling shares and the shareholders gain an ownership interest in the business in return. Debt financing can be raised either in the form of bank loans lent to the company or by the company issuing **bonds**, which are a type of investment where investors loan money to the company for a fixed period of time in return for the company paying them annual interest on their bonds – this interest payment is known as the **coupon** and the rate is known as the **coupon rate**. Both shares and bonds are also known collectively as **securities**.

In the case of a project that is financed with only equity and debt – and ignoring the effect of distortions from tax – the WACC formula is as follows:

$$\text{WACC} = \frac{(\text{total debt} \times \text{cost of debt}) + (\text{total equity} \times \text{cost of equity})}{(\text{total debt} + \text{total equity})}$$

The cost of equity is given as a percentage and is the rate of return the company pays to its equity investors (e.g. as dividends to shareholders). The cost of debt is also given as a percentage and, in its simplest form, is the interest rate on debt or the coupon rate on the company's bonds. The WACC will be covered in more detail in Part One of the ICSA qualifying programme.

Financial models can also be based on **scenario planning**, sometimes called 'scenario and contingency planning', where management considers a range of scenarios – possible stories, events, unexpected disasters or fortune – that might happen and how these might affect the business and plan accordingly. Royal Dutch Shell plc is an example of a company that famously uses scenario planning for its forecasts and business strategy – the company's management was prepared for the 1973 oil crisis, having anticipated it as one of six possible scenarios that could affect the oil industry, and were able to weather the shock rise in oil prices.

weighted average cost of capital (WACC)
The minimum return, expressed as a percentage, that a business must earn on an existing asset base to satisfy its creditors, owners, and other providers of capital (money) that their investment will deliver what they expect.

bonds
A type of investment where investors loan money to the company for a fixed period of time in return for the company paying them annual interest on their bonds.

time value of money
A concept which states that money received now is more valuable than money received in the future, because of the effect of inflation and other future uncertainties.

inflation
A general increase in prices which leads to a decrease in the purchasing power of money.

present value
A value representing what a monetary amount received in the future would be worth today (i.e. its value in the present).

discounted cash flow analysis
A way of assessing and analysing an investment project to estimate how much the entire investment would be worth today.

discounted cash flow
The present value(s) of an investment project's future expected cash flows.

net present value (NPV)
The difference between the present value of cash inflows and the present value of cash outflows.

Business valuation of projects – especially long-term projects that cover several accounting periods – is another type of financial modelling, which management can use to determine how attractive an investment opportunity is. The concept of the **time value of money** holds that money received now is more valuable than money received in the future – due to **inflation**, risk of future uncertainty or even the simple fact that money available now can be invested elsewhere – so you want to make sure that your appraisal of future cash flows and profits from the project is worth the money you will commit to investing in it.

To do this, we look at **present values** – the present value of a future monetary amount tells us what that future monetary amount would be worth today. This is the reverse of compounding. **Discounted cash flow analysis** is when you calculate the present value of an investment project's future expected cash flows to estimate how much the entire investment would be worth today.

The present value of £X cash flow received in n years' time at an interest rate of r% per annum is:

$$\text{Present value in n years' time} = £X \times (1 \div (1 + r)^n) = £X \times \frac{1}{(1 + r)^n}$$

The fraction $(1 \div (1 + r)^n)$ is known as the **discount factor**, and the **discounted cash flow** is the summation of the present values of all cash flows from year 1 to year n.

$$\text{Discounted cash flow} = \text{present value for year 1} + \text{present value for year 2} + \dots + \text{present value for year n}$$

The discounted cash flow formula can be used to calculate both cash inflows to the business, and cash outflows from the business. The **net present value (NPV)** is the discounted cash flow when any cash outflows (from costs or expenses) have been accounted for:

$$\text{Net present value} = \text{discounted cash inflows} - \text{discounted cash outflows}$$

NPV is useful for management because it is simple to make a decision based on the number the calculation produces. If NPV is positive, management usually decides to accept the project, as the investment will be worthwhile and increase the business's wealth in future. If NPV is negative, management will reject the project.

If there is more than one project being considered, the one with the highest NPV will increase business wealth the most, and this should be pursued.

3.4 Benefits and limitations

Different types of management accounting system have their advantages and disadvantages. We have already seen that proponents of ABC argue that its advantage is that identifying cost drivers helps to control costs. The disadvantage is that ABC can be costly and time-consuming; some argue that it is not as effective in cost control as its supporters say. Standard costing, however, is quick and can be cheaper – but the potential for significant variances between standard costs and actual costs means that it may not be the most accurate way either to budget or control costs.

4. Management accounting techniques

There are many accounting techniques that can be used for business analysis. The most fundamental include:

◆ activity-based costing

◆ cost-benefit analysis

◆ cost-behaviour analysis

◆ life cycle cost analysis

◆ net present value

◆ variance analysis

◆ forecasting.

There are many more (such as data mining) but they are outside the scope of this book.

4.1 Cost analysis

Cost analysis is simply a comparison of costs for analytical purposes. When the costs of a business strategy are being compared with anticipated results or anticipated benefits or profits, this is known as a **cost-benefit analysis**. Costs are classified according to their behaviour when being compared.

4.2 Cost behaviour

Cost behaviour is how the cost responds to changes in the level of the business activity. Fixed costs, as we have seen, remain the same regardless of the level of business activity or output, while variable costs do not.

4.3 Budgetary control statements

A **budget** is a plan of what management intends or wants to happen in the future regarding financial items such as sales (or income), costs, expenditure and profits. It differs from a forecast, which attempts to predict what will happen.

Budgetary control is the process of applying control over a business's activities and resources by preparing a budget and then comparing the business's actual performance against the targets set out in the budget. Management can take corrective action based on the comparison if necessary. An example is given in Figure 13.1.

Figure 13.1: Budgeted versus actual performance

	Budget		**Actual**	
Units sold or made	1,000 units		900 units	
	£		£	
Revenue	10,000		8,600	
Direct cost – raw materials	(4,000)	200 kg	(3,640)	170 kg
Direct cost – labour	(2,000)	50 hours	(1,740)	46 hours

cost analysis
A comparison of costs for analytical purposes.

cost-benefit analysis
A comparison of business strategy costs with anticipated results, or with anticipated benefits or profits, for analytical purposes.

cost behaviour
How a cost responds to changes in level of the business activity.

budgetary control
The process of applying control over a business's activities and resources by preparing a budget, and then comparing the business's actual performance against the targets set out in the budget.

Indirect cost – fixed overheads	(1,000)	(950)
Total production costs	(7,000)	(6,330)
Profit	3,000	2,270

Typically, a new budget is prepared once a year, but actual performance may be compared to the budget as often as every month. The **fixed budget** is the original plan for a period and is based on a planned volume of business activity – usually sales volume or turnover. This way, if actual performance differs, one can see if one reason for the difference between actual profit and budgeted profit for the period would be due to the difference between actual versus budgeted sales volume (or turnover).

If the actual performance that was measured turns out to be better than the budgeted target, management should try to ensure these improved results continue in future periods. If the actual performance is worse than budgeted targets, control measures should be taken if possible. If the differences were due to factors outside management's control, the budget or forecast should be revised.

4.4 Variance analysis

variance analysis
In management accounting, an evaluation of a business's performance by analysing variances.

variance
In management accounting, this is the difference between an actual amount and a budgeted (or standard costed) amount.

flexed budget
A budget with figures that have been recalculated proportionally to reflect the volume of actual production and sales, as opposed to original budget amounts.

CIMA defines **variance analysis** as: 'The evaluation of performance by means of variances, whose timely reporting should maximise the opportunity for managerial action.' A **variance** is the difference between an actual amount and a budgeted (or standard costed) amount.

To make variances useful in budgets, the budgeted figures should be **flexed** to the volume of actual production and sales, which means that budget targets should be recalculated proportionally according to actual results, as in Figure 13.2 below.

Figure 13.2: An example of a flexed budget

	Original budget	Flexed budget	Actual results	Difference (actual vs flexed)
Units sold or made	1,000 units	900 units	900 units	
	£	£	£	£
Revenue	10,000	9,000	8,600	400 (A)
Direct cost – raw materials	(4,000)	(3,600)	(3,640)	40 (A)
Direct cost – labour	(2,000)	(1,800)	(1,740)	60 (F)
Indirect cost – fixed overheads	(1,000)	(1,000)	(950)	50 (F)
Total production costs	(7,000)	(6,400)	(6,330)	
Profit	3,000	2,600	2,270	

In the example above, the (F) indicates a favourable variance (i.e. one where actual results were better than expected or budgeted) whereas (A) indicates an adverse variance (i.e. one where actual results were worse than expected or budgeted) this is sometimes indicated by (U) for unfavourable instead of (A), but they are the same thing.

There are a few different types of variance a business's management may look at. Some examples are:

◆ sales volume variance

◆ sales price variance

◆ direct material price variance

◆ direct material usage variance

◆ fixed/variable overhead variances.

The **sales volume variance** is the difference between the actual and budgeted number of units sold, multiplied by the budgeted price per unit. An unfavourable variance – a negative amount – generally indicates the actual volume of units sold was lower than the expected volume sold, assuming the budgeted price per unit was the actual selling price per unit.

Sales volume variance = (actual units sold – budgeted units sold) × budget unit price

In the example in Figure 13.2, we can see that not only was the actual volume of units sold lower than expected (900 units instead of 1,000), the price at which each unit was sold at was also different (roughly £9.56 instead of £10 per unit) so a different calculation would be needed. We can see that the **sales price variance** is an adverse one of £400 (£8,600 of revenue earned on 900 units sold, instead of the expected £9,000 revenue on 900 units) and is calculated as follows:

Sales price variance = (actual price per unit – budgeted price per unit) × quantity sold

However, the sales volume variance formula needs to be adjusted, because the actual selling price was not the same as that budgeted for.

There are two possible ways to calculate the sales volume variance where the actual sales volume and price were both different from expected or budgeted:

Sales volume variance = (actual units sold – budgeted units sold) × expected profit per unit

or, in the case of Figure 13.2 where the fixed overheads figure does not change regardless of how many units are sold or made, a better formula would be:

Sales volume variance = (actual units sold – budgeted units sold) × expected contribution margin

The contribution margin is defined as price per unit minus variable costs per unit – this means the variance will not be distorted by the unchanging fixed costs – and in this case, the expected contribution margin is the original budget contribution margin, which is equal to the original budget's expected sale price per unit less the expected variable costs per unit (i.e. £4 per unit, or (£10,000 – (£4,000 + £2,000)) ÷ 1,000 units = £4 per unit).

So, in the example of Figure 13.2, the sales volume variance is:

(Actual units sold – budgeted/expected units sold) × expected contribution margin

= (1,000 – 900) × £4 per unit = 100 units sold × £4 per unit = £400 adverse.

The **direct material price variance** is the difference between the actual cost of direct materials purchased or consumed, and the budgeted cost of the quantity purchased or consumed.

Direct material price variance = (actual cost – budgeted cost) × actual quantity used.

The budgeted cost can be replaced by the standard cost, if management is using a standard costing system and calculating variances based on standard costing rather than budgets. Either variance will give management an idea of how well the business is managing the purchase costs of direct materials.

A favourable direct material price variance may be due to the following:

◆ a reduction in the market price of direct materials

◆ the purchase of materials of lower quality (which may be reflected in adverse direct material usage variance later)

◆ the procurement staff negotiated better purchase prices, obtained discounts on larger orders, or put better practices into action (e.g. obtaining price quotations from multiple suppliers and choosing the cheapest).

An adverse direct material price variance may be due to the following:

◆ the market price of materials increased

◆ small order sizes meant that suppliers cancelled discounts

◆ poor procurement practices

◆ suppliers increased bargaining power

◆ higher quality materials were purchased (which may be reflected in favourable direct material usage variance later).

The **direct material usage variance** is a variance used in a standard costing system and represents the difference between the actual and expected quantity of units that was used to make the business's product.

Direct material usage variance = (actual quantity – standard quantity) × standard cost per unit.

With a quick and efficient feedback loop, this variance can be useful for identifying and rectifying anomalies in the procurement or production systems, and variances can be due to the following:

◆ the standard against which the actual quantity is measured needs correcting or updating

◆ production process problems that cause excess waste or scrap

◆ problems with the quality of raw materials purchased – or damage to these materials – resulting in more units being required in production

◆ a product process or design change where the amount of materials required wasn't changed accordingly.

We can now create a reconciliation between budgeted and actual profit for the example in Figure 13.2 – see Worked Example 13.2.

Worked example 13.2

See Figure 13.2 for the actual figures versus those in the original budget and flexed budget, and the resulting variances (most of which are from Figure 13.2, apart from sales volume variance and sales price variance which were calculated in the main body text). A reconciliation might look like this:

	£		£	
Budgeted profit as per Figure 13.2			3,000	
Sales volume variance	(400)	(A)		
Sales price variance	(400)	(A)		
			(800)	(A)
			2,200	
Direct materials price variance	(40)	(A)		
Direct labour cost variance	60	(F)		
Fixed overheads expenditure variance	50	(F)		
			70	(F)
Actual profit as per Figure 13.2			2,270	

Budgeted and standard costs may also include overheads (or a portion of overheads) in the cost, so management may want to have a look at overhead variances. These can be done for these variances:

◆ fixed (or variable) overhead expenditure

◆ fixed (or variable) overhead efficiency

◆ fixed (or variable) overhead capacity

◆ fixed (or variable) overhead volume

◆ any other fixed/variable overhead variances.

In this course, we will only cover two – the fixed overhead expenditure variance and the variable overhead expenditure variance.

The **fixed overhead expenditure variance** – sometimes called the fixed overhead spending variance – which appears in Worked Example 13.2 – is the difference between the actual amount spent on fixed overheads and the budgeted amount. Fixed overheads should be as budgeted as they are meant to be the same regardless of production output or sales – however, sometimes there is a variance.

Fixed overhead expenditure variance = actual fixed overhead cost – budgeted fixed overhead cost

As always, standard fixed overhead cost can be substituted for budgeted fixed overhead cost if necessary.

The **variable overhead expenditure variance** looks at the expenditure per hour that was incurred on variable overheads (such as indirect labour costs or electricity costs where electricity usage is dependent on business activity rather than fixed and unchanging).

Variable overhead expenditure variance = (actual variable overhead per hour – budgeted variable overhead per hour) × actual hours

4.5 Financial statements for management information

Management accounting information and variances are often presented in a similar manner to financial statements. Figures 13.1 and 13.2 show examples of budget comparisons to actual results and it can be noted that they are laid out in a similar fashion to a basic profit and loss statement.

Worked example 13.2 shows a reconciliation, by way of variances, between the actual profit for a period and the budgeted profit for the period. Favourable variances are added, while adverse variances are subtracted. The statement reconciling the two figures via variances is sometimes known as an **operating statement** and is one example of a financial statement for management accounting.

operating statement
The statement reconciling the actual figures and budgeted figures via variances in management accounting. It is sometimes also used (less commonly) as an alternative name for an income statement.

forecast
A plan of what management estimates will happen in future based on past data and current/ future trends.

4.6 Break-even analysis and forecasting

Further important and useful planning tools management can use are break-even analysis, cashflow forecasting and demand forecasting. **Forecasts** usually try to predict and assess what will happen over the next 12 months, although sometimes they look at timescales beyond that. Businesses need to look ahead and plan accordingly to survive the next year and well beyond.

Break-even analysis

As previously mentioned, the **break-even point** is the point at which a business's revenues are equal to its total costs – at this point, the business has not made a profit or a loss. Figure 13.3 illustrates this in a graph.

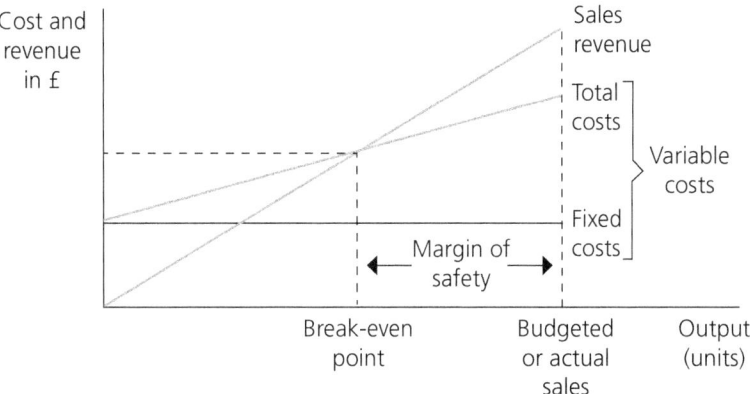

Figure 13.3: Break-even analysis graph

Break-even analysis is a technique used in forecasting at what point a business will break even and calculates a **margin of safety** – the amount at which revenues will exceed the break-even point – based on that, so that management can plan its activities accordingly. The margin of safety also allows the business to assess how risky the activities it plans to undertake are.

Cashflow forecasting

Businesses need cash to survive, and **cashflow forecasting** attempts to estimate or predict the amount of money the business expects to come in and pay out (i.e. the business's cashflows) in a forecast. This can cover the next 12 months or however many future accounting periods the business needs to make estimates for.

Cashflow forecasts are important for the following reasons:

◆ as an 'early warning system' that alerts management to any potential cash shortfalls, or to spot any problems customers may have paying the business

◆ to make sure the business can pay its staff, suppliers, tax authorities and shareholders as per the dividend policy

◆ to assess how the business can grow or expand into new markets, or how a potential product may perform in accounting periods to come

◆ to provide to external stakeholders who may require one (e.g. banks may want to see a cashflow forecast when considering extending a loan).

The cashflow forecast is therefore an important part of a management accountant's job, just like drawing up budgets. The simplest cash flow forecast will be a spreadsheet that estimates all cash inflows and outflows over a given period, whether that's a week, month or year, and calculates the predicted net cashflow at either the end of the period, or at regular intervals within the period.

Demand forecasting

To predict future demand for the business's products, a technique called **demand forecasting** is used, where management uses historical data, trends, **market research** (which involves surveying current and potential customers

break-even analysis
A method of forecasting at what point a business will break even (i.e. reach its break-even point) so that management can plan accordingly.

margin of safety
The amount at which revenues will exceed the break-even point, so that management can determine how risky a business undertaking will be.

about their needs regarding goods and services) and any other relevant information to estimate future customer demand – and therefore decide on pricing and business growth strategies, as well as assess the business's market and manage inventory according to likely demand. Demand forecasting can therefore also provide an idea of potential likely cash flows.

4.7 Potential consequences of inadequate planning

Poor financial management – and inadequate planning and analysis of internal information – causes many businesses to fail. For example, without demand forecasting, businesses risk making poor decisions about their products and target markets. Without cashflow forecasting, management cannot know where the business can expect to obtain cash from and without an idea of which level of output or sales the business expects to break even, a business will struggle to determine how to be profitable – and thus, how they can obtain the positive cashflow needed to maintain operations

Chapter summary

◆ Management accounting is the sourcing and analysis of financial and non-financial information for a business's management to help them run the business effectively and efficiently.

◆ When choosing a management accounting system, it is most effective to select one that integrates with the business's financial accounting system to increase the timeliness of management reports and eliminate redundant work or duplication.

◆ Like financial accounts, management accounts need to be presented in a format that is accurate; understandable; allows comparisons; and is either timely or up-to-date. However, unlike financial accounts, management accounts are not constrained by legislation on how to prepare or present them. They are primarily used by internal stakeholders and 'look forwards' to inform future strategy, as opposed to financial statements which 'look backwards' at an accounting period that has passed.

◆ Cost accounting looks at a business's expenses to determine the fixed and variable costs associated with making a product or providing a service sold by the business. The various methods of this are: standard costing, which estimates the planned unit cost of the product, component or service for the period in question; normal costing, which is like standard costing except actual values are used for direct costs of a unit but not the indirect costs; and actual costing, which goes one step further than normal costing and uses actual values to calculate both the direct and average indirect costs of a unit.

◆ Activity-based costing (ABC) is like actual costing but attempts to allocate indirect costs to products in a more proportional way.

◆ Life cycle costing looks at costs accumulated over the entire life of a product which may cover several accounting periods.

◆ Target costing is where the company plans its targets for price points, product cost and margins in advance, but cancels the project if these cannot be attained.

◆ Key performance indicators (KPIs) are values that can be used to evaluate how successful something has been in meeting performance or business objectives. These are often measured by comparing against one of four types of benchmark: internal benchmarks compare against another operating unit or function within the business, functional benchmarks compare and internal function against the best external practitioners of that function, generic benchmarking compares a process to a conceptually similar process or metric in another (often unrelated) business or industry, and competitive benchmarks compare against direct competitors.

◆ Balanced scorecards analyse financial, customer, learning and growth (or innovation), and internal business perspectives to help develop and monitor KPIs.

◆ Cost allocation is where a business identifies and assigns indirect costs to a cost object (something the business wants to separately measure costs for). Cost tracing is when direct costs are allocated to cost objects.

◆ Financial modelling involves creating a mathematical representation of a business's financial relations to examine how different economic situations or events would affect the business. Financial models can include a calculation of the weighted average cost of capital (WACC) which is the minimum return to satisfy its creditors, owners and other providers of capital, with cost of equity defined as the rate of return the company pays to its equity investors. Cost of debt is the interest rate on debt or the coupon rate on the company's bonds.

◆ Financial models can also be based on scenario planning where management considers a range of possibilities for what may happen in the future so they can be prepared should one of those possibilities occur.

◆ Financial models can also include business valuation of projects or investments to determine how attractive an investment is by looking at present values, found by working backwards from an investment project's future amount to see how much that would equate to today. Typically, these are assessed using discounted cashflows and net present values.

◆ Variance analysis compares the differences (called variances) between what was budgeted for and what the actual value turned out to be. Examples of variances include: sales volume variance; sales price variance, direct material price variance, direct material usage variance; and fixed/variable overhead variances.

◆ Forecasting is key. It allows a business to plan and make decisions to ensure future profitability and cashflow. To do this, management can utilise break-even analysis to calculate when a business will break-even and includes a margin of safety (the amount at which revenues should exceed the break-even point), cashflow forecasting to estimate the amount of money the business expects to come in and pay out and demand forecasting where historical data, trends, market research and any other relevant information are used to predict customer demand for a product or service.

Chapter fourteen
Introduction to financial decision making

CONTENTS

1. Introduction

This chapter outlines the principles of financial decision making. The ideas of corporate governance, value creation and sustainability will be introduced. This chapter also covers cost-volume-profit analysis and a consideration of the impact of a business's financial decisions on the environment and society.

2. Principles of financial decision making

Financial decision making is when management makes decisions about the business to achieve its objectives. The nature and importance of these decisions means the company secretary will often need to be involved in an administrative role.

Decisions are made about a range of topics and business functions, for example:

- investments the business should make (the investment decision)
- any long-term financing the business needs to raise (the financing decision)
- how profits should be distributed to shareholders (the dividend decision)
- short-term financing (working capital management).

2.1 Company (and management) objectives

There are several objectives a company's management (and therefore a company itself) may pursue when making decisions:

- maximising shareholder wealth;
- reinvesting in the company; or
- non-financial objectives.

Maximising shareholder wealth

In a capitalistic society, the main aim of a business is to maximise the wealth of its owners in the long term. In the case of a company limited by shares – whether those shares are publicly traded or privately owned – this would be known as maximising **shareholder wealth** (or **shareholder value**). To achieve this, the company therefore aims to maximise its combined value to maximise the returns paid out to shareholders, usually in the form of dividends (also known as distributions). The amount that is paid out to shareholders via dividends is governed by the company's dividend policy, which sets out the amount of dividend per share that is to be paid while taking into consideration the need to maintain adequate liquidity in the company or funds for future investment.

A company's dividend policy will depend on the level of growth it expects, as well as the nature of the company and the industry sector it operates in. Investors and potential investors may use the company's dividend policy – and any changes in this policy – when assessing how well the company is performing financially and therefore assessing how attractive an investment prospect the company is.

The main way businesses maximise their shareholder value – and therefore ensure shareholders receive the highest returns on capital they possibly can – is by maximising the business's profit in a period. The level of **risk** a business must take in pursuit of profit is driven by the goal of maximising shareholder wealth, and must therefore be incorporated in a business's strategy and decision making.

Reinvestment in company

While the main objective of a company's management is often to maximise shareholder value by maximising profit, it should not be the only objective. Profit is important, but changes in profits do not necessarily indicate current or future shareholder wealth. For example, profits that have been reinvested in the company may reduce profits and shareholder returns, but might be necessary for future growth. A company may, for instance, need to obtain capital to fund new developments by borrowing finance, issuing new shares or by reinvestment of its profits into the business – and it may take a while to generate returns.

If investors understand and have confidence in the ability and objectives of the company's management, they may be happy to accept a decrease in profitability in the short term so that their investment will pay off in the longer term. If the management of a publicly traded company communicates effectively with current and potential investors, the share price may even rise rather than fall – and the short-term decrease in profits can lead to an increase in share price, and therefore shareholder wealth.

shareholder wealth
Broadly speaking, this is the value of a company; the way this value is determined or calculated is outside the scope of this course.

shareholder value
The value a company delivers or returns to its shareholders. The way this is determined or calculated is outside the scope of this course.

risk
The possibility or probability of a loss or error being made, whether financial or non-financial.

Another possible reason for investing profits in the company rather than paying them out to shareholders is to maximise balance sheet or net asset values. The amount that the company is worth, after all liabilities have been paid, belongs to the shareholders, and it might well be in the company's interest to increase its net asset value – either as an indicator of its ability to generate future profits or to make the company less risky as regards bank lending (the more risky a company is as a finance prospect, the less likely the bank is to extend financing at a favourable rate – if it extends financing at all).

Non-financial objectives

The company might also want to pursue objectives that are not financial, such as:

◆ differentiating products and services so as to make them more attractive to customers than those of their competitors

◆ providing products and services of high quality

◆ innovation

◆ raising the skills of the workforce

◆ complying with the law

◆ sustainability, including maintaining a lower carbon footprint; or

◆ fair trade.

These non-financial objectives aim to help the business financially in the long term in some way, such as establishing the company as one that is more attractive to a particular type of customer or protecting or boosting the company's reputation (**reputation management**) or brand, which should therefore help to ensure long-term profitability. Financial decision making, therefore, can involve making decisions about non-financial objectives like those above as these can impact on a business's financial performance in the long term.

> **reputation management**
> An activity or activities carried out to create or maintain a desired public perception about a business, i.e. managing its reputation.

It is important to carefully consider costs and cash flows when making decisions, so information obtained from analysing financial accounts and management accounts comes in useful. Much of the analytical techniques a business's management can use will be covered in a later course.

2.2 Cost–volume profit (CVP) analysis

Cost–volume profit (CVP) examines how total revenues, total costs and operating profit changes as the following variables change:

> **cost–volume–profit (CVP) analysis**
> An analysis of how total revenues, total costs and operating profit changes as the following variables change: level of output, sale price, variable costs and/or fixed costs.

◆ level of output

◆ selling price

◆ variable costs

◆ fixed costs.

Another way of saying this is that CVP analysis looks at the behaviour of these financial measures when variables change. It is useful for answering questions on, for example, how revenues might be affected if the selling price changes or how costs might change if 500 more units were produced or what might happen if the company expands its business overseas.

The contribution margin

The contribution margin allows the business to determine how profitable individual products or services are. Management can use the contribution margin when deciding what price a product or service should sell for.

Contribution margin = price per unit – variable cost per unit

A contribution margin that is low – or even negative – is a good indicator that that product, business segment or service is not profitable. The contribution margin can also be used to resolve bottlenecks – if a business has limited resources, it will want to focus that resource towards its most profitable items, and can therefore use the contribution margin to help in its decision making.

The contribution

The **contribution** is the amount remaining after all variable costs have been subtracted from revenue. Whereas contribution margin refers to this amount per unit of product or service, the contribution is not necessarily per unit and represents the portion of revenue that is left to cover the fixed costs that arise during the period.

Contribution = revenue – variable costs

To make sure all costs and expenses related to revenue are recognised in the same accounting period as the revenue they relate to, one should calculate the business's contribution using the accrual basis. The profit earned during the period is whatever is left after fixed costs have also been subtracted from the contribution.

> **contribution**
> The amount remaining after all variable costs have been subtracted from revenue, and represents the amount left available to pay the business's fixed costs.

When deciding how to price products and services, the contribution is a useful concept for determining the lowest possible price point that can still cover all fixed costs. Therefore, working out the contribution (or even the contribution margin) can be useful for making decisions about the following:

- Discount sales – special deals on price should earn some contribution so that the business doesn't lose money on each sale, even with the discount on price.
- Budgets – management can forecast profit levels in subsequent accounting periods by estimating revenue, variable costs, and fixed costs.
- **Capital expenditures** – management can use the contribution to estimate how fixed asset purchases change the direct costs incurred, and thus how determine how profit changes (e.g. a machine purchase might reduce direct labour costs while increasing fixed costs).

> **capital expenditure**
> Expenditure relating to the purchase, repair or maintenance of fixed assets.

Contribution analysis can help management to get an idea of the number of product or services units the business must sell to cover a rise (even a small one) in fixed costs. Management can therefore use the knowledge gained from this analysis to either increase the contribution margin or reduce fixed costs – and thus increase the profitability.

Assumptions of CVP

When carrying out CVP analysis to make business decisions, one assumes the following are true:

❖   all costs, including manufacturing, administrative and overhead costs, can be accurately identified as either fixed or variable

❖   the selling price per unit is constant

❖   all units produced are sold

❖   changes in activity are the only factors that affect costs.

The advantages of CVP analysis is that it is reasonably simple and provides a detailed snapshot of activity within the business. This snapshot can be used – as we have seen above – to make decisions on pricing, profit forecasts, cost-reduction decisions and even capital spending.

However, CVP analysis has its limitations. Because of the assumptions above that require it to work, it can only provide approximate answers to both real and hypothetical problems. It must be carried out for each specific product, service or business segment, especially where pricing or costs involved are different – and in the case of some businesses with many product or service lines, such as restaurants where each item on the menu will have different direct costs associated with its production and sale, CVP analysis would be very difficult and complex to undertake.

Test yourself 14.1

Below is an example of a contribution income statement, which groups line items by cost behaviour to show the contribution or contribution margin.

	£
Revenue	7,000
Variable costs	(3,000)
Contribution	4,000
Fixed costs	(4,000)
Operating profit	0

Assume the above statement is when the break-even point is 50 units, the price per unit is £140, and variable cost per unit is £60.

- ◆ Calculate the contribution margin.

- ◆ Calculate (a) the contribution and (b) operating profit when 100 units are made and sold.

- ◆ Assuming revenue and variable costs remained the same, calculate the break-even point if fixed costs were halved.

2.3 The concept, purpose and benefits of integrated reporting

The business environment has changed rapidly in the twenty-first century. Increased globalisation and interconnectivity means that people, knowledge, finances and other forms of capital are more interlinked than ever before – and nowhere was this more evident than in the global financial crisis of around a decade ago. Combined with advances in technology, it became clear to many that new ways of doing business, of governing corporations and reporting need to take this hyper-connectivity into account – and **integrated reporting** or <IR> is one concept that has emerged as a possible way of meeting these needs.

What is integrated reporting?

According to former Governor of the Bank of England, Mervyn King: 'Integrated reporting builds on the practice of financial reporting, and environmental, social and governance (ESG) reporting, and equips organisations to strategically manage their operations, brand, and reputation to stakeholders and be better prepared to manage any risk that may compromise the long-term sustainability of the business.'

Integrated reporting is the production of an integrated report – a periodic, 'concise communication from the organisation' that is produced alongside the financial statements and should consist of:

- ◈ financial information
- ◈ governance and remuneration
- ◈ sustainability information
- ◈ management commentary.

This should detail an organisation's:

- ◈ value creation (in the short, medium and long term)
- ◈ corporate governance
- ◈ sustainability.

Value creation is the primary aim of any business, whether that's creating value for shareholders (i.e. maximising shareholder wealth) or creating value for customers in order to sell the business's products or services, and thus impact profitability.

integrated reporting
Also known as <IR>, this is a recent business approach which recommends the production of an integrated report alongside a business's financial statements.

value creation
The primary aim of any business – to create value for shareholders or customers to sell the business's products or services and increase profitability.

But value creation is not just financial. According to the website www.ValueBasedManagement.net: 'Traditional methods of assessing organisational performance are no longer adequate in today's economy. Stock price is less and less determined by earnings or asset base. Value creation in today's companies is increasingly represented in the intangible drivers like innovation, people, ideas, and brand.' Creating value is increasingly recognised by management as a better goal for companies and their long-term survivability and reputation, than simply meeting financial metrics of performance. Integrated reporting can help to communicate this to stakeholders.

corporate governance
The practice under which a company is directed and controlled, usually per the responsibility of the board of directors.

Corporate governance is the practice under which a company is directed and controlled. The board of directors is usually responsible for this. It includes providing effective leadership, setting the business's strategic aims, supervising how the business is managed, deciding how much board members and directors should be paid (remuneration) and reporting all of this to the company shareholders. As governance and remuneration practices will be part of the integrated report, it will be up to the business's management or organisation's board members to communicate their decisions on this effectively.

sustainability
The ability of a business to continue indefinitely while focusing on meeting the needs of the present without compromising the ability of future generations to meet their needs.

Sustainability is the ability of a business to continue indefinitely while focusing on meeting the needs of the present without compromising the ability of future generations to meet their needs. It can be broken down into three different types:

◆　economic (i.e. profit)

◆　environmental (i.e. the planet)

◆　social (i.e. people).

Purpose and benefits of integrated reporting

One of the most obvious benefits of integrated reporting is that it draws on a range of relevant information that is not just financial for the benefit of stakeholders. It also aims to encourage business leaders to think in a way that recognises the business's interconnectivity, and how its non-financial impacts are linked to its financial impacts. However, there is currently a lack of awareness of what <IR> is, as well as a lack of consensus of what exactly it will actually look like. Concerns over duplication of information, extra costs and the complexity of adopting a new reporting framework have also been cited by investors.

The International Integrated Reporting Council (IIRC) Framework states that: 'The more that **integrated thinking** (defined as management thinking that takes into account the connectivity and interdependencies between the range of factors that affect an organisation's ability to create value over time) is embedded into an organisation's activities, the more naturally will the connectivity of information flow into management reporting, analysis and decision making. It also leads to better integration of the information systems that support internal and external reporting and communication, including preparation of the integrated report.'

The purpose of integrated reporting, according to the IRC Framework, is to:

◆ Improve the quality of information available to providers of financial capital to enable a more efficient and productive allocation of capital.

◆ Promote a more cohesive and efficient approach to corporate reporting that draws on different reporting strands and communicates the full range of factors that materially affect the ability of an organisation to create value over time.

◆ Enhance accountability and stewardship for the broad base of capitals (financial, manufactured, intellectual, human, social and relationship and promote understanding of their interdependencies.

◆ Support integrated thinking, decision making and actions that focus on the creation of value over the short, medium and long term.

While the IIRC Framework aims to overcome the lack of accepted standards governing this type of reporting, it still needs to be tested in the field across a variety of organisations and provide guidance for both preparers and users of the reports.

3. The impact of financial decisions

As we have seen from the emergence of integrated reporting, it has been recognised that it is becoming increasingly important for organisations not to make business decisions based solely on financial information (economic sustainability) but considering the impact on the environment and society.

One approach has been that of the **corporate social responsibility (CSR)** movement, which has sprung up in recent years encouraging organisations to be more aware of how their business's actions impact on the rest of society, their stakeholders and the environment. Some companies have started detailing their CSR strategies in their annual reports, setting out how they will consider and deliver benefits to the environment and society while delivering sustainable economic performance.

corporate social responsibility (CSR)
An approach which examines and implements a way of doing business that is sustainable as well as beneficial to the environment and wider society.

Another example is decisions made about tax strategy in recent years that have sparked protests (such as the UK Uncut movement of the early 2010s) and have changed the way management decides on their tax strategies. The tax furore that followed the financial crisis put **reputation management** firmly under the spotlight – aggressive tax planning strategies being perceived negatively by the public and press has caused many companies to move away from them, and/or publish their own corporate tax strategies to justify why they have taken the actions on tax that they have.

Stop and think 14.1

Consider the business decisions the organisation you work for (or any other organisation you are familiar with) may have taken. Which of these have been influenced by environmental or social concerns? What

does the organisation hope to achieve with the decisions or strategy it has taken?

Chapter summary

◆ The objectives a company's management may pursue when making decisions: maximising shareholder wealth; reinvesting in the company to help drive future growth; and non-financial objectives.

◆ Cost–volume profit (CVP) analysis looks at how total revenues, total costs and operating profit change as level of output; selling price; variable costs; or fixed costs change. The break-even point is when revenue is equal to total expenses and the business has made neither a loss nor a profit.

◆ The contribution margin is what's left over when subtracting the variable cost of a unit from a unit's price. The contribution is what is left over when subtracting all variable costs from revenue and is not necessarily per unit. Both the contribution and the contribution margin can be used to help make decisions around pricing, budgets, and capital expenditure.

◆ CVP analysis assumes the following: all costs, including manufacturing, administrative and overhead, can accurately be identified as either fixed or variable; the selling price per unit is constant; all units produced are sold; changes in activity are the only factors that affect costs.

◆ An integrated report is a periodic report from an organisation consisting of the business's financial information, governance and remuneration, sustainability information and management commentary. It details value creation (in the short, medium and long term), corporate governance and sustainability. Integrated reporting benefits include providing stakeholders with a range of information that is not just financial, as well as encouraging management to think in a way that recognises a business's interconnectivity and how non-financial impacts are linked to financial impacts.

◆ The impact of financial decisions on the environment and society must also be taken into account. Some companies have started detailing corporate social responsibility (CSR) strategies in their annual reports. Integrated reporting, or <IR> aims to illustrate and communicate these non-financial impacts of the business to its stakeholders.

Test yourself answers

Chapter 1

Test Yourself 1.1

A mission statement communicates how an organisation plans on achieving its objectives and is very much focussed on the present (what the organisation is doing, how it's going to do it and why it's doing it) whereas a vision statement communicates where an organisation wants or aspires to be in the future.

Test Yourself 1.2

1. If one individual occupies both roles, it increases the chances of one individual dominating the board. Other board members may feel that they cannot raise objections or challenge constructively if one person is dominating discussions. This can lead to matters and issues not being thoroughly discussed and challenged, resulting in poor decisions made by the board that may have an adverse effect on the organisation and its stakeholders.

2. Non-executive directors can benefit a board by:
    - provide a balancing influence and help to minimise conflicts of interest
    - improving the effectiveness of a board by providing objective challenge and criticism in board meetings
    - acting as mentor to the chairperson and CEO, providing advice and guidance when issues arise
    - helping to make balanced and considered decisions on issues delegated to board committees (e.g. directors' pay and benefits packages).

3. A unitary board consists of executive and NEDs who make decisions as one body. A two-tier board structure separates the executive and non-executive directors with the supervisory board (consisting of the NEDs who represent the shareholders) overseeing the activities of the executive board.

Chapter 2

Test Yourself 2.1

1.   Internal stakeholders are individuals or groups within a business who are directly affected by its activities whereas external stakeholders are those outside the business who are interested in its performance and/or affected by its activities.

2.   Primary stakeholders are those who have a direct functional or financial interest in the business whereas secondary stakeholders have an influence on the business, but may not be directly involved in its day-to-day activities.

Test Yourself 2.2

1.   Consequences can include the organisation developing and implementing unrealistic or inappropriate business strategies that cause issues such as a decline in profitability, loss of market share, reputational damage, decreased level of sales or even cause the organisation to fail completely. Similarly, being slow to respond, not developing an appropriate response, or failing to respond at all may cause an organisation to miss out or eventually fail.

2.   PESTEL – political, political, economic, social/sociocultural, technological, environmental and legal factors. SWOT – strengths, weaknesses, opportunities and threats.

Chapter 3

Test Yourself 3.1

1.   The purposes of business law, as set out in the text are accountability, transparency, flexibility and autonomy, efficiency, certainty and predictability, ensuring certain persons act in the business's interests, dispute resolution, and preventing disaster and failure.

2.   The benefits of transparency are:

  ◆   It enables regulators and stakeholders to hold businesses to account. A business cannot be held to account if it fully conducts its business in secret.

  ◆   Businesses, knowing that they will be required to disclose certain information, will take steps to ensure that they are conducting themselves in a lawful and proper manner.

  ◆   It allows certain stakeholders to make informed decisions (e.g. shareholders when deciding whether to purchase shares, creditors when deciding whether to loan the business money).

3.   Laws should be sufficiently certain and predictable for several reasons:

  ◆   Businesses must be able to rely on the law and they cannot do this with confidence if the law is unclear or uncertain.

- Laws must adapt and evolve, but they should not be amended excessively frequently, nor changed without good cause.

- The application of business law should be predictable. This allows businesses to conduct themselves in a manner that does not breach the law, and so reduces the need to engage in costly litigation. If litigation does arise, clear and predictable law should allow for the dispute to be resolved more quickly and cheaply.

4. The three main forms of dispute resolution are (i) commencing legal proceedings in a court; (ii) taking a case to a tribunal; and (iii) using a form of alternative dispute resolution.

Test Yourself 3.2

1. The three meanings of the phrase 'common law' are:
   - those legal systems that have based their legal system on that of England;
   - the body of laws and decisions created by judges and applied via the doctrine of precedent; or
   - the unified system of law that arose following the Norman Conquest and still exists today.

2. The two meanings of the phrase 'civil law' are:
   - the body of law that pertains to civil wrongs (e.g. the law of torts, contract law) and do not impose criminal liability; and
   - those legal systems that are largely based on Roman law.

3. Criminal law refers to those laws that impose criminal liability on a person. Civil law refers to laws that do not impose criminal liability, but aim to provide a remedy to a person who has suffered loss due to a civil wrong committed by someone else.

4. Public law refers to laws that regulate the relationship between the state and persons within the state (e.g. human rights law, criminal law). Private law refers to laws that regulate the relationship between persons (e.g. company law, contract law, employment law).

Chapter 4

Test Yourself 4.1

1. A court with a first instance jurisdiction hears cases for the first time. Certain first instance decisions can be appealed and courts that can hear appeals are known as appellate courts. Most courts have some form of first instance and appellate jurisdiction.

2. The three categories of criminal offences are:
   - **Summary offences**: These are minor offences that are tried in a magistrates' court.

◆ **Offences triable on indictment only**: These are serious offences, so are usually heard in the Crown Court.

◆ **Offences triable either way**: Offences that have the potential to be minor or serious. Depending on their severity, they can be tried summarily in a magistrates' court or on indictment in the Crown Court.

3. The following statements are false:

◆ **County Court decisions can only be appealed to the High Court**: This is false because a County Court decision can be appealed to the Court of Appeal in certain cases.

◆ **The High Court only hears first instance cases**: This is not true because the High Court has both a first instance and appellate jurisdiction.

◆ **Decisions of the High Court can only be appealed to the Court of Appeal**: In limited cases, it is possible for an appeal to 'leapfrog' the Court of Appeal and go directly to the Supreme Court.

4. The Divisions of the High Court most applicable to businesses are:

◆ **The Chancery Division**: This Division hears a number of business-related cases (e.g. dissolution of partnerships) and has a Companies List, which focuses on cases involving insolvent companies.

◆ **The Queen's Bench Division**: This Division hears a number of business-related cases (notably cases in contract and tort) and it also has several specialist courts that focus on business matters (e.g. the Commercial Court, the Financial List).

Test Yourself 4.2

1. A tribunal panel typically consists of three persons, namely a chairperson (usually a Tribunal judge) and two laypersons (known as Tribunal members) who are not legally qualified, but have expertise in the relevant subject matter.

2. Tribunals hear more cases than courts and the potential advantages of tribunals are:

◆ tribunal cases are often cheaper and decided more quickly than court proceedings;

◆ tribunals are not subject to the mass of rules that courts are subject to, and are not bound by precedent, meaning that they can operate in a more flexible manner;

◆ it is easier to have a case heard before a tribunal than before a court;

◆ although many tribunal cases are open to the public, they tend to attract less publicity than court cases.

3. Cases are first heard by the relevant Chamber within the First-tier Tribunal. Decisions of this Chamber can be appealed to the relevant Chamber within the Upper Tribunal.

4. Decisions of the Upper Tribunal can be appealed to the Court of Appeal and, in limited cases, directly to the Supreme Court.

Test Yourself 4.3

1. The potential benefits of ADR over court proceedings are:

   ◈ ADR can be cheaper and quicker than commencing proceedings in a court;

   ◈ as certain forms of ADR focus more on the parties reaching an agreement, it is more likely to preserve the parties' relationship, thereby allowing them to do business again in the future;

   ◈ legal proceedings are played out in the public arena and any resulting publicity may have an adverse effect upon a company's reputation and/or share price, or provide the company's competitors with useful information.

2. The arbitrator will impose a legally binding decision on the parties to the dispute, so the dispute will be resolved. Conversely, a mediator will not impose a decision and will facilitate a dialogue between the parties, with the aim of resolving the dispute themselves. The downside of mediation is that a resolution may not be reached.

3. Conciliation is similar to mediation, in that the parties will appoint a conciliator in order to help them reach a mutually acceptable solution to their dispute. The difference is that the mediator facilitates dialogue, whereas the conciliator takes a much more active role and will lead the discussion and propose solutions to the dispute

Test Yourself 4.4

1. The six types of judges (in order of rank from highest to lowest) are (i) Justices of the Supreme Court; (ii) Lord/Lady Justices of Appeal; (iii) High Court judges/deputy High Court judges; (iv) circuit judges/deputy circuit judges; (v) recorders; and (vi) district judges/deputy district judges.

2. The law officers are the Attorney General and his deputy, the Solicitor General and they are both ministers. They are the government's chief legal advisers, with other roles including (i) superintending certain agencies (namely the Crown Prosecution Service and the Serious Fraud Office); (ii) providing permission to bring certain prosecutions; (iii) representing the government is important litigation; and (iv) referring unduly lenient sentences to the Court of Appeal.

3. The three principal occupations within the legal profession are solicitors, barristers, and legal executives. A fourth occupation, paralegals, have not achieved the formal level of recognition that the other three have and paralegals are not lawyers.

Chapter 5

Test Yourself 5.1

1. The two principal types of legislation are Acts of Parliament (also known as 'primary legislation') and subordinate legislation (also known as 'secondary' or 'delegated' legislation).

2.   The differences between the three types of bills are:

- Public Bills affect the general population.

- Private Bills affect specific persons, groups, organisations, or localities.

- Hybrid Bills affect the general population, but will have an increased effect upon specific persons, groups, organisations, or localities.

3.   For a Bill to become an Act, it will need to pass through Parliament, which consists of the House of Commons, the House of Lords and the monarch. Bills can be introduced into either House, but most are introduced into the House of Commons. In each House, the Bill will go through a series of stages and, if both Houses agree, the Bill will go to the monarch for Royal Assent.

4.   The three 'canons of interpretation' are:

- The literal rule provides that the words of a statute will be given their everyday, ordinary meaning.

- The golden rule provides that if a literal interpretation produces an absurdity, the relevant words may be given an alternative meaning, but it must be a meaning that the words can bear.

- The mischief rule interprets words based on the mischief or problem the statute was designed to remedy.

Test Yourself 5.2

1.   The three levels of precedent are:

- A binding precedent must be followed by courts that are bound by that precedent, unless the precedent can be distinguished.

- Certain precedents are not binding and so need not be followed, but they do constitute persuasive authority and may be followed.

- Certain cases provide no precedent value at all and need not be followed.

2.   The following are false:

- **Decisions of the inferior courts are not binding, but provide persuasive authority**: decisions of the inferior courts are not binding and also do not provide persuasive authority.

- **Decisions of the Crown Court bind magistrates' courts**: Crown Court decisions provide persuasive authority only.

- **The Divisional Courts and bound by decisions of the High Court**: the High Court is generally bound by the decisions of its Divisional Courts.

- **The Supreme Court is generally bound by its own decisions or those of the House of Lords**: the Supreme Court is not bound by its own decisions or those of the House of Lords.

3.   The *ratio decidendi* ('reason for deciding') refers to the reason(s) behind a decision in a case, and can be binding. *Obiter dicta* ('statements said by the way') refers to statements that are not part of the *ratio* and are not binding, but do provide persuasive authority.

Test Yourself 5.3

1. The financial institutions are the Court of Auditors and the European Central Bank. The political institutions are the European Council, the European Parliament, the Council of the EU, and the European Commission. The legal institution is the Court of Justice of the EU.

2. A preliminary ruling is a ruling by the Court of Justice, following a reference being made to that Court by a domestic court in which the domestic court seeks a ruling on a point of interpretation of EU law.

3. Directly applicable EU legislation is automatically incorporated into domestic law as soon as it is passed. Directly effective EU legislation is legislation that can be enforced in a domestic court.

4. The six types of EU legislation are (i) treaty provisions; (ii) Regulations; (iii) directives; (iv) decisions; (v) recommendations; and (vi) opinions.

Test Yourself 5.4

1. The EU and the ECHR are currently completely separate, and membership of one does not bring about membership of the other. However, the EU is in the process of acceding to the ECHR.

2. UK courts are not required to follow decisions of the ECtHR, but they are required to take them into account.

3. Section 3 of the HRA 1998 provides that '[s]o far as it is possible to do so, primary legislation and subordinate must be read and given effect in a way which is compatible with the Convention rights.' Section 3 is important because:

   ◆ it applies to legislation passed before and after the HRA 1998 came into force; and

   ◆ it takes priority over the doctrine of precedent, so a court that would be bound to follow a normally binding precedent need not follow that precedent if it feels that the precedent is incompatible with a Convention right.

4. A declaration of incompatibility is a declaration stating that the court is of the opinion that a legislative provision is incompatible with a Convention right. A declaration of incompatibility does not affect the validity, continuing operation or enforcement of the relevant provision. Accordingly, the court must still apply the law and a declaration does not compel Parliament to change the law (although it usually does).

Chapter 6

Test Yourself 6.1

1. The six principal sources of company law are legislation, case law, the constitution of the company, contract, European Union law, and the European Convention on Human Rights.

2. The principal piece of company law legislation in the UK is the Companies Act 2006.

3. Case law is important because:

   ◆ certain areas of company law are entirely created by case law;

   ◆ case law often establishes the scope and rules regarding the application of remedies and imposition of punishments;

   ◆ certain well-established case law rules are often implemented into legislation; and

   ◆ legislative rules are interpreted and applied via case law.

4. Contract is an important source of company law because it allows companies to create the rules which govern the transactions they enter into. Companies may enter into many contracts, so this is an extremely important source of law in practice.

Test Yourself 6.2

1. The two principal UK corporate governance codes are (i) the UK Corporate Governance Code; and (ii) the UK Stewardship Code.

2. The 'comply or explain' approach provides that listed companies must include in their annual report:

   ◆ a statement as to whether the company has complied with all the relevant provisions of the UK Corporate Governance Code; or

   ◆ a statement identifying which provisions were not complied with, the period within which they were not complied with, and the reasons for non-compliance.

3. The UK Corporate Governance Code applies to companies with a Premium listing, but other companies are free to comply or explain against the Code.

Chapter 7

Test Yourself 7.1

1. Examples of torts include negligence, product liability, wrongful interference with goods, occupiers' liability, nuisance, defamation, and the economic torts.

2. Examples of employment law topics are the status of employees and workers, employment rights, health and safety, discrimination law, unfair dismissal, wrongful dismissal, the rights of employees following the transfer of a business, and rights relating to collective action.

3. Commercial law concerns the body of laws that seek to regulate and facilitate the commercial dealings of businesses. Commercial law overlaps with contract law (as most businesses transact via contract) and consumer law (as many businesses deal with consumers).

4. The four principal ways in which a business can protect its intellectual property are by obtaining a patent, copyright, design right, and/or trade mark.

5. The tasks undertaken by the Competition and Markets Authority are:

    ◆   investigating breaches of EU and UK competition law;

    ◆   conducting marker studies and investigations into markets where a lack of competition could be adversely affecting consumers;

    ◆   prosecuting those who engage in cartel activity; and

    ◆   investigating mergers and could affect competition.

Chapter 8

Test Yourself 8.1

1. By Act of Parliament.

2. Legal personality and perpetual succession of ownership of assets separate from its investors.

3. By the Companies Act 2006.

Test Yourself 8.2

1. Private limited by shares.

    Public limited by shares.

    Private limited by guarantee.

    Private unlimited.

2. Private limited by shares.

3. To act within their powers.

    To promote the success of the company.

    To exercise independent judgement.

    To exercise reasonable care, skill and diligence.

    To avoid conflicts of interest.

    Not to accept benefits from third parties.

    To declare interests in any proposed transaction or arrangement.

4. Company.

    Directors.

    Members

Test Yourself 8.3

1. (a) Private limited by shares

    (b) Private limited by guarantee

    (c) Public company

2. Yes, referred to as sensitive words. Without approval names cannot imply national or international pre-eminence, connection to the government or royalty and certain specified words are also restricted

3. Incorporation of a company

Test Yourself 8.4

1. Rights to vote

   Rights to profit

   Rights to capital

   Rights to manage.
2. Pre-emption rights on allotment.
3. Tag along and drag along rights.
4. Grant of probate.

Test Yourself 8.5

1. [Memorandum and] articles of association
2. Shareholders'/Investors' agreement

Test Yourself 8.6

1. Directors or the company secretary at the request of a director.
2. Ordinary resolutions that change the constitution or share capital and all special resolutions.

Chapter 9

Test Yourself 9.1

1. Registers of directors, directors' residential addresses, secretaries, members, PSC and debenture holders (if any)
2. Registered office, SAIL address or on the central register for certain specified private company registers.
3. Everyone although only members can do so free of charge.

Test Yourself 9.2

1. Web filing or software filing using an approved software application.
2. Yes, filing penalties are automatically imposed on late filed accounts and may be imposed where amended articles have not been delivered after a request to do so.
3. Financial statements and confirmation statement

Test Yourself 9.3

1. Company name as registered, place of registration, registration number and registered office address.
2. No, it must also show its registered name on properties. The website should also contain the additional information required for headed stationery plus its VAT number, if registered.

Test Yourself 9.4

1. As the register are public documents non-statutory information should not be kept on the registers.

2. Individuals can provide a service address for inclusion on the public registers except where the register of directors' residential addresses or the register of members is kept on the central register in which case that information is currently publicly available.

Chapter 10

Test Yourself 10.1

1. Subject to the articles the quorum for meetings of the members or directors is two unless there is only one member or director in which case the quorum is one.

2. Provided there is authority in the articles, participants need not be in the same room provided they can hear and participate in the discussion, ask questions and participate in any vote.

3. Members' resolutions of a private company can be approved by circulating a written resolution to all members

4. Yes member(s) holding between them 5% of the total voting rights can request a resolution be put to a meeting or in the case of a private company circulated as a written resolution. In addition, 100 or more members of a public company may request a resolution is put to the next annual general meeting.

Test Yourself 10.2

1. Directors can hold management, board and committee meetings. Members could hold general, annual general, class and court meetings.

2. Name of company, date, time and place of the meeting, that the meeting is to an AGM, details of the business to be undertaken and members right to appoint a proxy who need not be a member.

3. To be validly approved the requisite majority for a written resolution must be obtained within 28 days of the resolution being circulated.

4. The notice and any supporting documents for a members meeting may be circulated in hard copy, electronically or via website. Electronic communication may only be used where actual consent has been obtained, website communication may be used where actual or deemed consent has been obtained.

5. Subject to the articles general meetings of a private or a non-traded public company may be held on 14 days' notice. The AGM of a public company must be held on 21 days' notice and the general meeting of a traded company may be held on 14 days' notice provided the special conditions set out in s. 307A have been met, otherwise 21 days' notice is required.

Test Yourself 10.3

1. Management, board and committee meetings.
2. Directors' meeting must be held on reasonable notice.
3. Yes.
4. The meeting can continue to discuss the matter before them, but no decision can be reached without a quorum being present.

Chapter 11

Test yourself 11.1

- rental income – this is revenue/income
- office rent – this is a cost/expense
- wages – this is a cost/expense
- bank interest received – this is revenue/income
- bank interest paid – this is a cost/expense
- interest on loan payment – this is a cost/expense
- purchase of T-shirts – this is a cost/expense
- accounting software expenditure – this is a cost/expense
- book royalties – this is revenue/income.

Test yourself 11.2

For John Shepard's business, using the figures in Worked Example 1.2,

1. Average fixed cost = Total fixed costs ÷ Quantity of goods produced
$$= 25 \div 40 = £0.63$$

2. Marginal cost = Change in total cost ÷ Change in quantity produced
$$= (£425 - £25) \div (40 - 0) = 400 \div 40 = £10$$

The cost of producing one more unit (the marginal cost) is £10. We know that Shepard has to pay his fixed costs (electricity and water of £25 a month) even if he produces nothing, so the change in total cost and quantity produced that we have used here is the change from when he was producing zero units to when he was producing 40 in a month.

Test yourself 11.3

Net profit = total revenue – total expenses

= (1,600,000 + 250,000) – (700,000 + 100,000 + 300,000 + 350,000 + 50,000)

= 1,850,000 – 1,500,000 = £350,000

Operating profit = sales − (COGS + operating expenses)

= 1,600,000 − (700,000 + (100,000 + 300,000 + 350,000))

= 1,600,000 − (700,000 + 750,000) = 1,600,000 − 1,450,000 = £150,000

EBIT = (sales + other income excl. finance income) − (COGS + operating expenses)

= (1,600,000 + 250,000) − (700,000 + (100,000 + 300,000 + 350,000))

= 1,850,000 − (700,000 + 750,000) = 1,850,000 − 1,450,000 = £400,000

EBITDA = EBIT + depreciation + amortisation = 400,000 + 25,000 + 75,000

= £500,000

Chapter 12

Test yourself 12.1

X plc – can only report under IFRS, rather than UK GAAP.

X Ltd – not listed on an EU stock exchange, and qualifies as a small entity, therefore can report under section 1A of FRS 102

Y Ltd – a large company, but not listed so can report under UK GAAP (FRS 102)

Z Ltd – qualifies as a micro-entity, and is also unlisted so can report under FRS 105.

Test yourself 12.2

Office building is a tangible fixed asset; petty cash is a tangible current asset; a bank overdraft is a current liability; commercial mortgage is a long-term (or non-current) liability; company cars are tangible fixed assets; patents are intangible fixed assets; trade creditors are current liabilities.

Test yourself 12.3

In very basic terms, if a company's equity is negative, it means that its total liabilities are greater than its total assets. (The accounting equation states that equity is equal to total assets minus total liabilities.) This means a company owes more money than the total value of things it owns, and is generally a bad sign. If a company went into liquidation (i.e. the business came to an end), the shareholders would owe money to the business's creditors. However, negative shareholder equity does not necessarily mean a business won't survive: if assets are generating cash before liabilities are due to be paid, then the business could carry on trading and return to a positive equity figure.

Test yourself 12.4

Horizontal analysis:

Total fixed assets	(105,000–100,000)/100,000 = 5% increase on 2017
Total current assets	(57,800–49,500)/49,500 = 16.77% increase on 2017
Total current liabilities	(24,900–27,800)/27,800 = 10.43% decrease from 2017
Long-term liabilities	(60,000-64,000)/64,000 = 6.25% decrease from 2017

Vertical analysis for 2017:

Total assets for 2017	= total fixed assets for 2017 + total current assets for 2017
	= 100,000 + 49,500 = 149,500

Therefore, as a percentage of total assets for 2017,

Total fixed assets	100,000/149,500 × 100 = 66.89%
Total current assets	49,500/149,500 × 100 = 33.11%
Total current liabilities	27,800/149,500 × 100 = 18.60%
Long-term liabilities	64,000/149,500 × 100 = 42.81%

Vertical analysis for 2018:

Total assets for 2018	= total fixed assets for 2018 + total current assets for 2018
	= 105,000 + 57,800 = 162,800

Therefore, as a percentage of total assets for 2018,

Total fixed assets	105,000/162,800 × 100 = 64.50%
Total current assets	57,800/162,800 × 100 = 35.50%
Total current liabilities	24,900/162,800 × 100 = 15.29%
Long-term liabilities	60,000/162,800 × 100 = 36.86%

Chapter 13

Test yourself 13.1

Answer 1 (Geth Prime):

Direct labour cost per unit = £15 × 0.1 = £1.50

Set-up cost per set-up = £600,000 ÷ 1200 = £500

Set-up cost per batch = £500 × 4 = £2,000

Set-up cost per unit = £2,000 ÷ 250 = £8

Handling cost per batch = £750,000 ÷ 500 = £1,500

Handling cost per unit = £1,500 ÷ 250 = £6

Other production overhead per machine hour = £945,000 ÷ 6,300 = £150

Other production overhead per unit = £150 × 0.06 = £9

Cost per unit = £35 + £1.50 + £8 + £6 + £9 = £59.50

Answer 2 (Geth Pyro):

Direct labour cost per unit = £10 × 0.05 = £0.50

Set-up cost per set-up = £600,000 ÷ 1200 = £500

Set-up cost per batch = £500 x 2 = £1,000

Set-up cost per unit = £1,000 ÷ 1,000 = £1

Handling cost per batch = £750,000 ÷ 500 = £1,500

Handling cost per unit = £1,500 ÷ 1,000 = £1.50

Other production overhead per machine hour = £945,000 ÷ 6,300 = £150

Other production overhead per unit = £150 x 0.012 = £1.80

Cost per unit = £20 + £0.50 + £1 + £1.50 + £1.80 = £24.80

Chapter 14

Test yourself 14.1

Contribution margin = price per unit – variable costs per unit = 140 – 60 = £80

When 100 units are made and sold,

(a) the contribution = revenue – variable costs

$\qquad$ = (140 × 100) – (60 × 100) = 14,000 – 6,000 = £8,000

(b) operating profit = revenue – (variable costs + fixed costs)

$\qquad$ = 14,000 – (6,000 + 4,000) = 14,000 – 10,000 = £4,000

Break-even point if fixed costs were halved: so fixed costs would now be £2,000, while all other costs (i.e. variable costs in this case) and price remained the same. This means the contribution margin remains the same. Therefore,

Break-even point in units = fixed costs ÷ (price – variable cost per unit)

or: Break-even point in units = fixed costs ÷ contribution margin

= 2,000 ÷ 80 = 25 units.

Directory of web resources

Organisations

Advisory, Conciliation and Arbitration Service
www.acas.org.uk

Bar Council
www.barcouncil.org.uk

Chartered Institute of Management Accountants
www.cimaglobal.com/

Chartered Institute of Legal Executives
www.cilex.org.uk

Companies House
www.gov.uk/government/organisations/companies-house

Company information
https://beta.companieshouse.gov.uk/

Company name checker
https://beta.companieshouse.gov.uk/company-name-availability

Forms
www.gov.uk/topic/company-registration-filing/forms

Guidance
www.gov.uk/government/collections/companies-house-guidance-for-limited-companies-partnerships-and-other-company-types

Competition & Markets Authority
www.gov.uk/government/organisations/competition-and-markets-authority

Confederation of British Industry
www.cbi.org.uk/

Court of Justice of the European Union
https://curia.europa.eu

Courts and Tribunals Judiciary
www.judiciary.gov.uk

Department for Business, Energy & Industrial Strategy
www.gov.uk/government/organisations/department-for-business-energy-and-industrial-strategy

Domain name registrars
ICANN
www.icann.org/

Nominet UK
www.nominet.uk/

Internic
www.internic.net/

European Business Register
www.ebr.org/

European Court of Human Rights
http://echr.coe.int

European Patent Office
www.epo.org/index.html

European Union
https://europa.eu

Financial Conduct Authority
FCA Handbook
www.handbook.fca.org.uk/handbook
Financial Conduct Authority
Financial Services Register
https://register.fca.org.uk/
Mutuals Public Register
www.fca.org.uk/firms/mutuals-public-register

Financial Reporting Council
www.frc.org.uk/
Audit resources
www.frc.org.uk/auditors
Corporate governance
www.frc.org.uk/directors/corporate-governance-and-stewardship
www.frc.org.uk/

HM Courts & Tribunals Service
 www.gov.uk/government/organisations/hm-courts-and-tribunals-service

HM Land Registry
www.gov.uk/government/organisations/land-registry

HM Revenue & Customs
www.gov.uk/government/organisations/hm-revenue-customs

Information Commissioner's Office
www.ico.org.uk

Institute of Chartered Accountants in England and Wales
www.icaew.com/

Institute of Chartered Accountants in Ireland
www.charteredaccountants.ie/

Institute of Chartered Accountants in Scotland
www.icas.com/

Institute of Chartered Secretaries and Administrators
www.icsa.org.uk/

Guidance material

www.icsa.org.uk/knowledge
https://ico.org.uk/

Institute of Directors
www.iod.com/

International Corporate Governance Network
www.icgn.org/

Judicial Committee of the Privy Council
www.jcpc.uk

Law society
www.lawsociety.org.uk/

Listing Rules
www.handbook.fca.org.uk/handbook/LR/

London Stock Exchange
www.londonstockexchange.com/home/homepage.htm

Admission and disclosure standards
www.londonstockexchange.com/companies-and-advisors/main-market/
documents/admission-and-disclosure-standards.pdf

AIM rules
www.londonstockexchange.com/companies-and-advisors/aim/publications/rules-
regulations/aim-rules-for-companies-march-2018.pdf

Dividend timetable
www.londonstockexchange.com/traders-and-brokers/rules-regulations/dividend-
procedure-timetable-2018.pdf

Panel on Takeovers and Mergers
www.thetakeoverpanel.org.uk/

Patent/Trademark Office
www.gov.uk/government/organisations/intellectual-property-office

Prudential Regulation Authority
www.bankofengland.co.uk/prudential-regulation

Stamp duty
www.gov.uk/topic/business-tax/stamp-taxes

Supreme Court of the United Kingdom
www.supremecourt.uk

Takeover Panel
www.thetakeoverpanel.org.uk

Trade Union Congress
www.tuc.org.uk/

UK Legislation
www.legislation.gov.uk/

UK Listing Authority
www.fca.org.uk/markets/ukla

UK Parliament
www.parliament.uk

Sectors of business activity

Centralised versus decentralised structures
www.cimaglobal.com/Documents/Student%20docs/2010%20syllabus%20docs/
E1/E1_fmarticle_nov2013.pdf

Charitable purposes
www.gov.uk/government/publications/charitable-purposes

Divisional organisational structure
http://smallbusiness.chron.com/advantages-disadvantages-divisional-
organizational-structure-611.html

Municipal enterprises
https://community-wealth.org/strategies/panel/municipal/index.html
www.theguardian.com/money/blog/2015/sep/26/return-age-of-municipality

Organisation types and legal structures
www.bgateway.com/business-guides/first-steps/form-a-company-or-business/
legal-structures-the-basics

Situational analysis
http://pestleanalysis.com/pestle-analysis-in-strategic-management/ www.
businessnewsdaily.com/5512-pest-analysis-definition-examples-templates.html
wps.pearsoned.co.uk/wps/media/objects/1514/1550600/ch08.ppt
https://articles.bplans.com/how-to-perform-swot-analysis/

Sectors of business activity
www.investopedia.com/terms/s/sector.asp#ixzz53bwDYyr2
Unitary and two-tier board structures
www.icfj.org/resources/who%E2%80%99s-running-company-guide-reporting-
corporate-governance/types-boards-directors

Vision, mission, core values and strategic planning
www.extension.iastate.edu/agdm/wholefarm/html/c5-09.html www.clearvoice.
com/blog/difference-between-mission-vision-statement-examples/ https://

onstrategyhq.com/resources/developing-your-strategy/ /www.bain.com/publications/articles/management-tools-mission-and-vision-statements.aspx

Publications

BTEC Higher National Business Study Guide, (Pearson custom publishing, 2011), ISBN10: 0857760033/ISBN13: 978-0857760036

CIMA Technical Information Service and Edwards-Nutton, S. *Standard Costing and Variance Analysis – Topic Gateway Series No. 24.* 2nd ed. [online PDF] (The Chartered Institute of Management Accountants, 2008). Available at: www.cimaglobal.com/Documents/ImportedDocuments/cid_tg_standard_costing_and_variance_analysis_mar08.pdf.pdf.

CIMA Technical Information Service and Murby, L. *Benchmarking – Topic Gateway Series No. 11.* 2nd ed. [online PDF] (The Chartered Institute of Management Accountants, 2008). Available at: www.cimaglobal.com/Documents/ImportedDocuments/cid_tg_benchmarking_july06.pdf.pdf.

Coyle, B and Hill, T: *Corporate Governance,* 6th ed. (CSQS), (ICSA Publishing Ltd, 2017).

Coyle, B., Atrill, P. and Sayers, J. *ICAEW Professional Stage Accounting Study Manual*, volumes 1 and 2. 5th ed. (ICSA Publishing Ltd, 2005).

Fernandes, N. *Finance for Executives: A Practical Guide for Managers*, (NPV Publishing, 2014) p. 32.

Frederick, D. *ICSA Study Text (CSQS) Financial Reporting and Analysis.* 2nd ed. (ICSA Publishing Ltd, 2014).

Horngren, C., Bhimani, A., Datar, S. and Foster, G. (2002). *Management and Cost Accounting.* 2nd ed. (Pearson, 2002).

International Accounting Standards Board, *Conceptual Framework for Financial Reporting 2010*, Chapter 1, para. F QC26.

International Integrated Reporting Council (2013). *The International <IR> Framework.* [online PDF] Available at: http://integratedreporting.org/wp-content/uploads/2015/03/13-12-08-THE-INTERNATIONAL-IR-FRAMEWORK-2-1.pdf.

Robertson, J. *ICSA Study Text (CSQS) Financial Decision Making.* 2nd ed. (ICSA Publishing Ltd, 2016).

The Institute of Chartered Accountants in England and Wales (2006). *ICAEW Professional Stage Business Finance Study Manual.* 6th ed. (The Institute of Chartered Accountants in England and Wales, 2006).

The Institute of Chartered Accountants in England and Wales *ICAEW Professional Stage Financial Reporting Study Manual.* 6th ed. (The Institute of Chartered Accountants in England and Wales, 2006).

The Institute of Chartered Accountants in England and Wales *ICAEW Professional Stage Business Management Study Manual.* 6th ed. (The Institute of Chartered Accountants in England and Wales, 2006).

Online publications

Accounting-Simplified.com (2014). *Direct Material Price Variance*. [online] Available at: http://accounting-simplified.com/management/variance-analysis/material/price.html#comment-1769467469.

AccountingCoach.com (date unknown). *Q&A: What is the accrual basis of accounting?* [online] Available at: www.accountingcoach.com/blog/acrrual-basis-accounting.

AccountingCoach.com (date unknown). *Q&A: What is the difference between normal costing and standard costing?* [online] Available at: www.accountingcoach.com/blog/normal-costing-standard-costing.

AccountingEdu.org (date unknown). *Cost accounting*. [online] Available at: www.accountingedu.org/cost-accounting.html.

aCOWtancy.com (date unknown). *B2b. Break-Even Point and Margin of Safety*. [online] Available at: www.acowtancy.com/textbook/acca-f5/b2-cost-volume-profit-analysis/break-even-point-and-margin-of-safety/notes.

BBC.co.uk (2014). *GCSE Bitesize Business Studies: Working Capital*. [online] Available at: www.bbc.co.uk/schools/gcsebitesize/business/finance/solvencyrev1.shtml.

Bragg, S. (2012). *Contribution definition*. [online] Available at: www.accountingtools.com/articles/what-is-contribution.html.

Bragg, S. (2017). *Cost allocation*. [online] Available at: www.accountingtools.com/articles/what-is-cost-allocation.html.

Bragg, S. (2017). *Direct material price variance*. [online] Available at: www.accountingtools.com/articles/what-is-the-direct-material-price-variance.html.

Bragg, S. (2017). *Financial forecasting methods*. [online] Available at: www.accountingtools.com/articles/financial-forecasting-methods.html.

Bragg, S. (2017). *Sales volume variance*. [online] Available at:

www.accountingtools.com/articles/2017/5/4/sales-volume-variance

Bragg, S. (2017). *Standard Costing*. [online] Available at: www.accountingtools.com/articles/2017/5/14/standard-costing.

Bragg, S. (2017). *Target Costing*. [online] Available at: www.accountingtools.com/articles/2017/5/14/target-costing.

Bragg, S. (2017). *Vertical Analysis*. [online] Available at: www.accountingtools.com/articles/2017/5/17/vertical-analysis.

Bragg, S. (2018). *Direct material usage variance*. [online] Available at: www.accountingtools.com/articles/what-is-the-direct-material-usage-variance.html.

BusinessDictionary.com (date unknown). *financial model.* [online] Available atwww.businessdictionary.com/definition/financial-model.html.

BusinessDictionary.com (date unknown). *sales volume variance.* [online] Available at: www.businessdictionary.com/definition/sales-volume-variance.html.

Chartered Institute of Management Accounting (date unknown). *What is management accounting?* [online] Available at: www.cimaglobal.com/Starting-CIMA/Why-CIMA/what-is-management-accounting/

College Accounting Coach (2007). *Explain what is Sales Price Variance & Sales Volume Variance.* [online] Available at: http://basiccollegeaccounting.com/2007/11/explain-what-is-sales-price-variance-sales-volume-variance/.

Diffen.com (2018). *Gross vs Net* [online] Available at: www.diffen.com/difference/Gross_vs_Net.

Economicsonline.co.uk (date unknown). Total costs [online image] Available at www.economicsonline.co.uk/Business_economics/Costs.html.

Encyclopædia Britannica Online (2008). *Cost.* [online] Available at: www.britannica.com/topic/cost#ref91518.

EY (2014). *Integrated reporting: Elevated value.* [online PDF] Available at: www.ey.com/Publication/vwLUAssets/EY-Integrated-reporting/$FILE/EY-Integrated-reporting.pdf.

Gordon, R. (2016). *Changes to accounting standards and regulations.* [Blog] Companies House blog on GOV.uk. Available at: https://companieshouse.blog.gov.uk/2016/02/29/changes-to-accounting-standards-and-regulations/.

Hillstrom, L. (date unknown). *Value Creation.* [online] Available at: www.referenceforbusiness.com/management/Tr-Z/Value-Creation.html.

icaew.com (2015). *The revised UK small companies regime.* [online] Available at: www.icaew.com/archive/technical/practice-resources/icaew-practice-support/practicewire/news/the-revised-uk-small-companies-regime.

icaew.com (date unknown) *The new UK GAAP.* [online] Available at: www.icaew.com/en/technical/financial-reporting/new-uk-gaap

icaew.com (date unknown). *What is corporate governance?* [online] Available at: www.icaew.com/technical/corporate-governance/overview/does-corporate-governance-matter.

Integrated-standards.com (date unknown). *What Is An Integrated Management System.* [online] Available at: http://integrated-standards.com/articles/what-is-integrated-management-system/.

International Integrated Reporting Council (2016). *Creating Value: The cyclical power of integrated thinking and reporting.* [online PDF] Available at: http://integratedreporting.org/wp-content/uploads/2016/11/CreatingValue_IntegratedThinking_.pdf

International Integrated Reporting Council (date unknown). *Integrated Reporting* [online] Available at: http://integratedreporting.org/.

InvestingAnswers.com (date unknown). *Discounted Cash Flow (DCF) Analysis.* [online] Available at: www.investinganswers.com/dictionary/discounted-cash-flow-dcf-analysis.

InvestingAnswers.com (date unknown). *Equity Financing.* [online] Available at:www.investinganswers.com/financial-dictionary/stock-market/equity-financing-1523.

Investopedia.com (date unknown). *Balanced Scorecard.* [online] Available at: www.investopedia.com/terms/b/balancedscorecard.asp

Investopedia.com (date unknown). *Bond.* [online] Available at: www.investopedia.com/terms/b/bond.asp.

Investopedia.com (date unknown). *Contribution Margin.* [online] Available at: www.investopedia.com/terms/c/contributionmargin.asp.

Investopedia.com (date unknown). *Financial Modeling.* [online] Available at: www.investopedia.com/terms/f/financialmodeling.asp.

Investopedia.com (date unknown). *Interest Coverage Ratio.* [online] Available at: www.investopedia.com/terms/i/interestcoverageratio.asp.

Investopedia.com (date unknown). *Sustainability.* [online] Available at: www.investopedia.com/terms/s/sustainability.asp.

Investorwords.com (2018). *Gross vs Net – What's the Difference?* [online] Available at: www.investorwords.com/article/gross-vs-net.html.

Jefferson, M. and Voudouris, V. (2011). *Oil scenarios for long-term business planning: Royal Dutch Shell and generative explanation, 1960–2010.* London Metropolitan Business School Centre for International Business and Sustainability Working Paper No. 18 [online PDF] Available at: https://mpra.ub.uni-muenchen.de/27910/1/MPRA_paper_27910.pdf.

Lewis, J. (date unknown). *Advantages & Disadvantages of Cost-Volume-Profit Analysis.* [online] Available at: http://smallbusiness.chron.com/advantages-disadvantages-costvolumeprofit-analysis-35135.html.

Lexicon.FT.com (date unknown). *Definition of corporate social responsibility (CSR). Financial Times.* [online] Available at: http://lexicon.ft.com/Term?term=corporate-social-responsibility--(CSR).

McClure, B (date unknown). *A Clear Look At EBITDA.* [online] Available at: www.investopedia.com/articles/06/ebitda.asp.

Moneyterms.co.uk (date unknown). *Operating Profit* [online] Available at: https://moneyterms.co.uk/operating-profit/.

Murray, J. (2017). *Cost vs. Expense – What is the Difference?* [online] Available at: www.thebalance.com/cost-vs-expense-what-is-the-difference-3974582.

O'Neill, D. (2017). *FRS 102 Section 1A Quick Guide.* [online] Available at: http://uk.frs102.com/blog/frs-102-section-1a-quick-guide/.

Operations management – types of cost. [online] Available at: http://textbook.stpauls.br/Business_Textbook/Operations_management_student/page_28.htm.

Parikh, V. (2012). *Advantages and Disadvantages of Management Accounting.* [online] Available at: www.letslearnfinance.com/advantages-and-disadvantages-of-management-accounting.html.

Peavler, R. (2017). *Learn to Calculate a Breakeven Point with This Formula.* [online] Available at: www.thebalance.com/how-to-calculate-breakeven-point-393469.

Perez, W. (2017). *Learn About Business Entities.* [online] Available at: www.thebalance.com/business-entities-3193420.

Spacey, J. (2016). *22 Management Accounting Techniques.* 2nd ed. [online] Available at: https://simplicable.com/new/management-accounting-techniques.

Spacey, J. (2017). *4 Types of Benchmarking.* [online] Available at: https://simplicable.com/new/types-of-benchmarking.

The Economist (2008). *Scenario planning.* [online] Available at: www.economist.com/node/12000755.

Thwink.org (2014). *Sustainability.* [online] Available at: www.thwink.org/sustain/glossary/Sustainability.htm.

TradeGecko.com (2017). *What is demand forecasting and how can it help your business?* [online] Available at: www.tradegecko.com/blog/what-is-demand-forecasting-and-how-can-it-help-your-business.

Universalclass.com (date unknown). *How to Perform a Cost Analysis.* [online] Available at: www.universalclass.com/articles/business/basic-methods-and-calculations-of-financial-and-cost-analysis.htm.

ValueBasedManagement.net (2016). *Summary of the Value Creation Index (VCI).* [online] Available at: www.valuebasedmanagement.net/methods_valuecreationindex.html.

Welch, I. (2013). *The Benefits and Downsides of Integrated Reporting.* [online] Available at: www.theaccountant-online.com/comments/the-benefits-and-downsides-of-integrated-reporting.

Wikipedia.com (2017). *Cash flow forecasting.* [online] Available at: https://en.wikipedia.org/wiki/Cash_flow_forecasting.

Wimbledon, J. (2016). *The importance of good financial management and planning.* [online] Available at: www.simplybusiness.co.uk/knowledge/articles/2016/03/consequences-poor-financial-management-business/.

Wolters Kluwer CCH Tagetik (date unknown). *Cost allocation.* [online] Available at: www.tagetik.com/uk/glossary/cost-allocation#.WnxGb5PFKu5.

Woodruff, J. (2018). *What is A Management Accounting System?* Bizfluent [online] Available at: https://bizfluent.com/facts-5460765-management-accounting-system.html.

Zaleschuk, M. (2015–2017, exact date unknown). *You only need 4 KPIs to measure performance!* [online] Available at: www.propels.ca/you-only-need-4-kpis-to-measure-performance/.

Glossary

Abridged accounts A condensed version of the annual accounts which small and medium-sized companies (according to the specified size criteria) are allowed to file with the register of companies. They may not be used as a substitute for the full annual accounts for the circulation to members.

Absorption cost In management accounting, the cost of all the resources used to produce an item of output or activity.

Accounting equation This represents the dual effect of accounting, where total equity (or capital) equals net assets (i.e. total assets minus total liabilities).

Accounting period A period of time during which the business's accounting records or financial statements were recorded.

Accounting standards Rules and guidelines setting out proper accounting practice for the benefit of those who prepare, analyse and use an entity's financial statements.

Accrual (or accrued expense) An adjustment in the accounts or books to reflect an expense payment that falls due in an accounting period but is paid after the period ends

Accruals basis (accrual accounting) A way of accounting for transactions by recording them in the accounting period they are earned or incurred, regardless of when money is paid or received.

Accruals concept An accounting concept stating that revenue and expenses should be recorded in the accounting period in which they occur, regardless of when the money is received or paid for them.

Acid test ratio Another name for the quick ratio (also liquidity ratio).

Act of Parliament Issued by Parliament, Acts are the supreme form of domestic law in the UK.

Activity-based costing (ABC) In management accounting, a method of cost accounting to determine the total cost of producing an item or output.

Actual costing In management accounting, a method of cost accounting that uses the actual direct costs and indirect costs to estimate or calculate the total cost of production of an item or output.

Administration order Court order to appoint an administrator to manage the affairs of a company in financial difficulty.

Administrator A person appointed by the court to manage a company in financial difficulties to protect creditors and, if possible, avoid liquidation. The administrator has the power to remove and appoint directors. A person who administers the estate of a deceased person in the absence of any executors.

Agency A relationship under which one person (the principal) appoints another person (the agent) to undertake some act on the principal's behalf.

Agent Someone who is authorised to carry out business transactions on behalf of another (the principal), who is thereby bound by such actions.

Allotment The issue of shares.

Allottee A person or company to whom shares have been allotted.

Alternate director A person appointed by a director to represent them, usually at board meetings, and who assumes the responsibilities and duties of their appointor when acting in their place.

Amortisation The depreciation of an intangible asset.

Annual accounts, annual report and accounts The accounts which are prepared to fulfil the directors' duty to present audited accounts to members in respect of each financial year. Annual accounts of limited companies must be filed with the Registrar of Companies.

Annual general meeting (AGM) A general meeting of the company's members, which must be held in each calendar year within 15 months of the previous AGM. Under Companies Act 2006, private companies are (generally) no longer required to hold AGMs, although the requirement remains for public companies.

Annual return Statement under Companies Act 2006, s. 854 which has been replaced by the confirmation statement from 1 July 2016.

Appeal A challenge to a legal decision in a case (usually by the person who lost the case).

Arbitration A form of ADR under which the parties refer their dispute to an arbitrator who will impose a legally binding decision upon the parties.

Articles of association The constitutional document setting out the internal regulations of the company. Unless modified or excluded, the specimen articles in the relevant version of Table A/model articles have effect.

Asset An item a business owns that either generates cash or has the potential to.

Audit The independent examination of, and expression of opinion on, the company's accounts. All persons or firms offering audit services must be registered auditors and belong to one of the recognised accountancy bodies.

Balance sheet Another name for the statement of financial position.

Balanced scorecard A method of analysing a business, both internally and externally to determine KPIs and/or benchmarks.

Basis of apportionment The way of apportioning an amount between business/production departments using a method that seems the most reasonable or fair.

Bearer shares Shares that can be transferred simply by passing the certificate from one person to the next. The 'bearer' of the certificate having title to the shares represented by it. Bearer shares are no longer legal in the UK.

Benchmarking A way of determining targets and comparatives by gathering and evaluating relevant data. Once set, benchmarks can be used to measure areas of performance (or underperformance).

Bill A draft piece of legislation which, if passed by Parliament, becomes an Act of Parliament.

Bonds A type of investment where investors loan money to the company for a fixed period of time in return for the company paying them annual interest on their bonds.

Bonus issue Issue of additional shares to existing shareholders, in proportion to their current holding, already paid up in full out of the distributable reserves of the company.

Books An informal term for the ledgers and books of prime entry.

Books of prime entry In bookkeeping, these are used to record a business's financial transactions before they are fed through to one of the ledgers.

Book debts Amounts owed to a company resulting from its trading activities, usually in the form of unpaid invoices rendered to customers.

Break-even analysis A method of forecasting at what point a business will break even (i.e. reach its break-even point) so that management can plan accordingly.

Budget A plan of what management intends or wants to happen in the future regarding financial items.

Budgetary control The process of applying control over a business's activities and resources by preparing a budget, and then comparing the business's actual performance against the targets set out in the budget.

Call A formal notice issued by a company requiring shareholders to pay all or part of the amounts unpaid on partly paid issued shares.

Capital The money or money's worth used by a company to finance its business. *See also* working capital.

Capital expenditure The amount of money spent in relation to the purchase, repair or maintenance of fixed assets.

Carriage in/inwards The cost, paid for by the business rather than the supplier, of delivering purchases to the business.

Carriage out/outwards The cost of delivering goods to customers that is paid for by the business and not the customer.

Case law The body of laws that are created by the judges and applied via the doctrine of precedent.

Cash Money in banknotes or coins (cash in hand), or money sitting in a bank account (cash at bank).

Cash basis (cash accounting) A way of accounting for transactions by recording them as and when they happen, or whenever the cash is paid or received.

Cash equivalents Money in a form that can be converted quickly into cash, such as cheques.

Cash flow/Cashflow The cash (money) flowing into and out of the business.

Cash flow forecasting A way of estimating or predicting the amount of money the business expects to come in and pay out (i.e. its cashflow) in a forecast.

Cash flow statement/statement of cash flows A statement showing how much cash the business is generating from its operations.

Cash inflow/outflow Money coming into/out of the business.

Centralised structure Authority for decision-making rests with the senior management in this structure.

Certificate of incorporation A certificate issued by the Registrar of Companies on receipt of specified constitutional and other documents of the company. The company assumes its identity as a legal person on the date of incorporation shown on the certificate.

Chain of command This defines who reports to whom in an unbroken line from the very top of the organisation (senior management) to the bottom (operations).

Charge A means by which a company offers its assets as security for a debt. A charge is a general term that includes, but is not limited to, a mortgage. A fixed charge relates to a specific asset or assets. A floating charge relates to whatever assets of a specified class are in the company's possession at the time the charge crystallises (if it does so).

Civil law Civil law can refer to (i) the body of law that pertains to civil wrongs (e.g. the law of torts, contract law) and do not impose criminal liability, or; (ii) those legal systems that are largely based on Roman law.

Claimant A person who commences a civil legal action.

Class rights Where a company has more than one class of shares, the rights attached to those different classes of shares.

Closing capital/closing balance sheet amount The reconciliation showing how the capital in the business has changed over an accounting period. The closing balance sheet amount should equal the net assets at the end of the period (i.e. the capital the business 'closes' the period with).

Commencement Order A form of subordinate legislation that brings an Act of Parliament, or parts of it, into force on a specified date.

Common law Common law can refer to (i) those legal systems that have based their legal system on that of England; (ii) the body of laws and decisions created by judges and applied via the doctrine of precedent, or; (iii) the unified system of law that arose following the Norman Conquest and still exists today.

Common seal A seal bearing a company's name for affixing to legal documents.

Company An association of persons which, on incorporation, becomes a legal entity entirely separate from the individuals comprising its membership. In the Companies Act 2006, 'company' is restricted to companies registered under that Act or previous Companies Acts.

Company secretary An officer of the company with a number of statutory duties, such as to sign the confirmation statement and accompanying documents, and usually charged with a range of duties relating to the company's statutory books and records, filing requirements, etc. Under the Companies Act 2006, private companies are no longer required to appoint a company secretary.

Company voluntary arrangement An arrangement under the Insolvency Act 1986 between the company and its members.

Company limited by guarantee A company owned by the members (known as guarantors) instead of shareholders.

Company limited by shares Shareholders usually receive a share of any profits the business makes (dividends). Shares can be kept private or, if a public limited company, offered to the general public and traded on the stock exchange.

Comply or explain The obligation placed upon listed companies to state in their annual reports how they have applied the UK Corporate Governance Codec and explain any areas of non-compliance.

Compulsory liquidation Winding up of a company by order of the winding-up court.

Conciliation A form of ADR under which the parties refer their dispute to a conciliator who will lead a dialogue between the parties and help them to resolve their dispute by suggesting solutions.

Confirmation Statement A form filed each year with the Registrar of Companies, confirming that specified information about the company's directors, secretary, registered office, shareholders, share capital, notified to Companies House is correct or that any changes to the information are being notified at the same time as the confirmation statement. Replaced the annual return from 1 July 2016.

Consolidated financial statements (group accounts) Financial statements of a group of companies presented as if they are a single entity.

Contract An agreement between two or more legal persons creating a legally enforceable obligation between them.

Contribution The amount remaining after all variable costs have been subtracted from revenue, and represents the amount left available to pay the business's fixed costs.

Contribution margin Allows the business to determine how profitable individual products or services are. This can help determine what price to sell them for in the future.

Corporate director A corporate entity that is appointed as a director of another company. Quite common within groups of companies.

Corporate social responsibility (CSR) The measures taken by a business to assess and take responsibility for their effect on the environmental and social wellbeing of the wider society influenced by their activities.

Cost An amount that has to be spent to buy or obtain something. A cost is not always financial.

Cost accounting A management accounting method that looks at all of a business's expenses to determine the actual fixed and variable costs associated with making the product, or providing the service, that the business sells.

Cost analysis A comparison of costs for analytical purposes.

Cost behaviour How a cost responds to changes in level of the business activity.

Cost benefit analysis A comparison of business strategy costs with anticipated results, or with anticipated benefits or profits, for analytical purposes.

Cost centre A department or business segment to which costs, particularly indirect costs or overheads, can be allocated for management accounting purposes.

Cost driver A factor that causes an activity that creates indirect costs or overheads.

Cost object In management accounting, this is anything a business wants to separately measure costs for. This can be a cost centre, but is not always.

Cost of debt The interest rate on debt or the coupon rate on the company's bonds.

Cost of equity The rate of return that a company pays to its equity investors (e.g. as dividends to shareholders).

Cost of goods sold (COGS) Also known as cost of sales.

Cost of sales Expenses relating directly to the make or manufacture of the products sold by the business in the course of its trade.

Cost–volume–profit (CVP) analysis An analysis of how total revenues, total costs and operating profit changes as the following variables change: level of output, sale price, variable costs and/or fixed costs.

Credit Either (a) in bookkeeping, an entry recording an amount of money received or owed by a business as one half of a transaction's double entry (CR for short); or (b) the state of a business receiving goods or services before paying for them while being trusted to pay what they owe in the future.

Creditors (payables) The people/other businesses the business owes money to.

Creditors' turnover The amount of time in days the business takes to pay its suppliers and/or creditors.

Creditor A person or company owed money.

Creditors' voluntary winding up Insolvent winding up of a company by resolution of its members.

CREST Operated by Euroclear UK & Ireland Limited, CREST is the major UK securities settlement system for UK equities, government bonds and a range of other securities providing simultaneous and irrevocable transfer of cash and securities for all sterling and euro payments and real-time settlement.

Criminal law Criminal law refers to those laws that impose criminal liability on a person.

Current asset An asset that a business can expect to convert to cash over the course of a year.

Current liability A liability or debt which a business expects to settle (i.e. pay off in full) over the course of a year.

Current ratio A ratio which measures how adequately a business's current assets can cover its current liabilities.

Debenture A written acknowledgement of a debt owed by a company, often – but not necessarily – secured. It is common practice for a debenture to be created by a trust deed by which company property is mortgaged to trustees for the debenture holders, as security for the payment of interest and capital.

Debt An amount of money owed by one person a debtor owes to another, being the creditor.

Debit In bookkeeping, this is an entry recording an amount of money paid by or owed to a business as one half of a transaction's double entry (DR for short).

Debtors (receivables) The people/other businesses that owe money to the business.

Debtors' turnover (trade receivables collection period/debtor days) The amount of time in days the business's average customer and/or debtor takes to pay the business.

Decentralised structure Authority for decision making is distributed across a larger group within the organisation. For example, day-to-day operational decisions may be delegated to middle and lower-level managers, leaving only major decisions to the remit of senior management.

Declaration of incompatibility A declaration stating that the court is of the opinion that a legislative provision is incompatible with a ECHR right.

Defamation A collective term for the torts of libel and slander.

Deferred income Money or income received for goods or services before they have been delivered.

Department for Business, Energy and Industrial Strategy (BEIS) The government department responsible for the administration of company law. The Companies Act confers certain powers on the Secretary of State. Formerly called the Department for Business, Innovation and Skills (BIS).

Depreciation This is an allocation of the cost of an asset over its useful life, and is accounted for as an expense in a business's accounts even though no actual money has been spent or received.

Director An officer of the company responsible for determining policy, supervising the management of the company's business and exercising the powers of the company. Directors must generally carry out these functions collectively as a board.

Directors' report A statement attached to the annual accounts containing certain information laid down in the Act.

Direct applicability EU legislation that is directly applicable is automatically incorporated into domestic law as soon as it is passed.

Direct effect EU legislation that can be enforced in a domestic court is said to have direct effect.

Discounted cash flow The present value(s) of an investment project's future expected cash flows.

Discounted cash flow analysis A way of assessing and analysing an investment project to estimate how much the entire investment would be worth today.

Distributable reserves Profit retained by a company which may be distributed to its members.

Distribution The transfer of some or all a company's assets (usually cash) to its members, generally by way of dividend or on a winding up.

Distributions Another name for dividends.

Distribution costs In an income statement, these are expenses involved in distributing a business's goods or services.

Dividend The money a company pays to its shareholders out of its profits and/ or reserves, usually either annually or every six months.

Dormant company A company which has not traded or has ceased trading and has no accounting transactions that need to be entered in its financial records.

Double-entry bookkeeping A method of bookkeeping based on the concept that every economic transaction has two parts – a positive entry and a corresponding negative entry, and will therefore affect two ledger accounts.

Dual effect of accounting The principle on which double-entry bookkeeping and the accounting equation are based (i.e. that every economic transaction has two parts and that this dual effect should be recorded in two places).

Earnings The money earned by the business, either as profit or income.

EBIT Earnings before interest and tax. Most of the time it is the same as the operating profit.

EBITDA (earnings before interest, tax, depreciation and amortisation) A way of measuring a company's profitability without the effects of financing, tax or accounting treatments taken into account.

Entity A person, organisation or business with a separately identifiable and legal existence.

Equity Another name for capital; alternatively, it can refer to shares or shareholdings.

Expenditure This is money spent (on an item, or a service, etc) by a business.

Expense This is an amount paid for an item or service that is being, or has been, used in the business. It often refers to a payment – or expenditure – that a business makes regularly over a specific time period.

Fiduciary Having a position of trust, such that the power and authority conferred by the position must be exercised solely in the interest of the person with whom the fiduciary relationship exists. Trustees are in a fiduciary position, as are solicitors in relation to their clients. Directors have a fiduciary duty to the company, obliging them to act always in good faith and not to derive a personal profit from their position.

Finance costs (finance expenses/charges) Expenses relating to the financing of a business, such as bank charges or interest paid on loans and overdrafts.

Financial modelling A way of analysing a business by using financial models to estimate economic outcomes, forecast future profits and cash flows, and make decisions and recommendations.

Financial statements (or accounts) These are a summary of an entity's performance over a given time period (often a year), and its financial position at the end of that period.

Financial year The period in respect of which the company's profits and loss account is drawn up; it need not coincide with the fiscal or calendar year and need not be a period of 12 months.

First instance The first time a case is heard by a court, it is said to be heard at first instance.

Fixed asset (non-current assets) An asset (tangible or intangible) that a business owns for long-term use, rather than to sell to customers

Fixed charge Security, usually for a loan, over a specific asset such as a building or equipment.

Fixed cost A cost or expenditure amount that is unchanged (fixed) regardless of how much work is done or how much output is produced.

Flexed budget A budget with figures that have been recalculated proportionally to reflect the volume of actual production and sales, as opposed to original budget amounts.

Float (imprest) An amount (often the maximum) that a business holds in petty cash.

Floating charge Security, usually for a loan, over a class of assets the individual components of which vary over time, such as stock or book debts.

Forecast A plan of what management estimates will happen in future based on past data and current/future trends.

Formation *See* registration.

FTSE 100 The largest 100 companies in the UK, as measured by market capitalisation.

FTSE 350 The largest 350 companies in the UK, as measured by market capitalisation.

Function The main departments of a business (e.g. finance, human resources, sales, operations).

Gazette Official publication for formal announcements. Published daily by the TSO on behalf of the National Archive

Gearing A measure of the ratio between a business's borrowings (debt) and its share capital and reserves (equity).

Generally accepted accounting practice (GAAP) A set of accounting standards that establish how financial statements for companies must be prepared in the jurisdiction that the company is governed by.

General meeting Any general meeting of the company's members that is not an annual general meeting.

Going concern A business that is a going concern has no intention to liquidate, or be brought to an end, and is likely to operate for the 'foreseeable future' (usually meaning at least the next 12 months).

Goods Another name for products, or items to be sold by the business in the course of its trade.

Gross In finance, this generally refers to the total amount before anything is deducted. Opposite of net.

Gross profit The amount made from total sales (or revenue, or turnover) minus the cost of sales. It is used to measure how much profit a business is making on its products or services before any incidental business costs or expenses are taken into account.

Gross profit margin This is a way of measuring a business's profitability by expressing gross profit as a percentage of sales or revenue.

Groupthink A psychological phenomenon that can occur when the desire for harmony, conformity and consensus within a group results in irrational or dysfunctional decision-making processes (e.g. suppressing dissenting opinion, not allowing group members to constructively challenge decisions or propose alternatives and isolating themselves from outside opinion).

Guarantee A formal agreement under which a guarantor undertakes to meet the contractual obligations of one person to another in the event of default. A company limited by guarantee is one in which the liability of the members is limited to a specified amount in a winding up.

Hierarchy Another term for chain of command.

Holding company A company which has subsidiaries.

Horizontal analysis A type of financial statement analysis performed by comparing an item against previous periods using the figures on the same horizontal line in that financial statement.

Hybrid Bill A Bill that affects the general population, but will have an increased effect upon specific persons, groups, organisations, or localities.

IFRS This stands for International Financial Reporting Standards and is the set of internationally agreed financial reporting and accounting standards that all types of entity can use.

Imprest Another name for float.

Income (revenue/turnover) The money a business receives.

Incorporation The act and process of legally creating a company or corporate entity.

Indirect cost (overhead) A cost or expense that is necessary to operate the business, but which does not relate directly to the production or sale of the business's products or services.

Inflation A general increase in prices which leads to a decrease in the purchasing power of money.

Insider dealing Buying or selling shares on the basis of an unfair advantage derived from access to price-sensitive information not generally available. Insider dealing is a criminal offence.

Insolvency The situation in which a company or individual can no longer pay back the money owed to outside lenders (e.g. a loan from a bank or other financial institution).

Institutional investors Powerful shareholders such as banks, pension funds, and insurance companies that invest significant sums in the stock market on their own behalf and on behalf of their customers/clients.

Intangible asset An asset which is a non-physical or abstract item (i.e. intangible), such as patents, copyrights, trademarks and goodwill.

Integrated reporting Also known as <IR>, this is a recent business approach which recommends the production of an integrated report alongside a business's financial statements.

Interest Money paid at a particular rate (i.e. the interest rate) by a business or individual for the use of money lent (i.e. monetary debt) to that business or individual.

Interest cover (interest coverage ratio) A way of measuring how many times the business's profits could cover its own interest expenses.

Interest payable The interest that a business must repay on a financial liability such as a loan or overdraft.

Interest rate The rate at which interest is paid on a debt.

Interest receivable The interest income earned by a business. Often this is bank interest paid on the money the business holds in a bank account.

Inventory Items the business intends to sell in the course of its trade.

Inventory turnover (inventory days or stock turnover) This measures in number of days on average that an item stays in inventory before it is sold. Not to be confused with inventory turnover ratio.

Inventory turnover ratio A ratio which measures the number of times inventories are 'turned over' each year (i.e. replaced with new stock for the business to sell). Not to be confused with inventory turnover.

Investment An asset owned by a business (or a person) that generates income, such as shares, other businesses or rental properties.

ISDX The trading facility operated by Icap Group to facilitate trading in securities not on the Stock Exchange.

Issued capital *See* share capital.

Judgement creditor A creditor who has obtained a court order in their favour.

Key Performance Indicator (KPI) A measurable value that demonstrates how effectively a company is meeting performance or business objectives.

Ledger In bookkeeping, one of the main books in which a business's financial data is recorded.

Legislation Laws that derive from Parliament.

Liability This is a monetary amount the business owes and therefore needs to pay for.

Limited company The most common form of company, in which the liability of members for the debts of the company is limited – either to the amount of share capital for which they have applied (a company limited by shares) or to a specific amount guaranteed in the event of a winding up (a company limited by guarantee).

Limited liability partnership (LLP) A corporate body where the members have limited liability but undertake the management themselves rather than appointing directors to manage the company on their behalf.

Limited liability The separation of ownership by the members from liability for commercial debts incurred by and in the name of the corporate entity. Any loss suffered by the members being limited to the amount they have agreed to pay for their shares or in the case of a guarantee company the nominal guarantee provided.

Life cycle costing A management accounting system that keeps track of, and adds up, the actual costs attributable to each product from the start of the product being created to its end (i.e. over its 'life cycle').

Liquidity The ability of an asset or a business to either produce cash when needed, or be quickly and easily converted to cash.

Liquidity ratio Another name for the quick ratio.

Listed company A company whose shares are listed by the Financial Services Authority on the Official List of the UK and admitted for trading on the London Stock Exchange or PLUS Listed markets.

Liquidation The process under which a company ceases to trade and realises its assets for distribution to creditors and then shareholders. The term 'winding up' is synonymous.

Loan An amount of money (e.g. lent by a bank). Loans often charge interest which must be repaid alongside the loan itself.

Long-term liability A liability or debt that a business will settle (i.e. pay in full) in more than one year's time. Also known as a non-current liability.

Loss This occurs when the profit figure is negative, which is when a business's expenses exceeds the income it received.

Management accounting system A business system or process which collects internal financial data from business operations such as sales data, shifts in inventory and changes in raw materials costs, then analyses the information in reports for management to use.

Marginal cost A figure representing how total costs change as output changes.

Margin of safety The amount at which revenues will exceed the break-even point, so that management can determine how risky a business undertaking will be.

Market capitalisation A company's share price multiplied by the number of shares it has issued.

Market value The price that an asset can be sold for through the relevant marketplace (e.g. a stock exchange, an auction, an estate agent or retailer).

Materiality A concept that describes whether an item's omission or misstatement could influence the decision taken by users of financial statements, or cause those financial statements to not faithfully represent the economic substance of the information contained.

Mediation A form of ADR under which the parties refer their dispute to a mediator, who will facilitate a dialogue between the parties so that they can resolve the dispute themselves

Members A subscriber to the memorandum of association and any other person who agrees to be a member and whose name is entered in the register of members.

Members' voluntary winding up Solvent winding up of a company by resolution of its members.

Memorandum of association A constitutional document setting out details of the subscribers on incorporation.

Micro, small- and medium-sized enterprises Categories for defining the size of an organisation. The criteria differs between countries, but as a general rule, these are categorised into <10 employees (micro), <50 employees (small) and <250 employees (medium).

Model Articles The specimen articles of association for a company limited by shares incorporated under the Companies Act 2006. Unless specifically modified or excluded, the version of the Model Articles in force at the time of a company's incorporation automatically applies to the company.

Natural directors Companies are required to have at least one natural director, by which is meant a human being rather than a corporate entity.

Net In finance, this generally refers to the amount after deductions are made. Opposite of gross.

Net assets The amount of assets that are left in the business after all liabilities have been accounted for.

Net asset value The value of what's left in the business after the value of all liabilities have been subtracted from the value of all assets. For the valuation of a listed company, the net asset value can also refer to net assets per share.

Net present value (NPV) The difference between the present value of cash inflows and the present value of cash outflows.

Net profit The amount left when all costs have been taken into account. Used to see how well the business is performing overall.

Net profit margin A way of measuring a business's profitability by expressing net profit as a percentage of sales or revenue.

Net sales Technically, this is the sales figure minus any returns or refunds. However, it is occasionally used in place of sales or turnover.

Nominal value The face value of a share as set out in the company's memorandum and articles. Also known as ordinary value.

Non-current asset Another term for fixed asset.

Non-current liability Another term for long-term liability.

Non-operating income Income received by a business that is not from its trade.

Obiter dicta 'Statement said by the way'; anything said by a judge in a case that is not part of the ratio.

Officer Includes a director, manager or (where appointed) the secretary of a company. Not everyone with the title of manager is sufficiently senior to be regarded as an officer, who must have a level of supervisory control which reflects the general policy of the company. Also includes the company's auditor.

Opening capital (opening balance sheet amount) The closing capital figure from the previous accounting period (i.e. the amount of capital the business 'opens' the period with).

Operating (operating expenses/running costs) The costs and expenses that relate to the operating of the business, but not necessarily directly to the manufacture or making of the business's products or services to be sold.

Operating margin Another name for operating profit margin.

Operating profit The amount of profit that is left after cost of sales and operating expenses are deducted from total income (or revenue, or turnover).

Operating profit margin A way of measuring a business's profitability by expressing operating profit as a percentage of sales or revenue.

Operating statement The statement reconciling the actual figures and budgeted figures via variances in management accounting. It is sometimes also used (less commonly) as an alternative name for an income statement.

Ordinary resolution A resolution at a general meeting carried by a simple majority of votes cast.

Ordinary shares The most common form of share in a company, giving holders the right to share in the company's profits in proportion to their holdings and the right to vote at general meetings (although non-voting ordinary shares are occasionally encountered).

Ordinary value Another term for a share's nominal value.

Paid-up capital Refers to the amounts paid up on any issued shares.

Partnership A business run by two or more persons where the owners share ownership (partners) and have unlimited liability for the businesses debts.

Passporting The right of a company registered in a EEA state to do business in another EEA state without obtaining further authorisation.

Petty cash A small amount of physical cash a business keeps on hand in a drawer or a safe, rather than in the bank, to make small cash payments when necessary.

Person with Significant Control (PSC) An individual owning or exercising control over 25% or more of a company's equity shares or voting rights.

Pre-emption rights Preferential right of existing members to purchase new shares to be issued or existing shares being offered for sale by way of transfer by an existing member.

Preference shares Shares carrying the right to payment of a fixed dividend out of profits before the payment of an ordinary dividend or the preferential return of capital or both.

Premium Listing A company whose shares have a Premium Listing is subject to additional rules and is expected to meet the highest standards of regulation and governance.

Present value A value representing what a monetary amount received in the future would be worth today (i.e. its value in the present).

Prima facie On the face of it, at first sight.

Private company A company that is not a public company.

Private Bill A Bill that affects specific persons, groups, organisations, or localities.

Private law Laws that regulate the relationship between persons (i.e. the state is usually not a party to the legal proceedings).

Probate The law relating to wills and the dealing of a deceased person's assets.

Product An item that the business makes and/or sells as part of its trade.

Profit The amount by which the revenue the business generates is greater than the business's expenses (or costs paid) for a trading period.

Profit and loss account This is either (a) another term for income statement or (b) another name for the retained earnings account that appears in a line on the balance sheet.

Profit and loss statement Another name for the income statement, also sometimes known as the profit and loss account or a P&L statement.

Profit margin A ratio, expressed as a percentage, used to measure and analyse a business's profitability.

Pro rata In proportion, rateably.

Prospectus Any prospectus, notice, circular, advertisement or other invitation to the public to subscribe for purchase of a company's shares or debentures.

Proxy A person authorised by a member to vote on his behalf at a general meeting. A proxy need not also be a member of the company.

Prudence The accounting principle of ensuring that financial information and recorded transactions should neither overstate/overestimate assets, income and profits nor understate/underestimate liabilities, expenses and losses.

Public Bill A Bill that affects the general population.

Public company (plc) A company which meets specified requirements as to its minimum share capital and which is registered as a public company. Only public companies can offer shares and debentures to the public.

Public law Laws that regulate the relationship between the state and persons within the state.

Quasi-loan A loan where a company reimburses the director's creditor.

Quick ratio (acid test/liquidity ratio) A way of measuring short-term liquidity.

Ratio analysis A type of financial analysis to evaluate a business's operating and/or financial performance over time.

Ratio decidendi 'Reason for deciding'; the reasons behind a decision of a court, which can be binding on other courts.

Redeemable shares Shares which are issued as redeemable may be bought back by the company at a future date.

Receiver(s) A person or a company appointed by a court to manage the finances of a bankrupt business or person.

Reconciliation The process that works arithmetically between two sets of recorded figures to check (or confirm) that they are correct. The trial balance is one example of a reconciliation.

Registrar of Companies The official responsible for maintaining the company records filed under the requirements of the Companies Act.

Registration Process by which companies are created by filing (or registering) several specified documents at Companies House.

Regulatory information service (RIS) An information provider approved by the FSA to disseminate information to the market.

Reserve An amount a business can use for future payments and/or emergencies in excess of what is already needed for day-to-day operations.

Resolution A decision at a meeting reached by a majority of members voting.

Retained earnings The profit/net earnings after dividends have all been paid that a company has left to pay its debts or reinvest in the business.

Retirement by rotation The annual standing down of directors (usually one third) for re-election by members at an annual general meeting.

Return on assets (ROA) A ratio indicating how efficient a business is at using its assets to generate profit.

Return on equity (ROE) A ratio indicating how able a business is at generating profits from the shareholders' investment in the business

Return of capital An amount paid back to members being a repayment of the principal originally invested. A return of capital will occur if shares are redeemed or otherwise purchased by the issuing company.

Revenue (turnover) The money a business receives.

Rights of audience The right to advocate proceedings in a particular court.

Risk The possibility or probability of a loss or error being made, whether financial or non-financial.

Sales The money a business receives from trading. Often used interchangeably in a company's accounts with income, revenue or turnover.

Sales returns Sales made to customers that were later refunded.

Securities This is the collective name for items that can be publicly traded on a stock exchange.

Service contract A director's contract of employment.

Selling costs (selling expenses/selling and marketing expenses) All expenses involved in marketing and selling (and sometimes transporting/distributing) a business's goods or services.

Semi-fixed cost (semi-variable cost) A cost which has a fixed cost part and a variable cost part.

Separate legal personality The company is set up as a legal 'person' to delineate the actions of company from that of its owners.

Service This means either (a) paying the costs of debt (i.e. servicing debt) or (b) an item that is not a physical/tangible good that is sold as part of a business's trade.

Shadow director A person, not appointed as a director, managing or directing the affairs of a company or who directs the actions of the directors.

Share A unit of ownership of the company, representing a fraction of the share capital and usually conferring rights to participate in distributions. There may be several kinds of shares each carrying different rights. Shares are issued at a fixed nominal value, although the company may actually receive a larger amount, the excess representing share premium. Members may not be required to subscribe the full amount immediately, in which case the shares are partly paid. The members then await calls, which require them to pay further amounts until the shares are fully paid.

Shareholder A member holding shares of a company with a share capital. The most common form of company member.

Share premium The excess value of a share over its ordinary value (or nominal value).

Share capital The capital of a company contributed or to be contributed by members. Nominal capital represents the nominal value of the shares issued and excludes any premium paid.

Silo effect Members of a discrete department communicate and collaborate efficiently within their group but have limited interaction with other departments.

Situational analysis A collection of methods used to analyse an organisation's internal and external environment to understand its capabilities, potential customers, and factors that may influence or impact upon its activities.

Special resolution A resolution required either by the Companies Act or a company's articles which must be carried by at least 75% of the members voting at a general meeting. Such resolutions tend to be required where the proposal would change the nature of the relationship between a company and its members, such as an amendment to the articles.

Standard costing In management accounting, this is a method of cost accounting that uses pre-determined expected costs (known as **standards**) for both direct and indirect costs to estimate the total cost of production of an item or output.

Statute law The body of law represented by legislation, and thus occurring in authoritative written form. Statue law contrasts with common law, over which it takes precedence.

Start-up costs The expenditures made in starting a business, or costs that need to be considered in starting a business. Also known as pre-trade expenses.

Statement of cash flows (cash flow statement) A statement showing how much cash the business is generating from its operations.

Statement of income and retained earnings (statement of retained earnings) A statement that reconciles the changes that have taken place over an accounting period in the retained earnings account.

Statement of financial position (balance sheet) A statement providing a snapshot of the business's financial position at a point in time, usually at the end of an accounting period.

Statement of profit or loss (income/P&L statement) A statement showing a business's financial performance over a specified period.

Statute law Laws created by Parliament.

Stock Either (a) another name for inventory or finished goods or (b) another name for company shares and/or bonds.

Stock exchange A financial market in which shares, bonds and other securities can be bought and sold.

Stocks and shares Another name for securities.

Stock transfer form Document used to transfer ownership of shares from one person (transferor) to another (transferee).

Subordinate legislation Legislation made by a person or body that Parliament has conferred law-making powers upon.

Subscriber A person who subscribes to the memorandum of association and agrees to take up shares in the company on incorporation.

Subsidiary One company controlled by another which usually holds a majority of the issued shares.

Sustainability The ability of a business to continue indefinitely while focusing on meeting the needs of the present without compromising the ability of future generations to meet their needs.

Table A The specimen articles of association for a company limited by shares incorporated under former Companies Acts. Unless specifically modified or excluded, the version of Table A in force at the time of a company's incorporation automatically applies to the company.

Takeover The process under which one company acquires control of another usually by acquiring all the shares.

Target costing A management accounting system where a company plans in advance its targets for the price points, product costs, and margins it wants to attain for a new product. If the targets cannot be met, production is cancelled.

Tangible asset An asset with a physical, touchable (i.e. tangible) form, such as land, buildings, plant and equipment, and physical inventory.

Three-way proxy A proxy form, which must be used by a listed company, which allows a member to instruct his proxy how to vote on each resolution.

Time value of money A concept which states that money received now is more valuable than money received in the future, because of the effect of inflation and other future uncertainties.

Total assets The sum of all assets the business holds.

Total cost The total expense a business incurs to reach a particular level of output.

Total fixed costs The amount remaining when total variable costs are subtracted from total costs.

Total liabilities The sum of all liabilities the business owes, both current and long-term.

Tort A form of civil wrong, with examples including negligence, nuisance and defamation.

Transfer Process where ownership of shares passes from one person to another usually by way of a sale.

Transferee A person acquiring shares by way of transfer.

Transferor A person disposing of shares by way of transfer.

Trade payables Another name for creditors that relate to a business's trade.

Trade payables collection period Another name for creditors' turnover, or creditor days.

Trade receivables Another name for debtors that relate to a business's trade.

Trade receivables collection period Another name for debtors' turnover, or debtor days.

Trial balance A statement, created from the business's bookkeeping system, of all the debits and credits representing the business's financial transactions over an accounting period.

UK Corporate Governance Code The code on corporate governance that applies to UK listed companies. It is a voluntary code rather than a legal requirement.

Unit cost (average cost) The total cost per unit produced.

Unlimited personal liability The owner of the business is personally responsible for any debts and liabilities accrued by the business.

Value creation The primary aim of any business – to create value for shareholders or customers to sell the business's products or services and increase profitability.

Variable cost This is a cost that varies with how much work is done or how much output is produced.

Variable overhead expenditure variance The difference between the actual amount spent on variable overheads and the budgeted amount.

Variance In management accounting, this is the difference between an actual amount and a budgeted (or standard costed) amount.

Variance analysis In management accounting, an evaluation of a business's performance by analysing variances.

Vertical analysis A type of financial statement analysis performed by comparing an item using figures within the same vertical column of figures on that financial statement.

Weighted average cost of capital (WACC) The minimum return, expressed as a percentage, that a business must earn on an existing asset base to satisfy its creditors, owners, and other providers of capital (money) that their investment will deliver what they expect.

Winding up The process of liquidating the assets of a limited company. The company will stop doing business and employing people and assets are used to pay off its debts with any money left going to shareholders. The company won't exist once it has been dissolved (either 'struck off' or 'liquidated') and removed from the companies register at Companies House.

Work in progress (WIP) This is a business's product which is in the process of being made or manufactured for trade, but is not yet finished or ready for sale.

Working capital The amount that a business requires to meet its short-term financial obligations and commitments.

Working capital cycle The time taken by a business to convert its net current assets and current liabilities into cash.

Working capital ratio Another name for the current ratio.

Year-end adjustment An accounting adjustment made at the end of the financial year where necessary before the financial statements are prepared.

Index

Lightning Source UK Ltd.
Milton Keynes UK
UKHW052230020220
357980UK00012B/168